GREG PAK · GIANNIS MILONOGIANNIS · IRMA KNIIVILA

RONIN ISLAND ™

VOLUME ONE
TOGETHER IN STRENGTH

RONIN ISLAND Volume One, December 2019. Published by
BOOM! Studios, a division of Boom Entertainment, Inc. Ronin
Island is ™ & © 2019 Pak Man Productions, Ltd. Originally
published in single magazine form as RONIN ISLAND No.
1-4. ™ & © 2019 Pak Man Productions, Ltd. All rights reserved.
BOOM! Studios™ and the BOOM! Studios logo are trademarks
of Boom Entertainment, Inc., registered in various countries
and categories. All characters, events, and institutions
depicted herein are fictional. Any similarity between any of the
names, characters, persons, events, and/or institutions in this
publication to actual names, characters, and persons, whether
living or dead, events, and/or institutions is unintended and
purely coincidental. BOOM! Studios does not read or accept
unsolicited submissions of ideas, stories, or artwork.

BOOM! Studios, 5670 Wilshire Boulevard, Suite 400, Los
Angeles, CA, 90036-5679. Printed in China. First Printing.

ISBN: 978-1-68415-459-3, eISBN: 978-1-64144-576-4

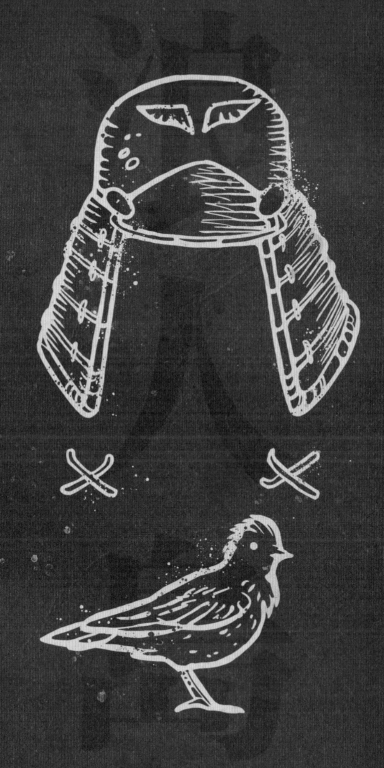

WRITTEN BY
GREG PAK

ILLUSTRATED BY
GIANNIS MILONOGIANNIS

COLORED BY
IRMA KNIIVILA

LETTERED BY
SIMON BOWLAND

COVER BY
GIANNIS MILONOGIANNIS
WITH COLORS BY **MSASSYK**

SERIES DESIGNER
MICHELLE ANKLEY

COLLECTION DESIGNER
MARIE KRUPINA

ASSOCIATE EDITOR
AMANDA LAFRANCO

EDITOR
CAMERON CHITTOCK

SENIOR EDITOR
ERIC HARBURN

RONIN ISLAND™

CREATED BY **GREG PAK** AND
GIANNIS MILONOGIANNIS

CHAPTER ONE

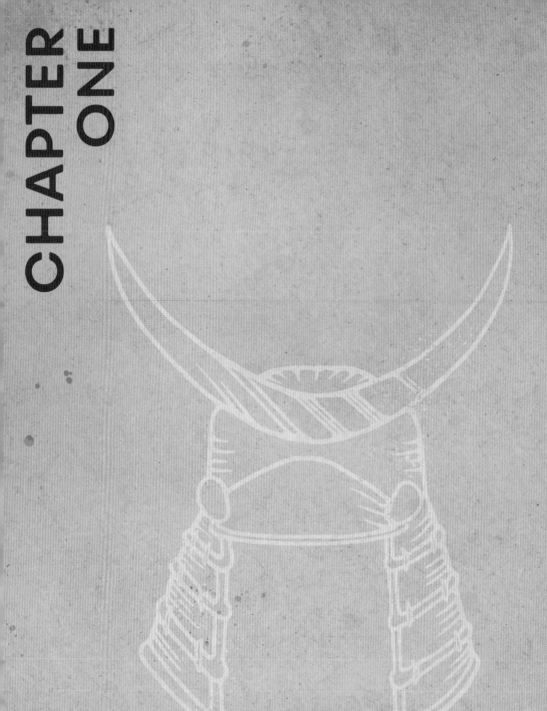

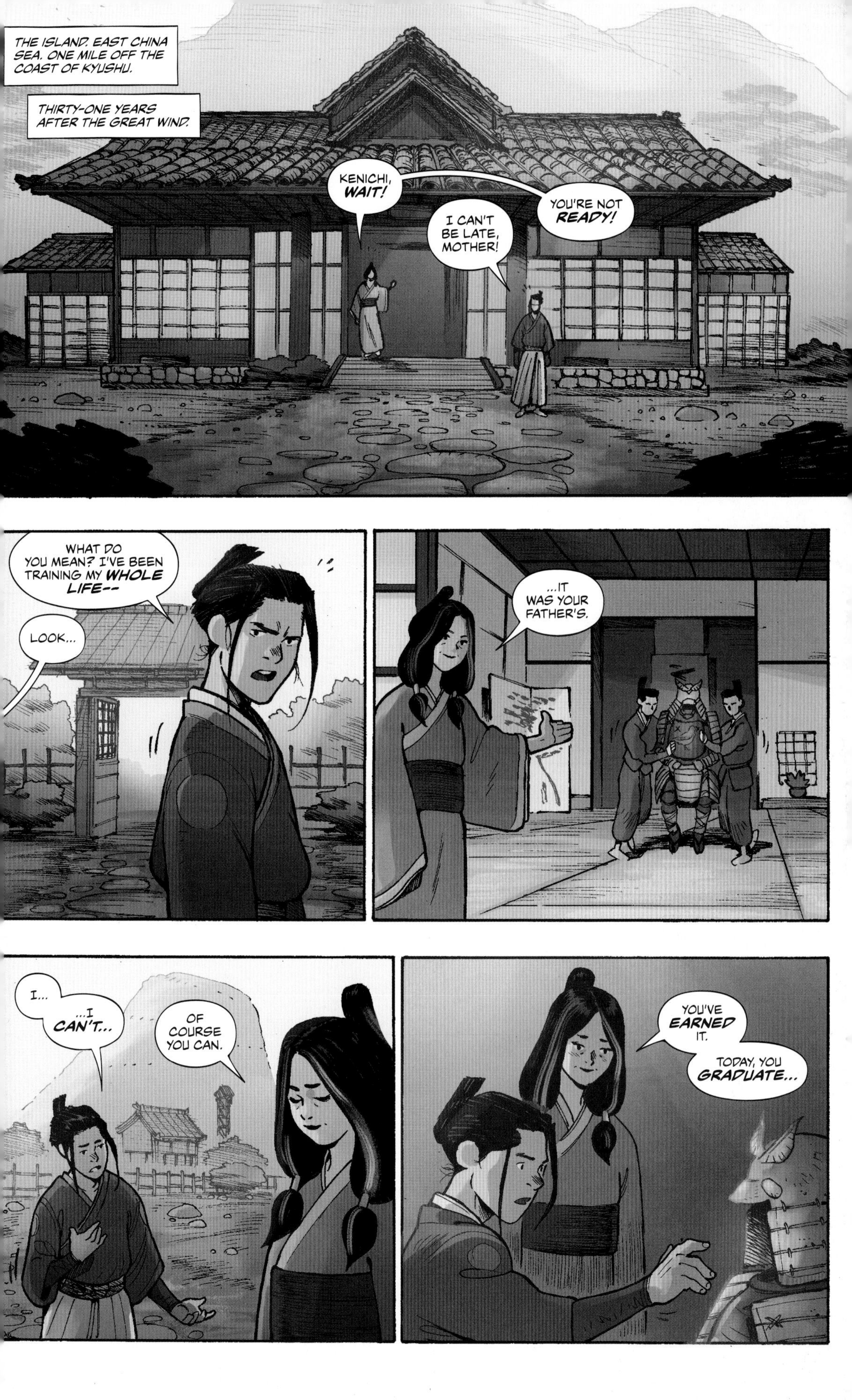
THE ISLAND. EAST CHINA SEA. ONE MILE OFF THE COAST OF KYUSHU.
THIRTY-ONE YEARS AFTER THE GREAT WIND.
KENICHI, WAIT!
I CAN'T BE LATE, MOTHER!
YOU'RE NOT READY!
WHAT DO YOU MEAN? I'VE BEEN TRAINING MY WHOLE LIFE--
LOOK...
...IT WAS YOUR FATHER'S.
I...
...I CAN'T...
OF COURSE YOU CAN.
YOU'VE EARNED IT.
TODAY, YOU GRADUATE...

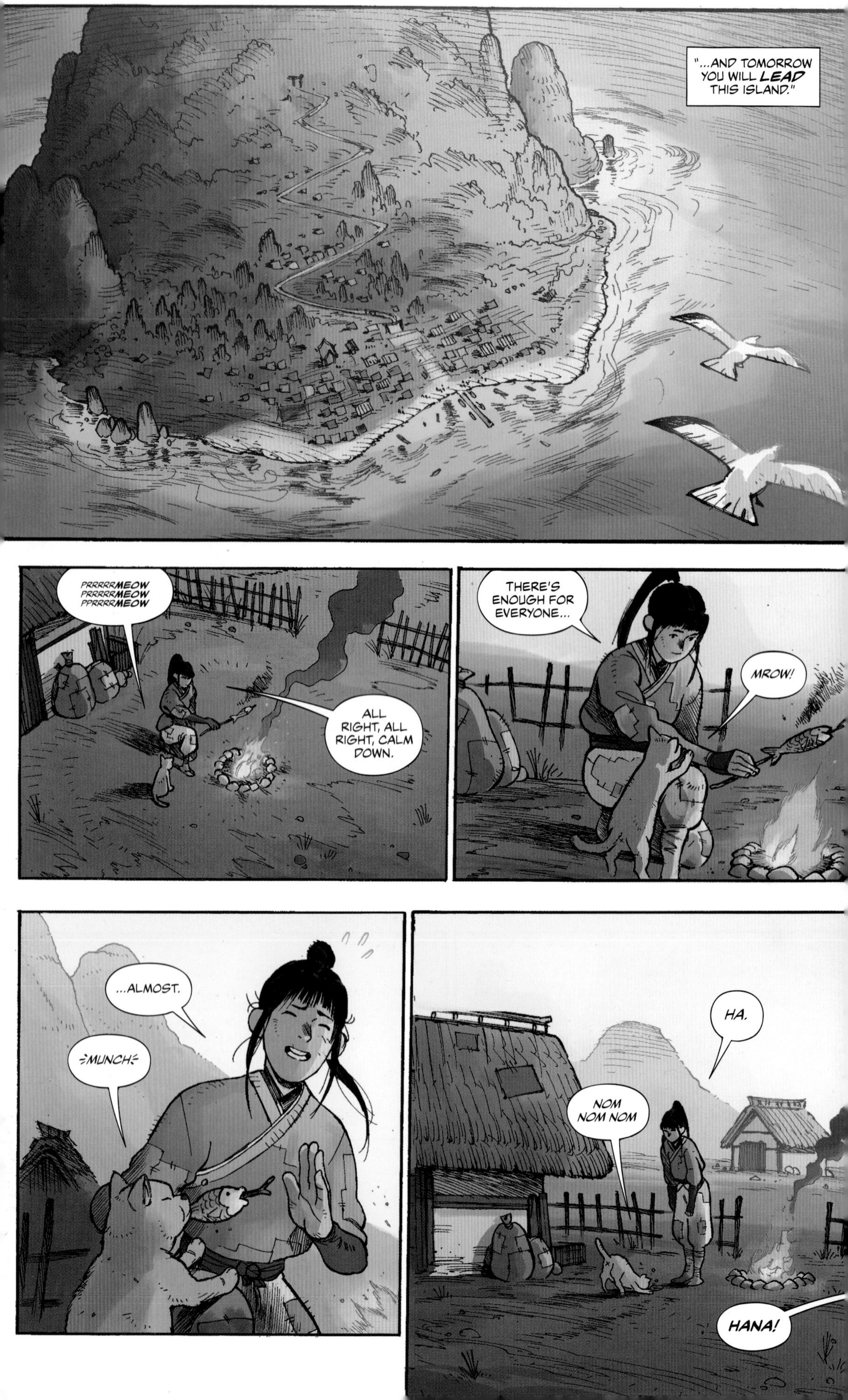
"...AND TOMORROW YOU WILL LEAD THIS ISLAND."
PRRRRRMEOW PRRRRRMEOW PPRRRRMEOW
ALL RIGHT, ALL RIGHT, CALM DOWN.
THERE'S ENOUGH FOR EVERYONE...
MROW!
...ALMOST.
MUNCH
HA.
NOM NOM NOM
HANA!

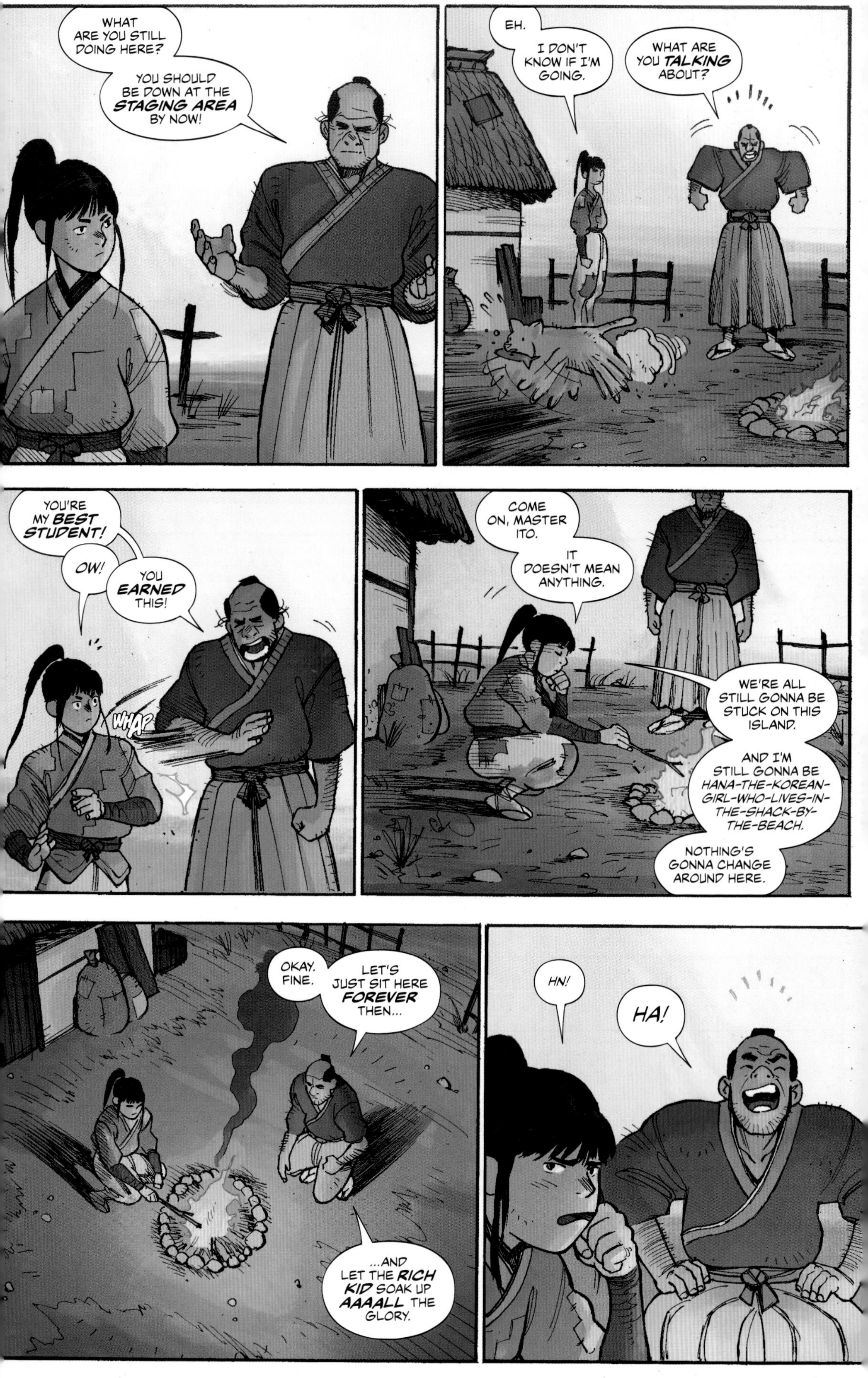

WHAT ARE YOU STILL DOING HERE?
YOU SHOULD BE DOWN AT THE STAGING AREA BY NOW!
EH.
I DON'T KNOW IF I'M GOING.
WHAT ARE YOU TALKING ABOUT?
YOU'RE MY BEST STUDENT!
OW!
YOU EARNED THIS!
WHAP
COME ON, MASTER ITO.
IT DOESN'T MEAN ANYTHING.
WE'RE ALL STILL GONNA BE STUCK ON THIS ISLAND.
AND I'M STILL GONNA BE HANA-THE-KOREAN-GIRL-WHO-LIVES-IN-THE-SHACK-BY-THE-BEACH.
NOTHING'S GONNA CHANGE AROUND HERE.
OKAY. FINE.
LET'S JUST SIT HERE FOREVER THEN...
...AND LET THE RICH KID SOAK UP AAAALL THE GLORY.
HN!
HA!

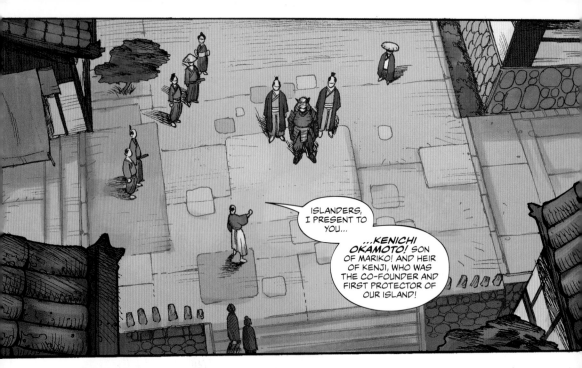

ISLANDERS, I PRESENT TO YOU...

...KENICHI OKAMOTO! SON OF MARIKO! AND HEIR OF KENJI, WHO WAS THE CO-FOUNDER AND FIRST PROTECTOR OF OUR ISLAND!

AND... ...HANA!

OVER TO YOU, ELDER JIN.

THANK YOU, MASTER ITO.

TODAY OUR TOP STUDENTS COMPETE FOR THE HONOR OF FIRST IN CLASS.

ONE OF THE MOST TREASURED TRADITIONS IN OUR SHORT HISTORY.

FOR WE WOULD NOT STAND HERE AS THE ONLY SURVIVORS OF THE GREAT WIND IF OUR FOUNDERS HAD NOT STRIVEN FOR EXCELLENCE...

...BUT ALWAYS REMEMBERED THE ISLAND WAY.

TOGETHER IN STRENGTH.

TOGETHER IN STRENGTH.

YOU LOOK LIKE YOU JUST ROLLED OUT OF BED.

YOU LOOK LIKE A BABY PLAYING DRESS UP.

THIS IS EMBARRASSING.

CAN'T YOU TAKE ANYTHING SERIOUSLY?

READY...

SURE. KICKING YOUR ASS.

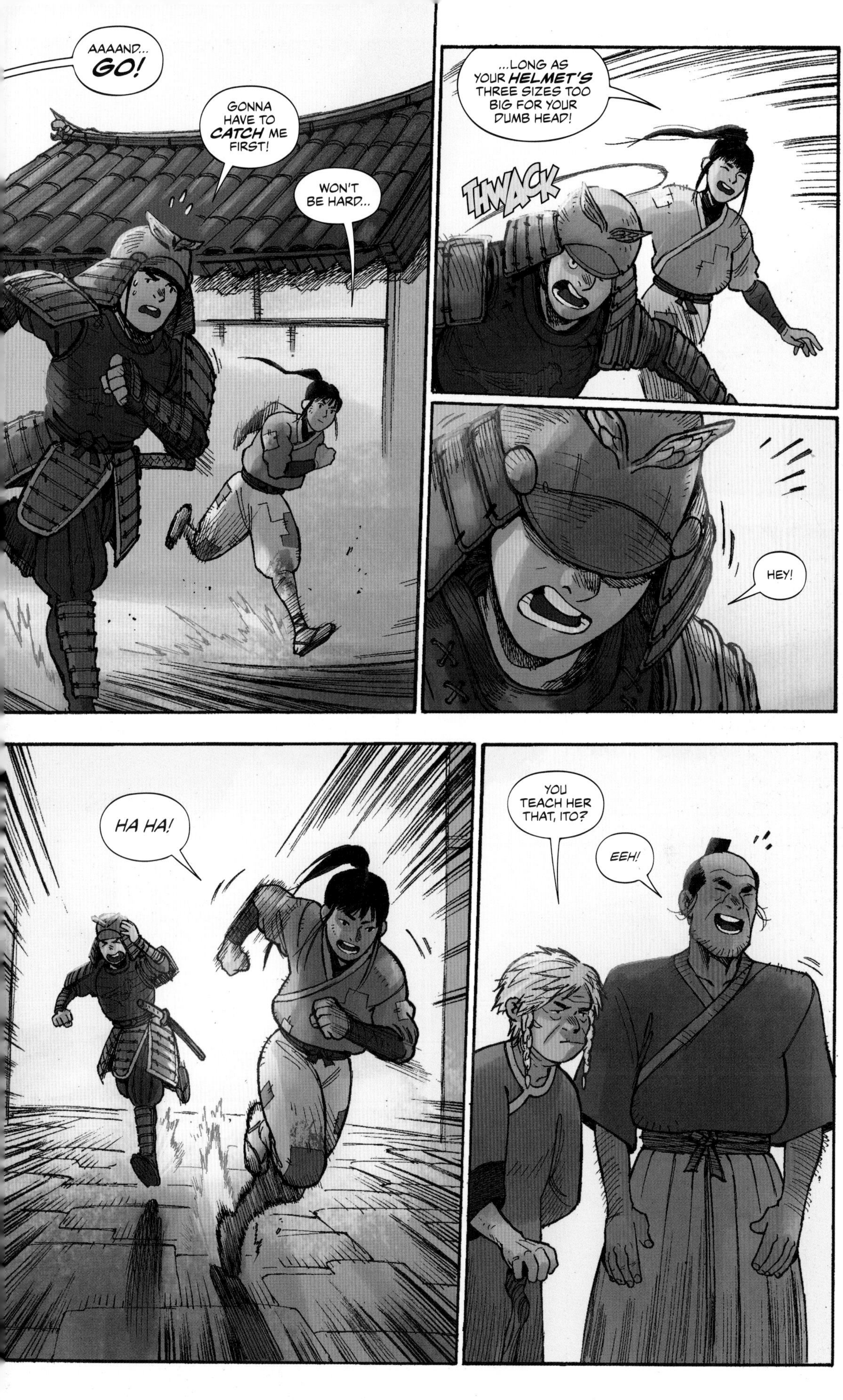
AAAAND... GO!
GONNA HAVE TO CATCH ME FIRST!
WON'T BE HARD...
...LONG AS YOUR HELMET'S THREE SIZES TOO BIG FOR YOUR DUMB HEAD!
THWACK
HEY!
HA HA!
YOU TEACH HER THAT, ITO?
EEH!

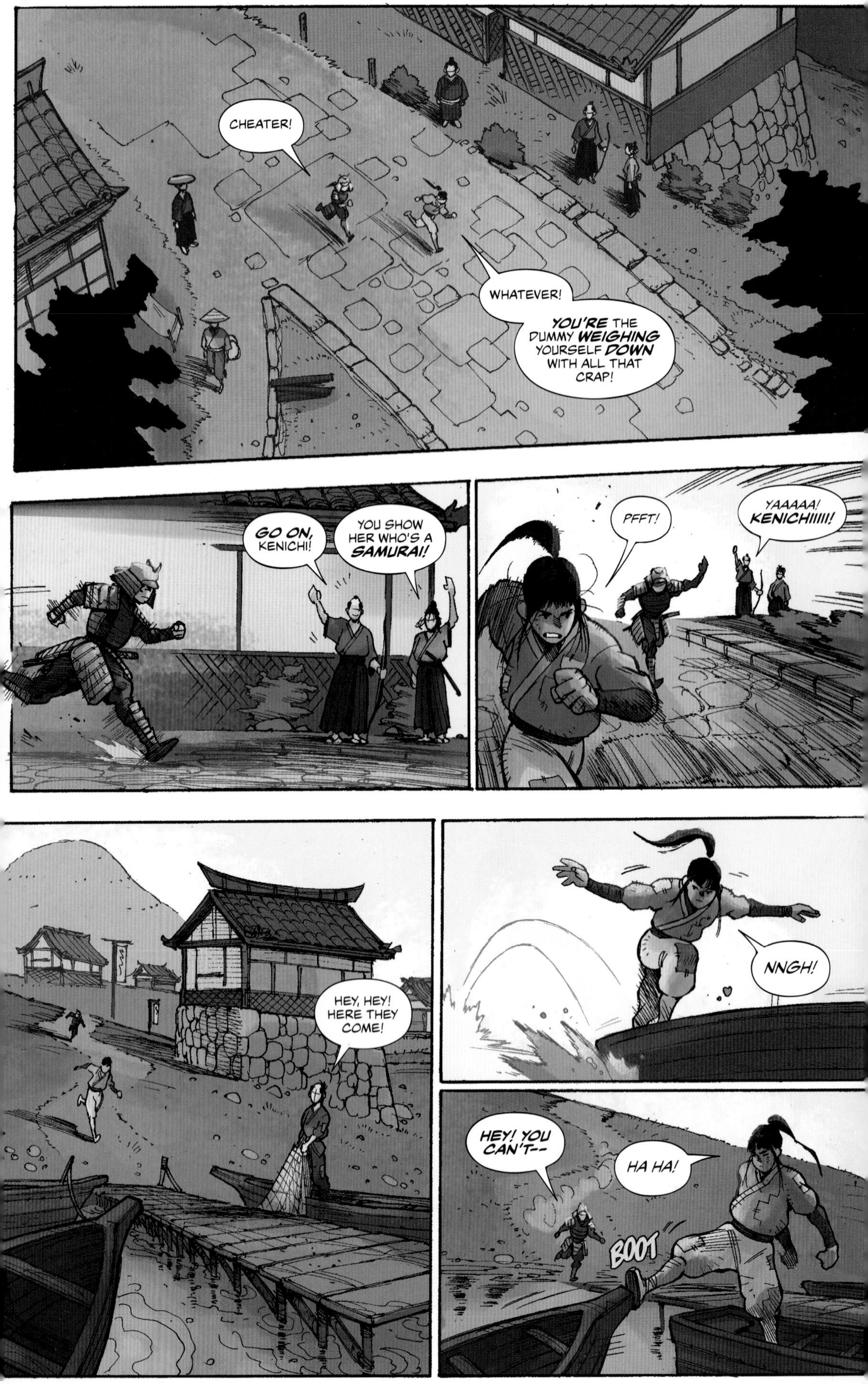
CHEATER!
WHATEVER!
YOU'RE THE DUMMY WEIGHING YOURSELF DOWN WITH ALL THAT CRAP!
GO ON, KENICHI!
YOU SHOW HER WHO'S A SAMURAI!
PFFT!
YAAAAA! KENICHIIIIII!
HEY, HEY! HERE THEY COME!
NNGH!
HEY! YOU CAN'T--
HA HA!
BOOT

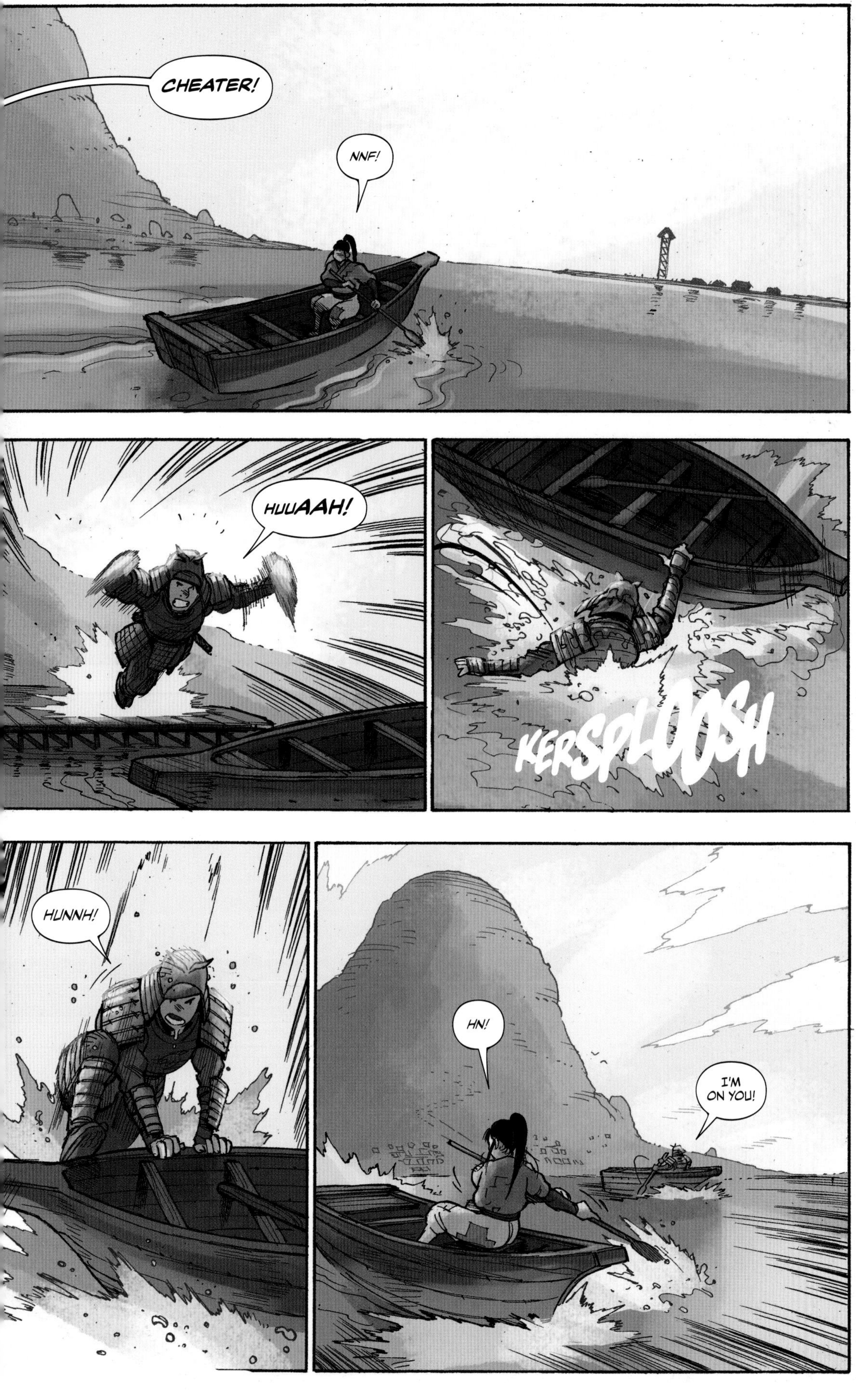
CHEATER!
NNF!
HUUAAH!
KERSPLOOSH
HUNNH!
HN!
I'M ON YOU!

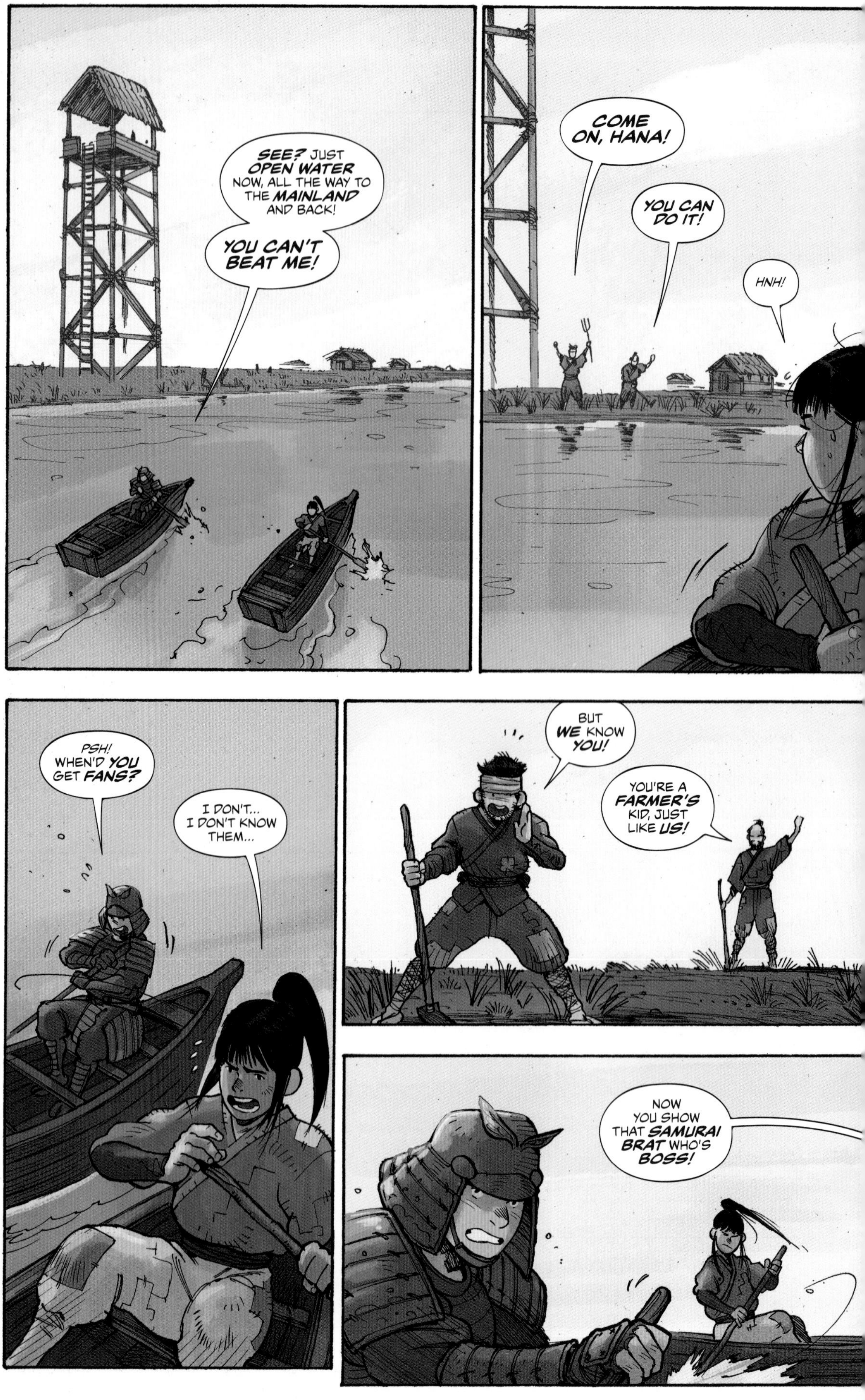

SEE? JUST OPEN WATER NOW, ALL THE WAY TO THE MAINLAND AND BACK!
YOU CAN'T BEAT ME!
COME ON, HANA!
YOU CAN DO IT!
HNH!
PSH! WHEN'D YOU GET FANS?
I DON'T... I DON'T KNOW THEM...
BUT WE KNOW YOU!
YOU'RE A FARMER'S KID, JUST LIKE US!
NOW YOU SHOW THAT SAMURAI BRAT WHO'S BOSS!

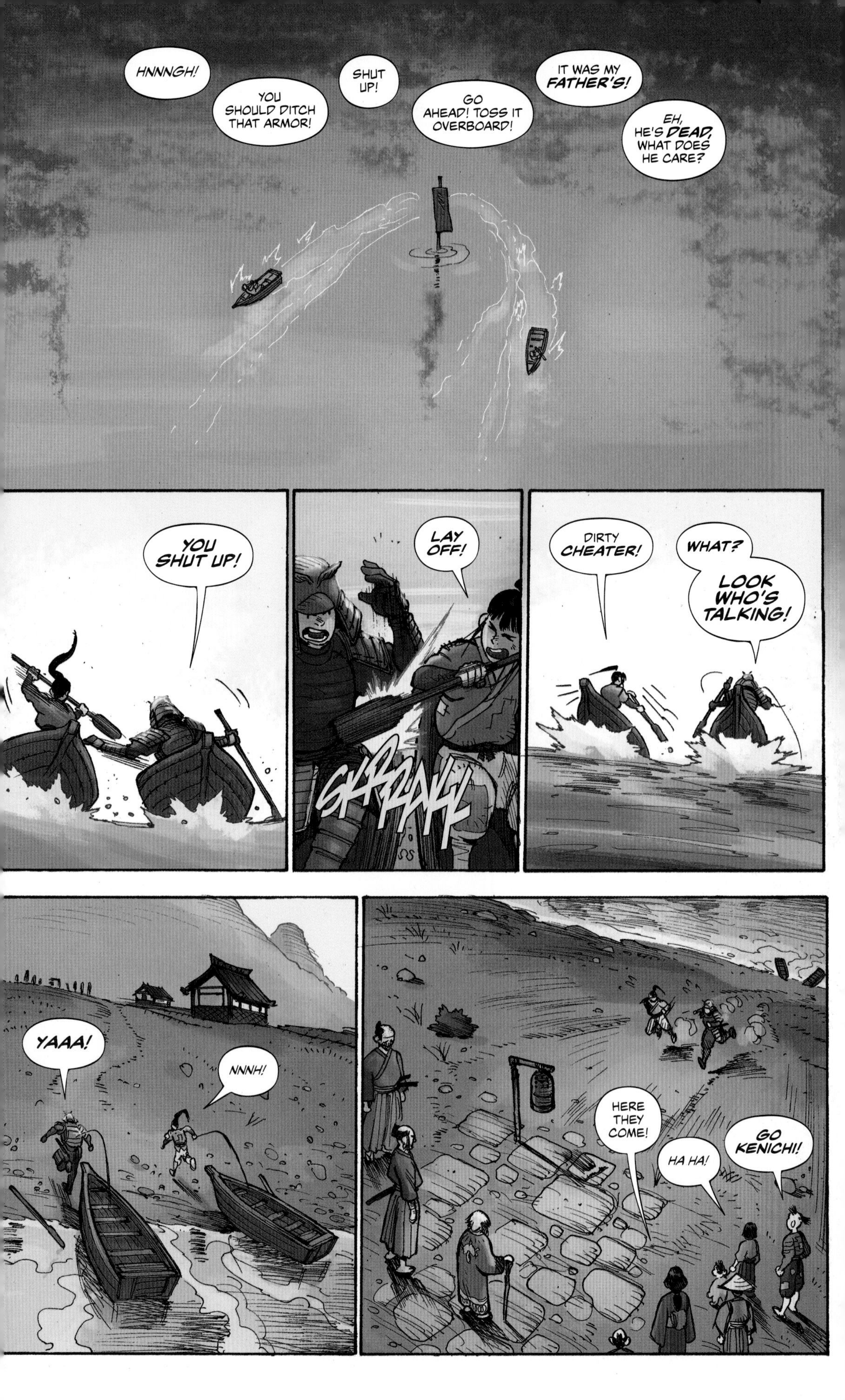
HNNNGH!
YOU SHOULD DITCH THAT ARMOR!
SHUT UP!
GO AHEAD! TOSS IT OVERBOARD!
IT WAS MY FATHER'S!
EH, HE'S DEAD, WHAT DOES HE CARE?
YOU SHUT UP!
LAY OFF!
SKRAK!
DIRTY CHEATER!
WHAT?
LOOK WHO'S TALKING!
YAAA!
NNNH!
HERE THEY COME!
HA HA!
GO KENICHI!

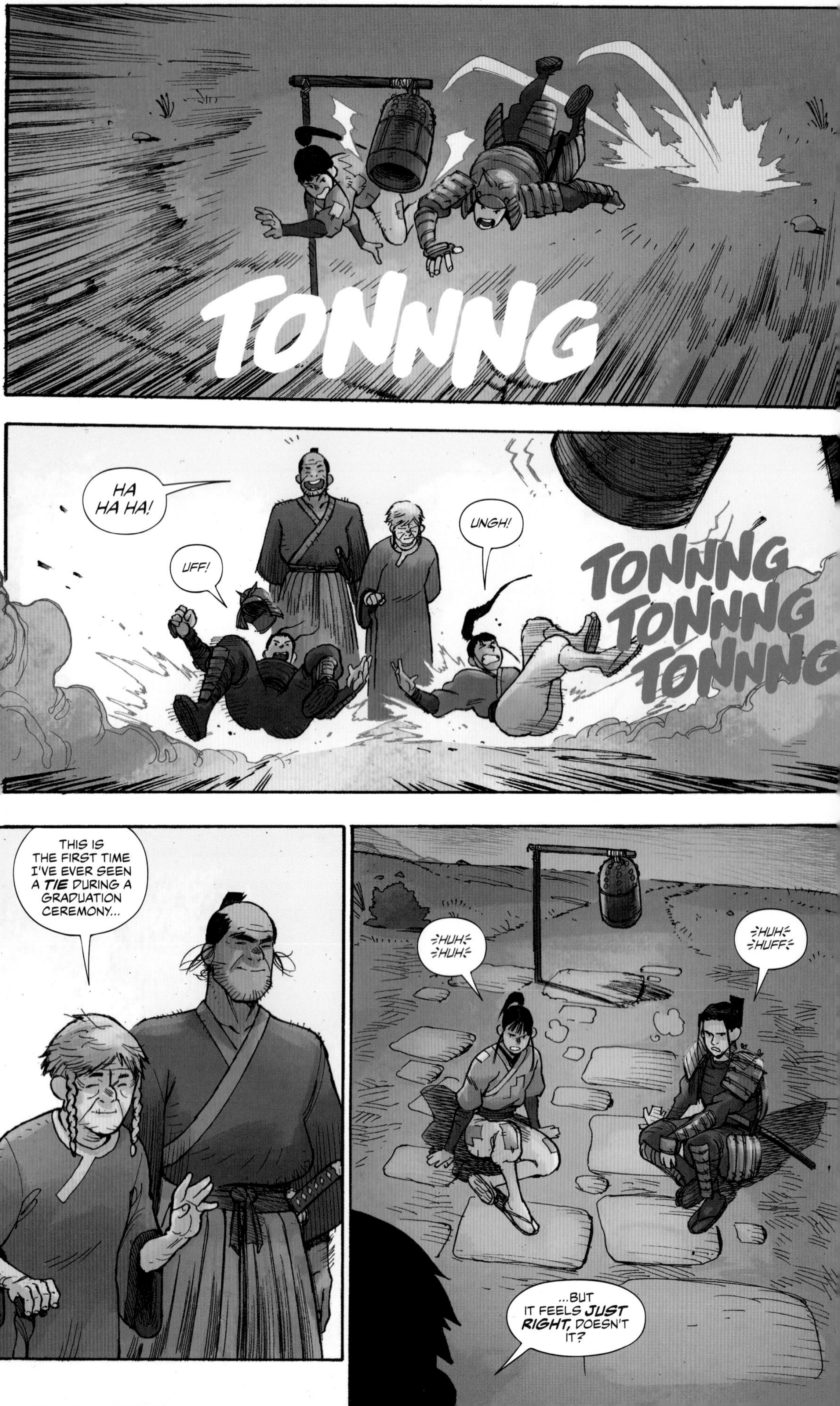
TONNNG
HA HA HA!
UFF!
UNGH!
TONNNG TONNNG TONNNG
THIS IS THE FIRST TIME I'VE EVER SEEN A TIE DURING A GRADUATION CEREMONY...
HUH HUH
HUH HUFF
...BUT IT FEELS JUST RIGHT, DOESN'T IT?

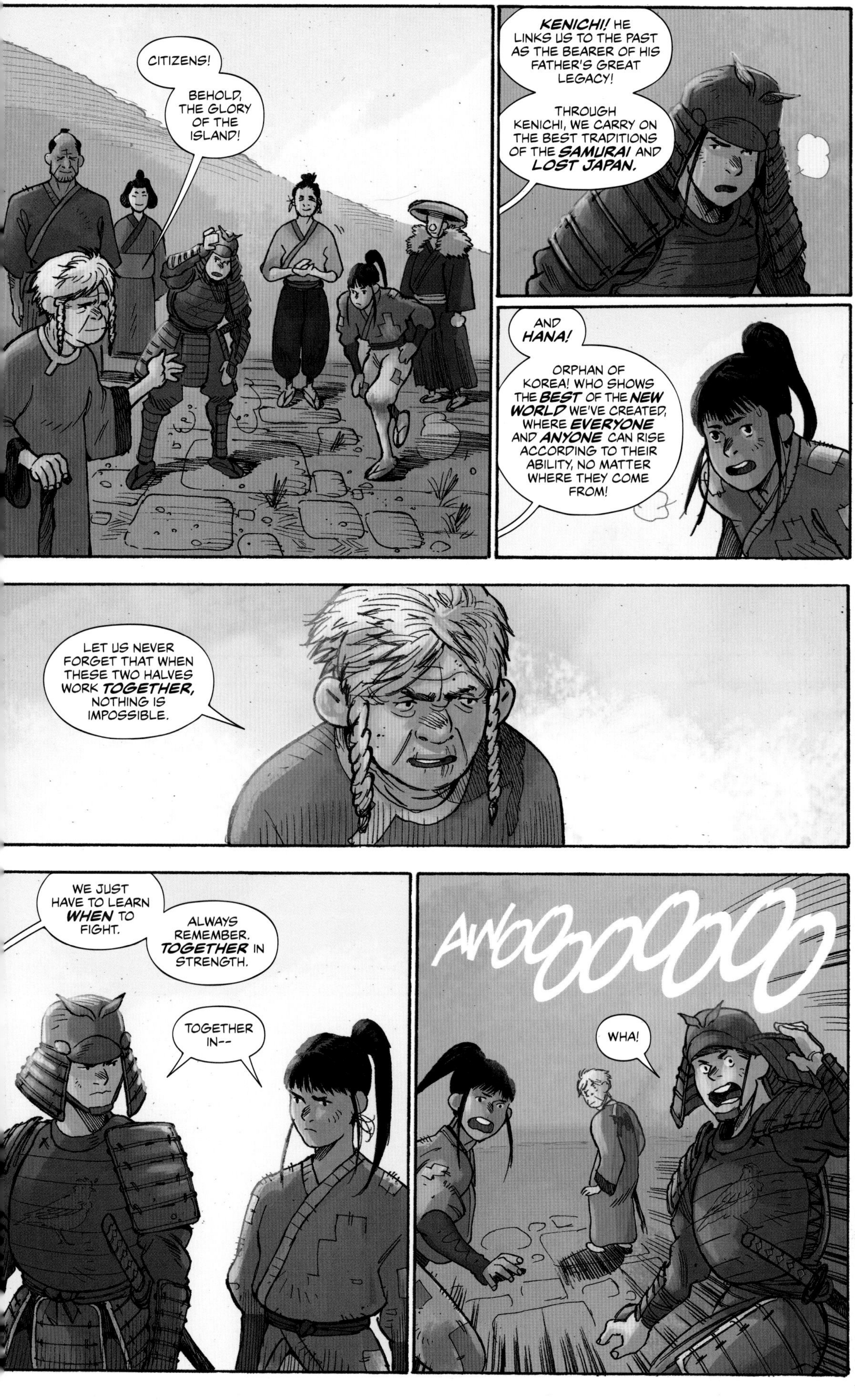
CITIZENS!
BEHOLD, THE GLORY OF THE ISLAND!
KENICHI! HE LINKS US TO THE PAST AS THE BEARER OF HIS FATHER'S GREAT LEGACY!
THROUGH KENICHI, WE CARRY ON THE BEST TRADITIONS OF THE SAMURAI AND LOST JAPAN.
AND HANA!
ORPHAN OF KOREA! WHO SHOWS THE BEST OF THE NEW WORLD WE'VE CREATED, WHERE EVERYONE AND ANYONE CAN RISE ACCORDING TO THEIR ABILITY, NO MATTER WHERE THEY COME FROM!
LET US NEVER FORGET THAT WHEN THESE TWO HALVES WORK TOGETHER, NOTHING IS IMPOSSIBLE.
WE JUST HAVE TO LEARN WHEN TO FIGHT.
ALWAYS REMEMBER. TOGETHER IN STRENGTH.
TOGETHER IN--
AWOOOOOOOOO
WHA!

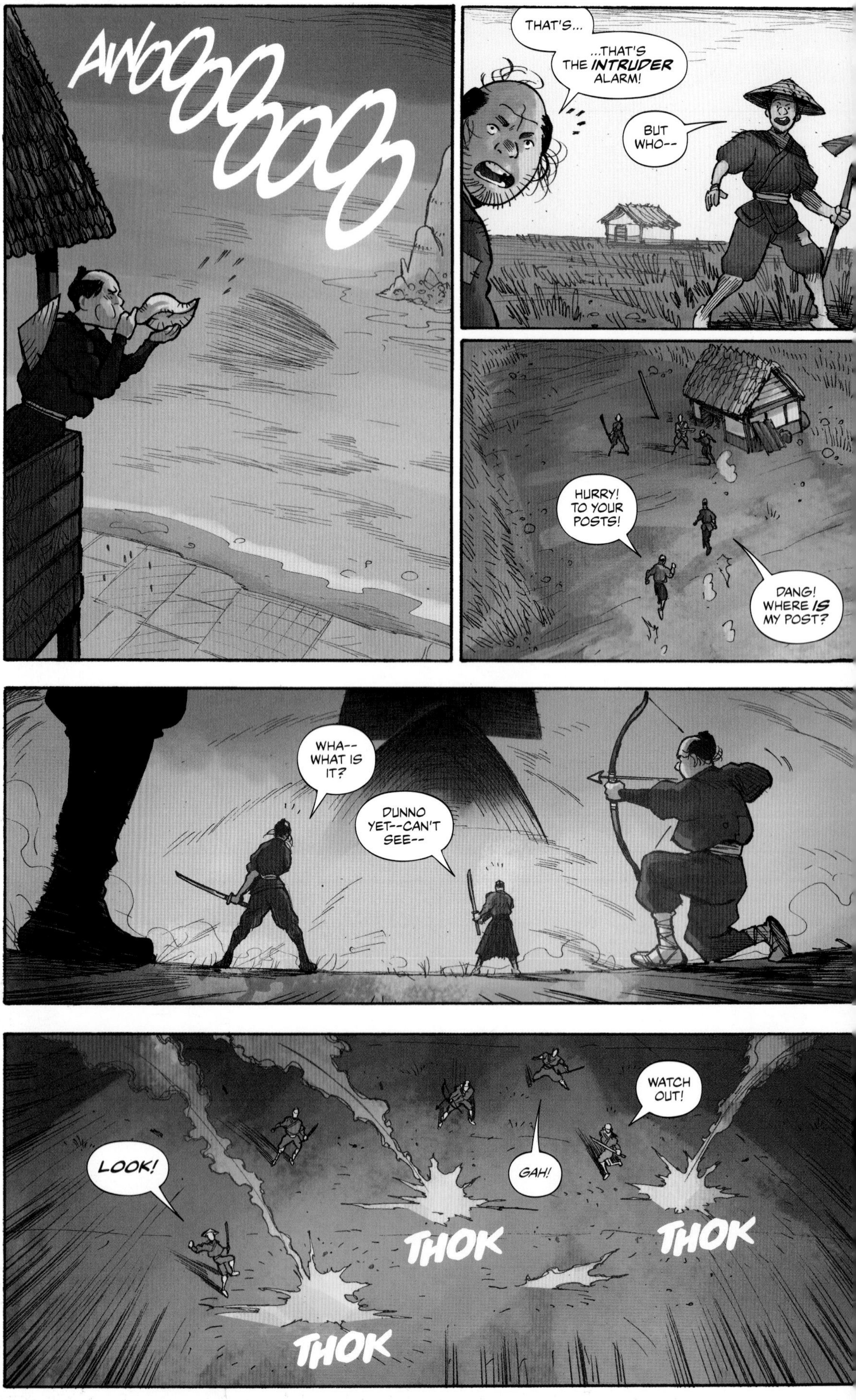
AWOOOOOOOO
THAT'S...
...THAT'S THE INTRUDER ALARM!
BUT WHO--
HURRY! TO YOUR POSTS!
DANG! WHERE IS MY POST?
WHA-- WHAT IS IT?
DUNNO YET--CAN'T SEE--
WATCH OUT!
GAH!
LOOK!
THOK
THOK
THOK

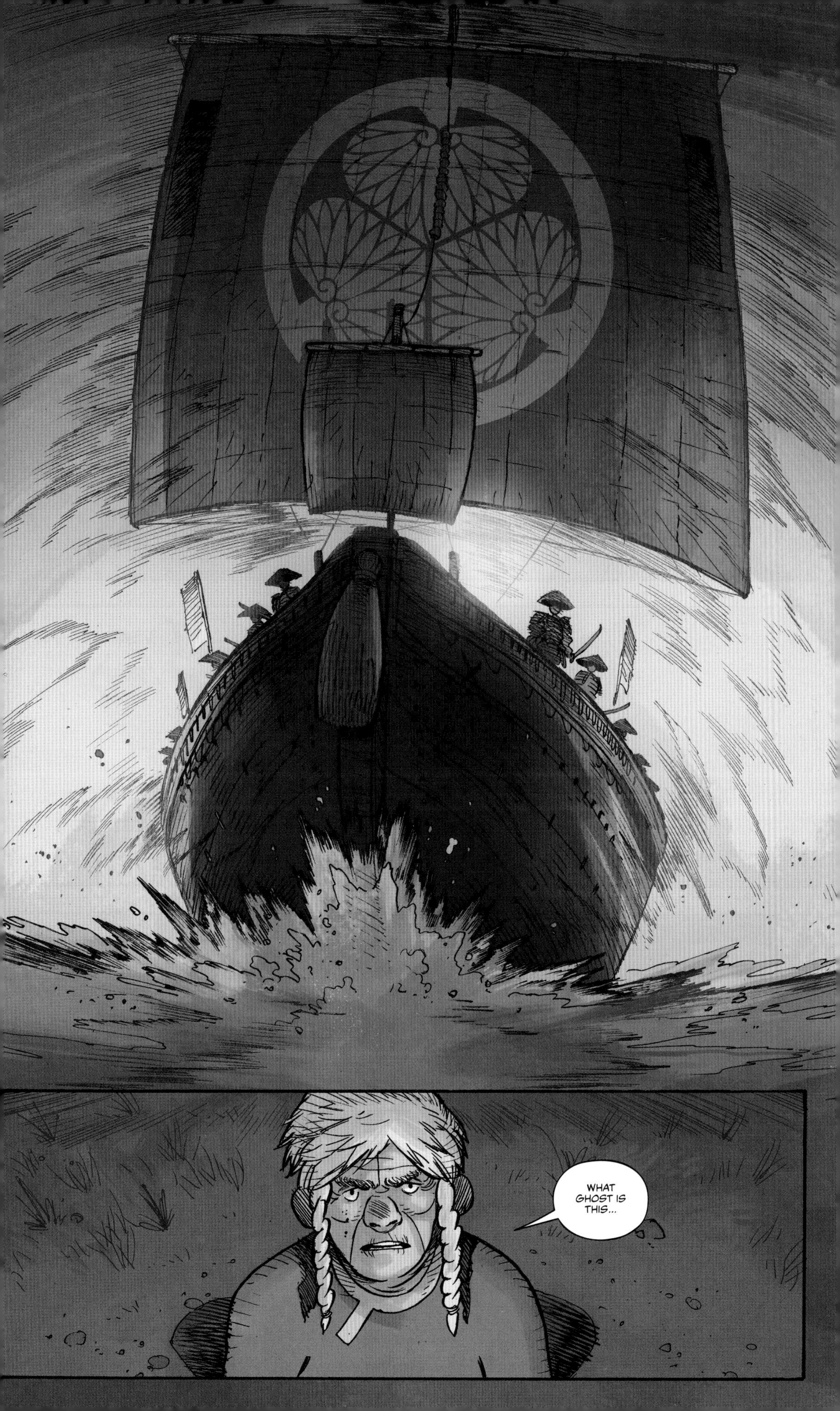
WHAT GHOST IS THIS...

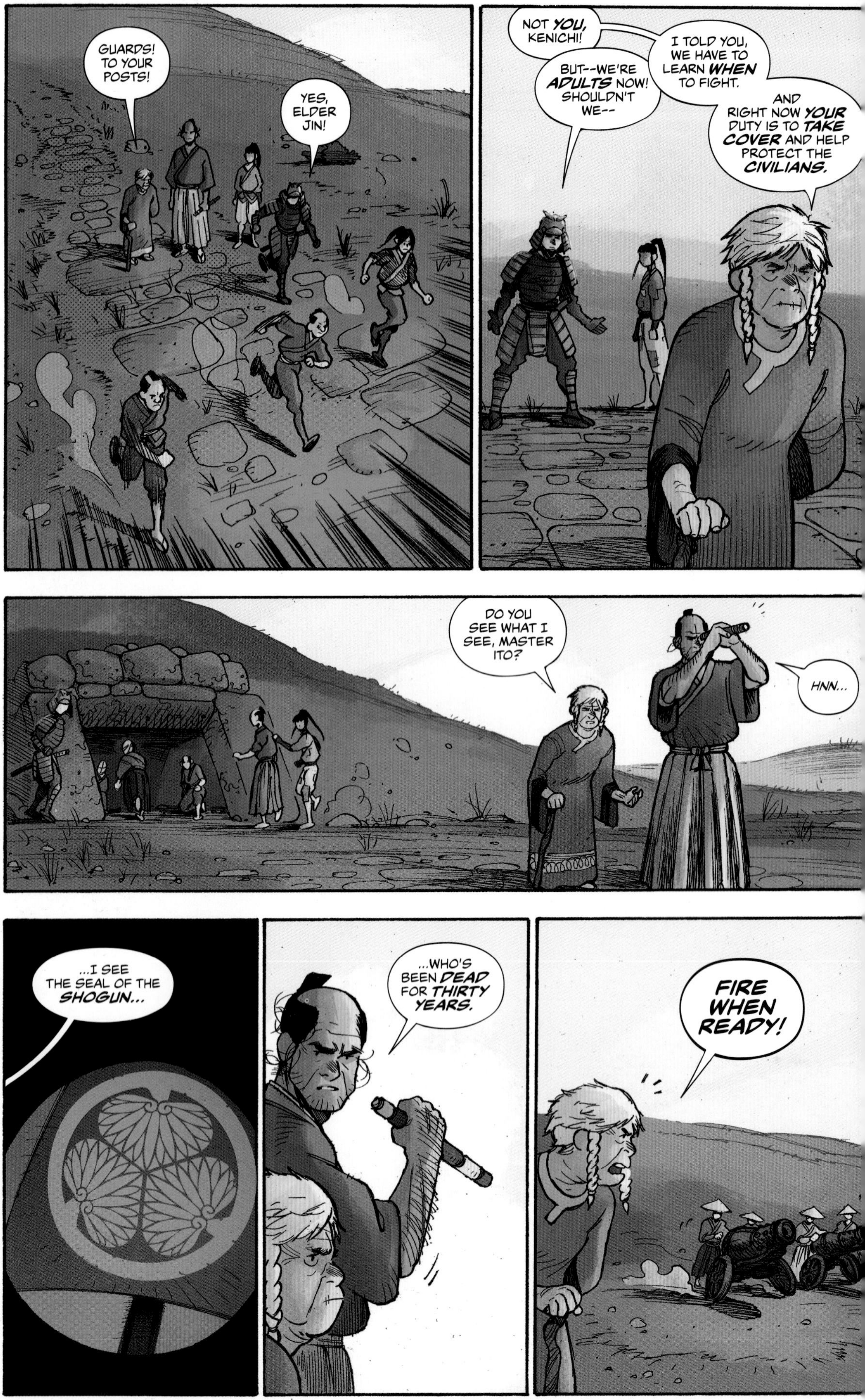
GUARDS! TO YOUR POSTS!
YES, ELDER JIN!
NOT YOU, KENICHI!
BUT--WE'RE ADULTS NOW! SHOULDN'T WE--
I TOLD YOU, WE HAVE TO LEARN WHEN TO FIGHT.
AND RIGHT NOW YOUR DUTY IS TO TAKE COVER AND HELP PROTECT THE CIVILIANS.
DO YOU SEE WHAT I SEE, MASTER ITO?
HNN...
...I SEE THE SEAL OF THE SHOGUN...
...WHO'S BEEN DEAD FOR THIRTY YEARS.
FIRE WHEN READY!

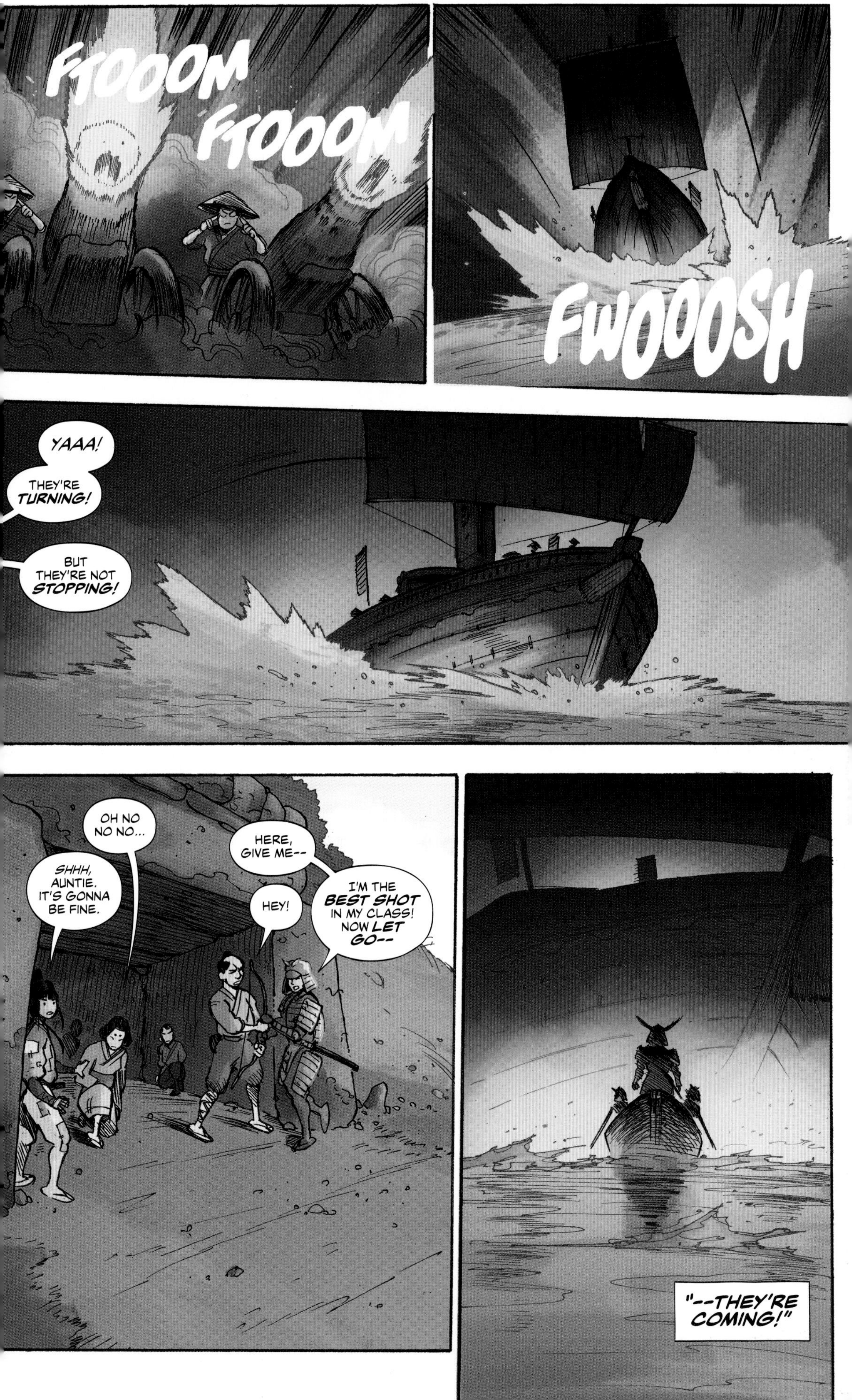
FTOOOM
FTOOOM
FWOOOSH
YAAA!
THEY'RE TURNING!
BUT THEY'RE NOT STOPPING!
OH NO NO NO...
SHHH, AUNTIE. IT'S GONNA BE FINE.
HERE, GIVE ME--
HEY!
I'M THE BEST SHOT IN MY CLASS! NOW LET GO--
"--THEY'RE COMING!"

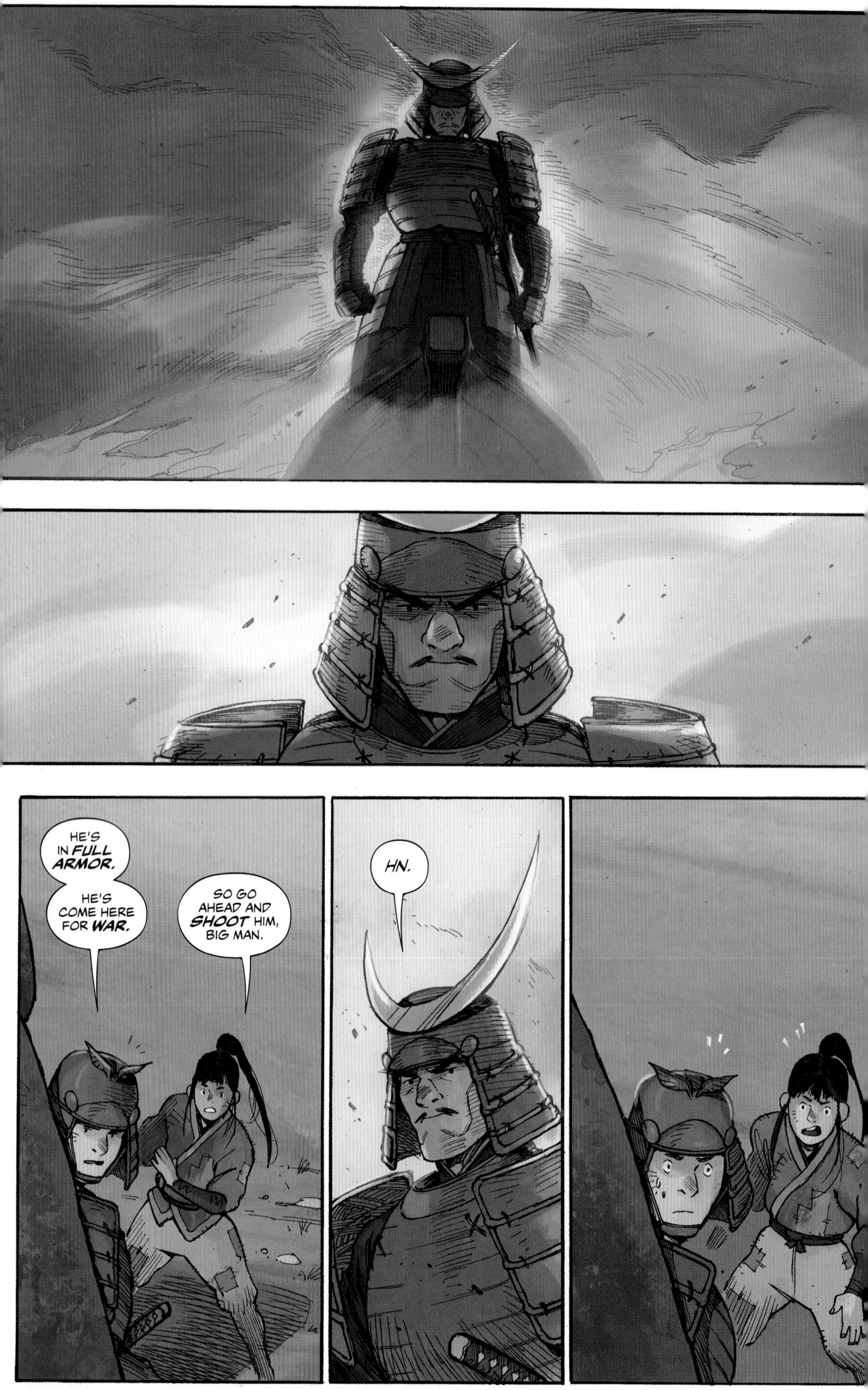

HE'S IN FULL ARMOR.
HE'S COME HERE FOR WAR.
SO GO AHEAD AND SHOOT HIM, BIG MAN.
HN.

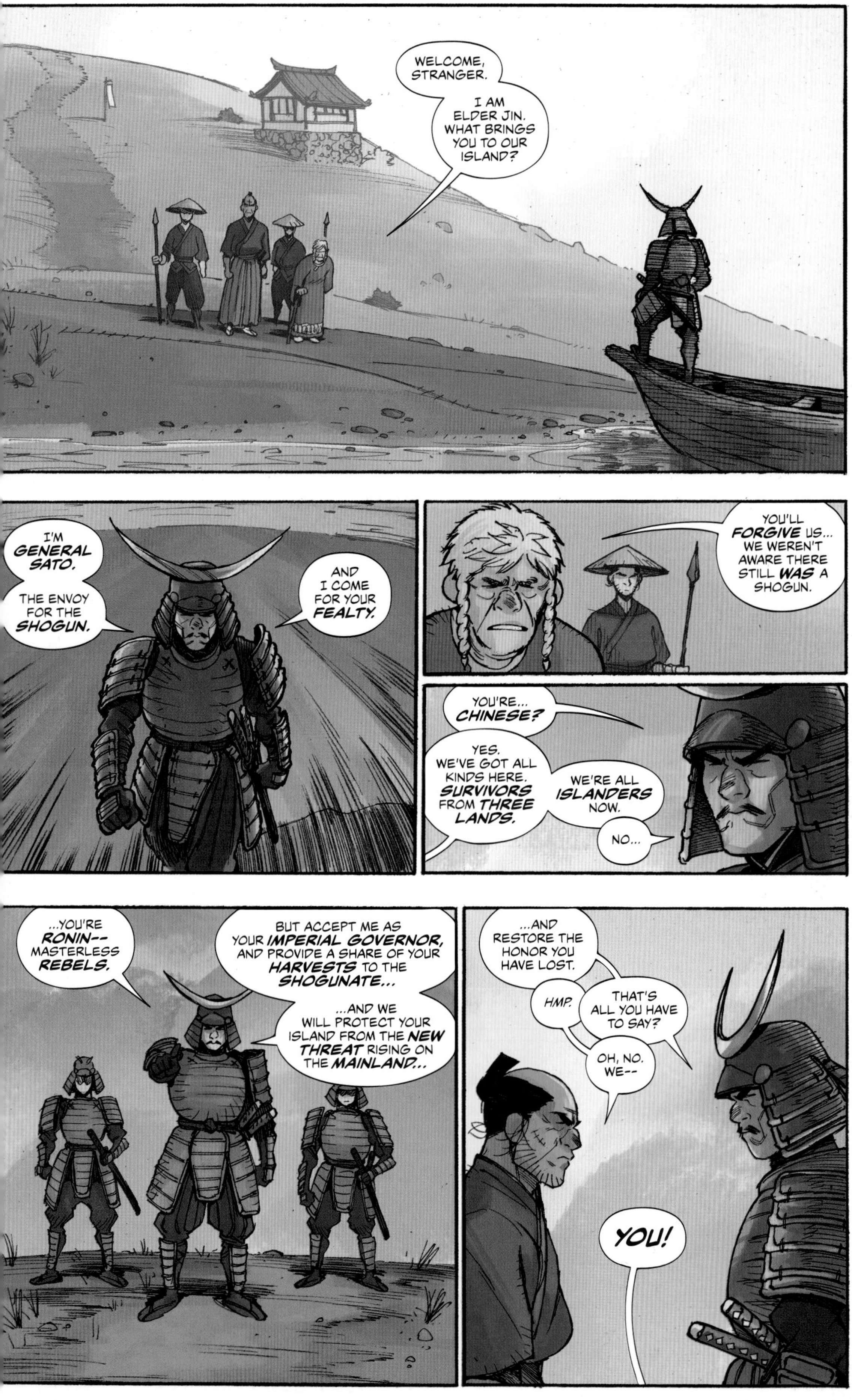
WELCOME, STRANGER.
I AM ELDER JIN. WHAT BRINGS YOU TO OUR ISLAND?
I'M GENERAL SATO.
THE ENVOY FOR THE SHOGUN.
AND I COME FOR YOUR FEALTY.
YOU'LL FORGIVE US... WE WEREN'T AWARE THERE STILL WAS A SHOGUN.
YOU'RE... CHINESE?
YES. WE'VE GOT ALL KINDS HERE. SURVIVORS FROM THREE LANDS.
WE'RE ALL ISLANDERS NOW.
NO...
...YOU'RE RONIN-- MASTERLESS REBELS.
BUT ACCEPT ME AS YOUR IMPERIAL GOVERNOR, AND PROVIDE A SHARE OF YOUR HARVESTS TO THE SHOGUNATE...
...AND WE WILL PROTECT YOUR ISLAND FROM THE NEW THREAT RISING ON THE MAINLAND...
...AND RESTORE THE HONOR YOU HAVE LOST.
HMP.
THAT'S ALL YOU HAVE TO SAY?
OH, NO. WE--
YOU!

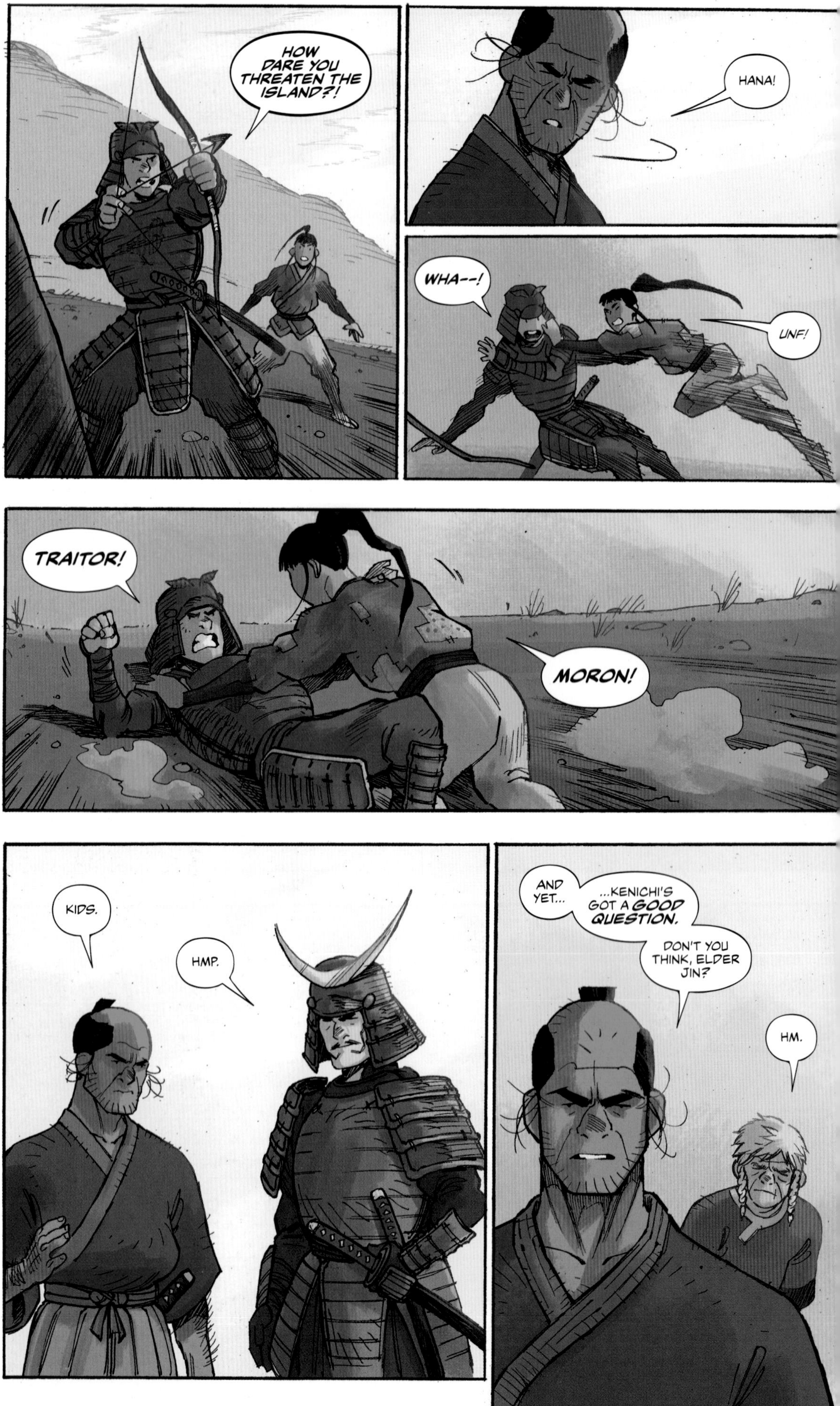
HOW DARE YOU THREATEN THE ISLAND?!
HANA!
WHA--!
UNF!
TRAITOR!
MORON!
KIDS.
HMP.
AND YET...
...KENICHI'S GOT A GOOD QUESTION.
DON'T YOU THINK, ELDER JIN?
HM.

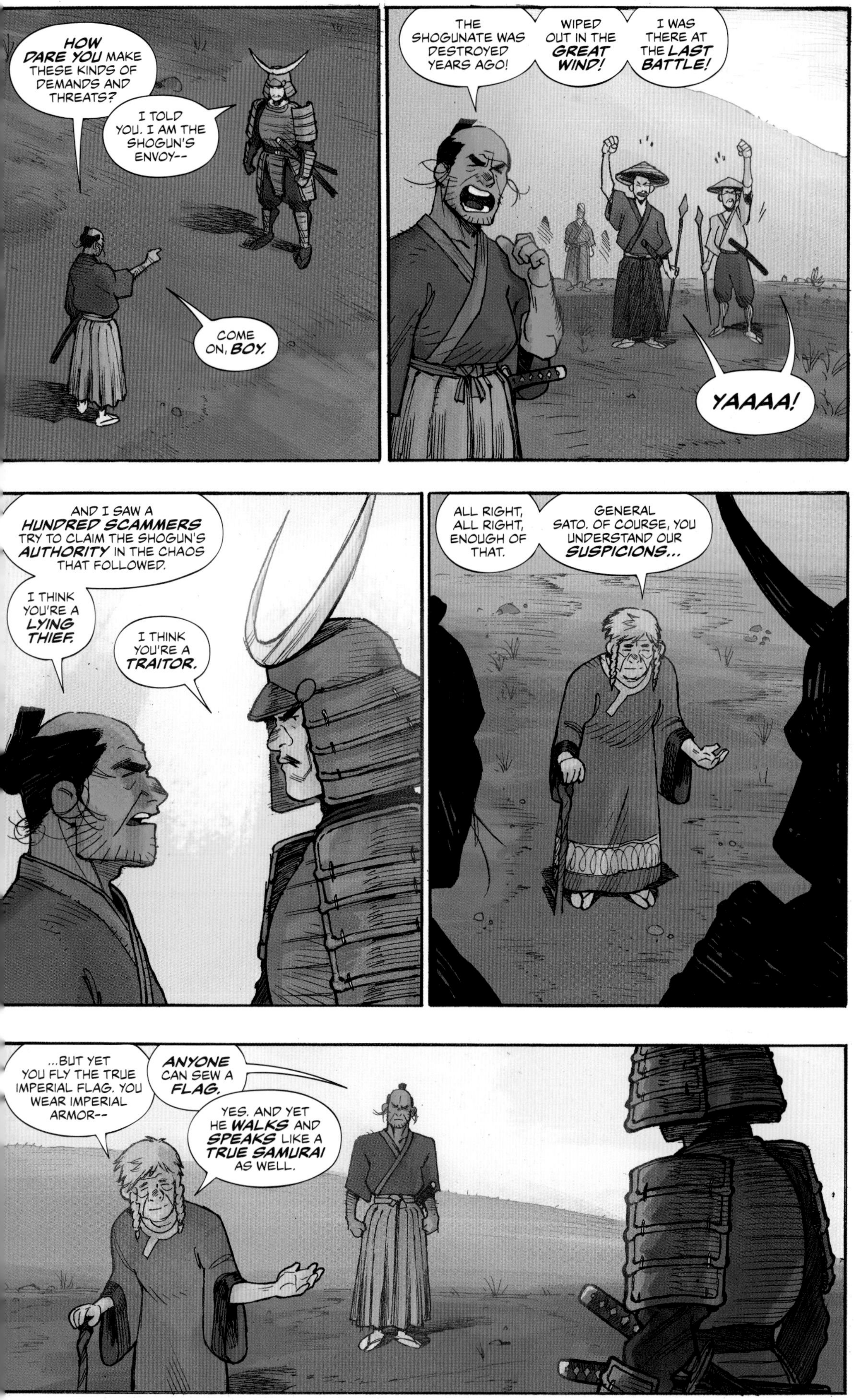
HOW DARE YOU MAKE THESE KINDS OF DEMANDS AND THREATS?
I TOLD YOU. I AM THE SHOGUN'S ENVOY--
COME ON, BOY.
THE SHOGUNATE WAS DESTROYED YEARS AGO!
WIPED OUT IN THE GREAT WIND!
I WAS THERE AT THE LAST BATTLE!
YAAAA!
AND I SAW A HUNDRED SCAMMERS TRY TO CLAIM THE SHOGUN'S AUTHORITY IN THE CHAOS THAT FOLLOWED.
I THINK YOU'RE A LYING THIEF.
I THINK YOU'RE A TRAITOR.
ALL RIGHT, ALL RIGHT, ENOUGH OF THAT.
GENERAL SATO. OF COURSE, YOU UNDERSTAND OUR SUSPICIONS...
...BUT YET YOU FLY THE TRUE IMPERIAL FLAG. YOU WEAR IMPERIAL ARMOR--
ANYONE CAN SEW A FLAG.
YES. AND YET HE WALKS AND SPEAKS LIKE A TRUE SAMURAI AS WELL.

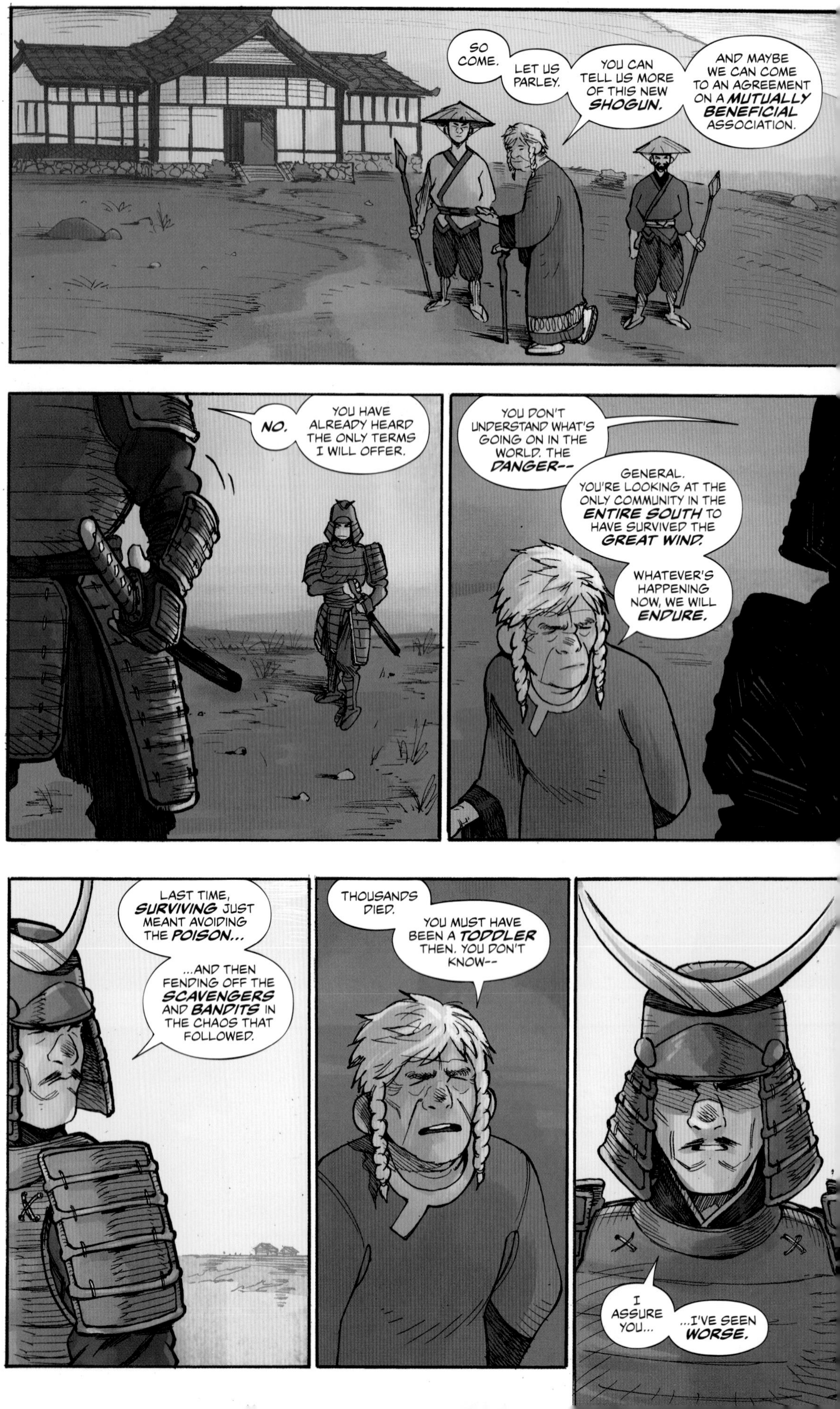
SO COME.
LET US PARLEY.
YOU CAN TELL US MORE OF THIS NEW SHOGUN.
AND MAYBE WE CAN COME TO AN AGREEMENT ON A MUTUALLY BENEFICIAL ASSOCIATION.
NO.
YOU HAVE ALREADY HEARD THE ONLY TERMS I WILL OFFER.
YOU DON'T UNDERSTAND WHAT'S GOING ON IN THE WORLD. THE DANGER--
GENERAL. YOU'RE LOOKING AT THE ONLY COMMUNITY IN THE ENTIRE SOUTH TO HAVE SURVIVED THE GREAT WIND.
WHATEVER'S HAPPENING NOW, WE WILL ENDURE.
LAST TIME, SURVIVING JUST MEANT AVOIDING THE POISON...
...AND THEN FENDING OFF THE SCAVENGERS AND BANDITS IN THE CHAOS THAT FOLLOWED.
THOUSANDS DIED.
YOU MUST HAVE BEEN A TODDLER THEN. YOU DON'T KNOW--
I ASSURE YOU...
...I'VE SEEN WORSE.

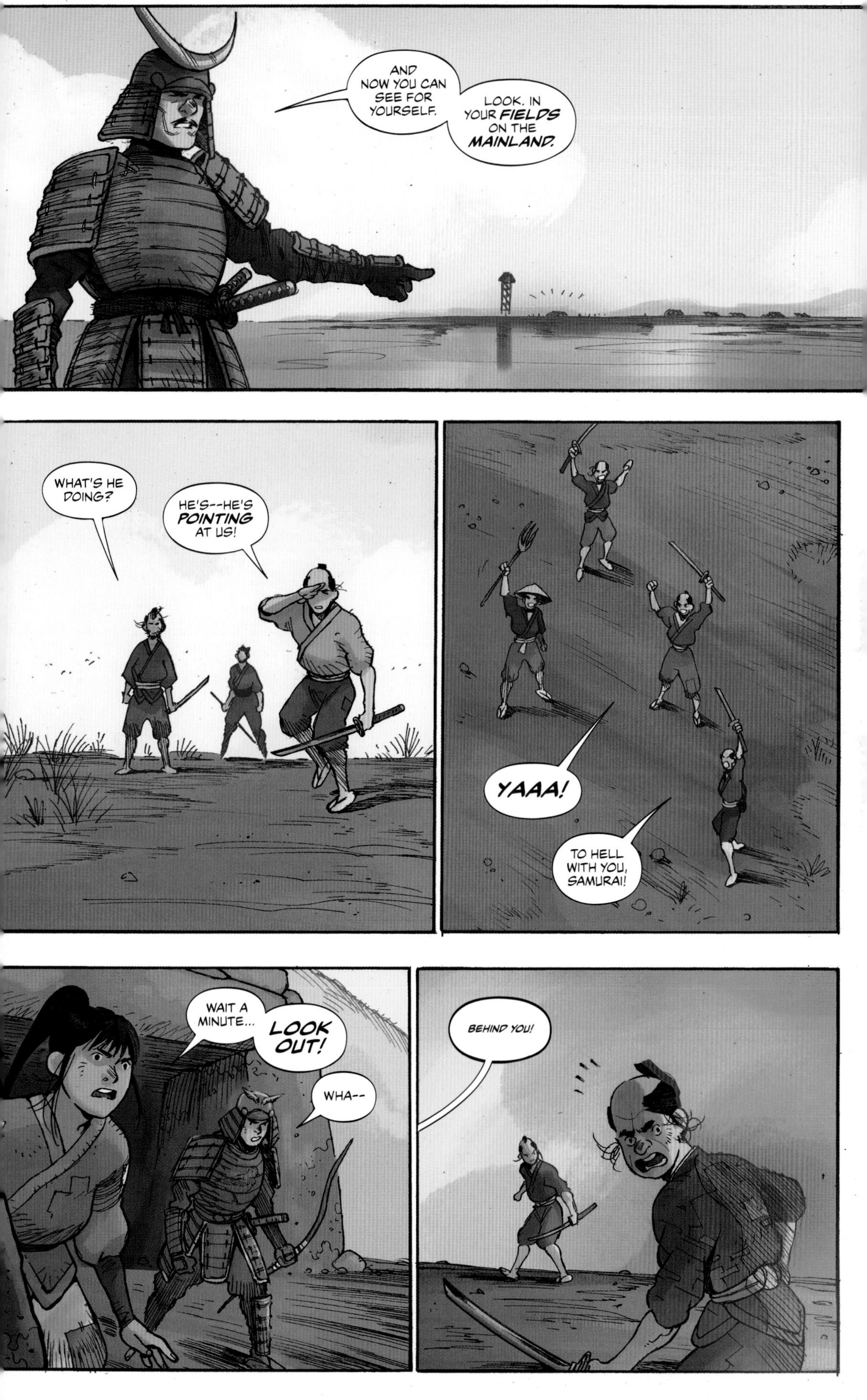
AND NOW YOU CAN SEE FOR YOURSELF.
LOOK. IN YOUR FIELDS ON THE MAINLAND.
WHAT'S HE DOING?
HE'S--HE'S POINTING AT US!
YAAA!
TO HELL WITH YOU, SAMURAI!
WAIT A MINUTE...
LOOK OUT!
WHA--
BEHIND YOU!

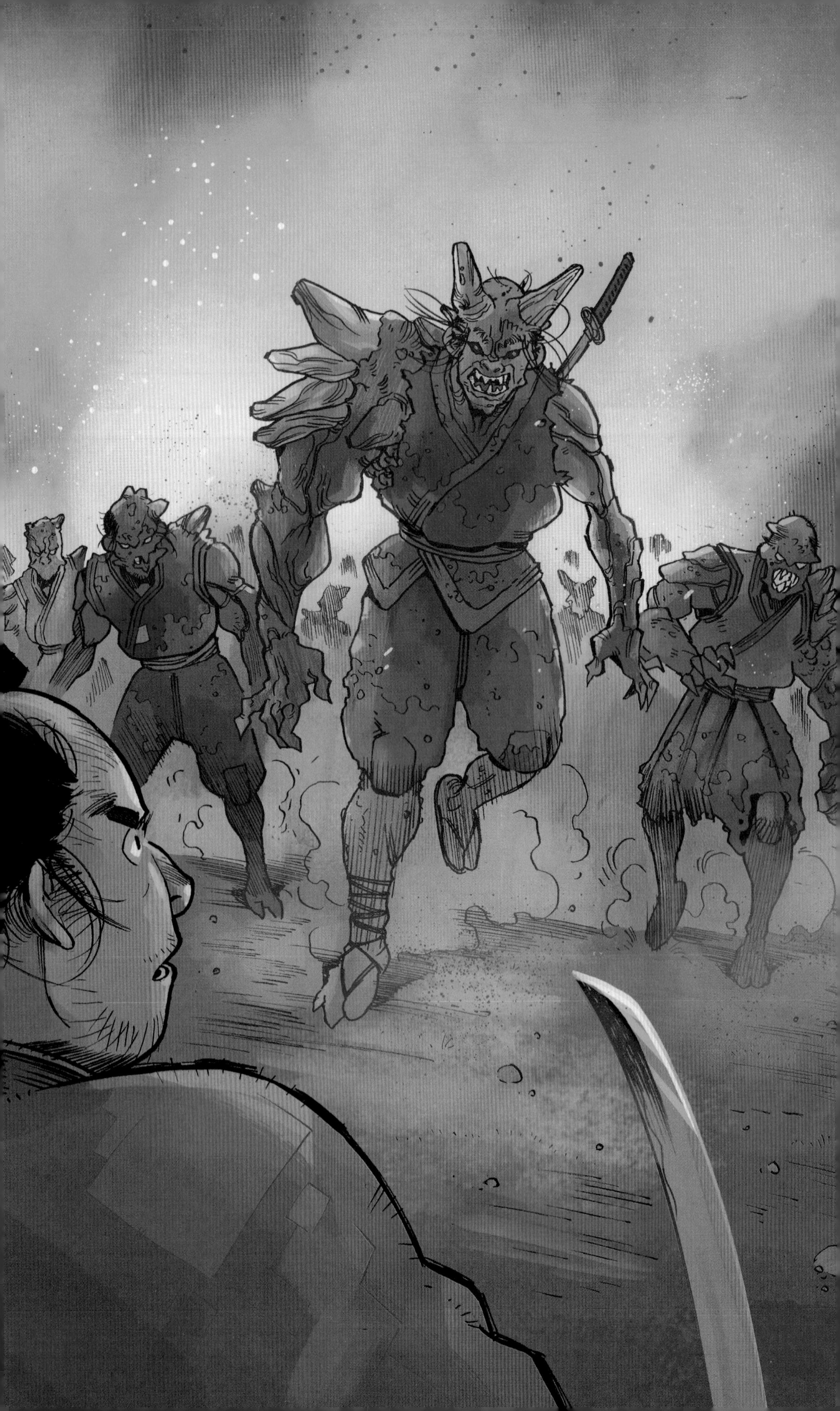

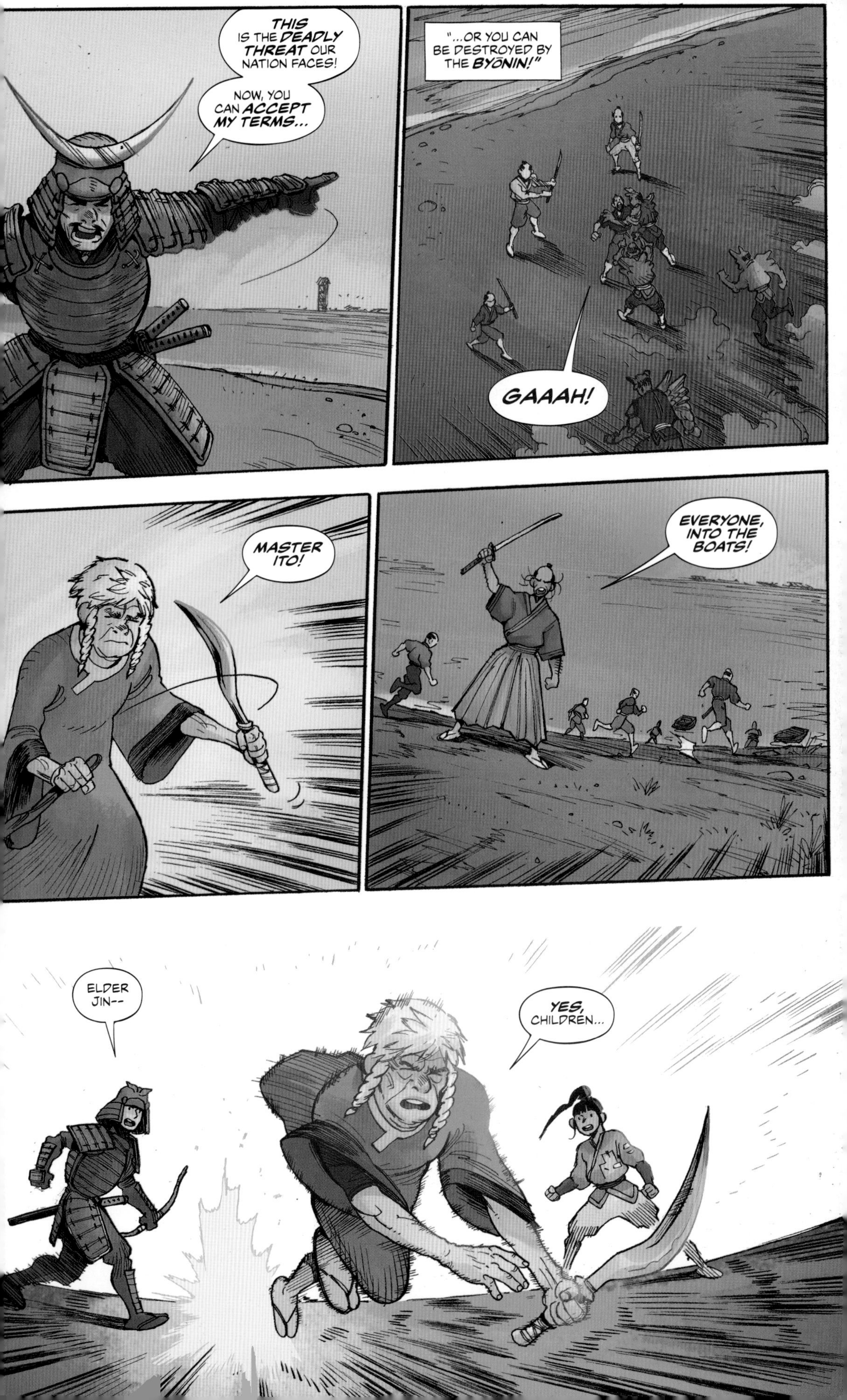
THIS IS THE DEADLY THREAT OUR NATION FACES!
NOW, YOU CAN ACCEPT MY TERMS...
"...OR YOU CAN BE DESTROYED BY THE BYŌNIN!"
GAAAH!
MASTER ITO!
EVERYONE, INTO THE BOATS!
ELDER JIN--
YES, CHILDREN...

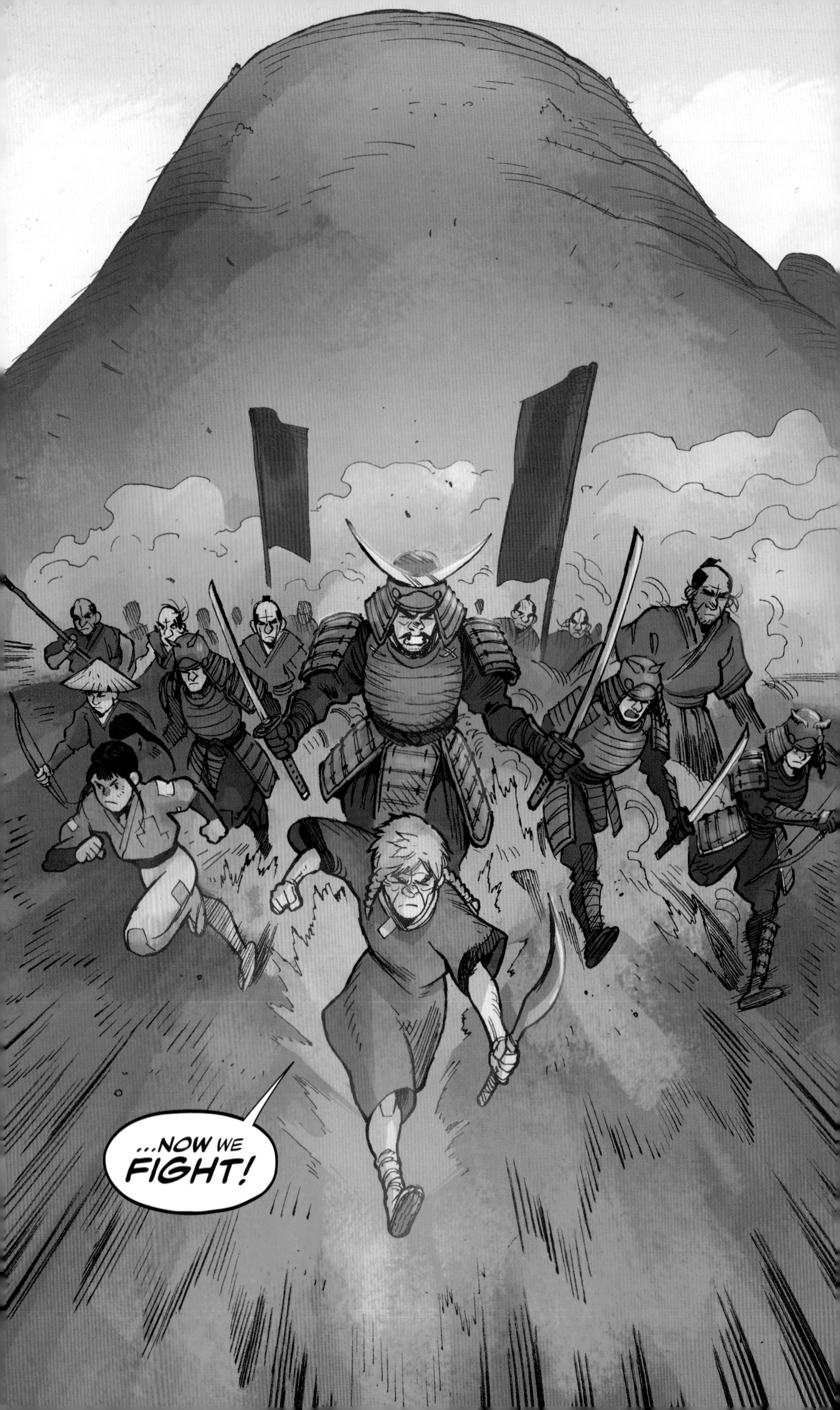
...NOW WE FIGHT!

Issue One Cover by **Ethan Young**

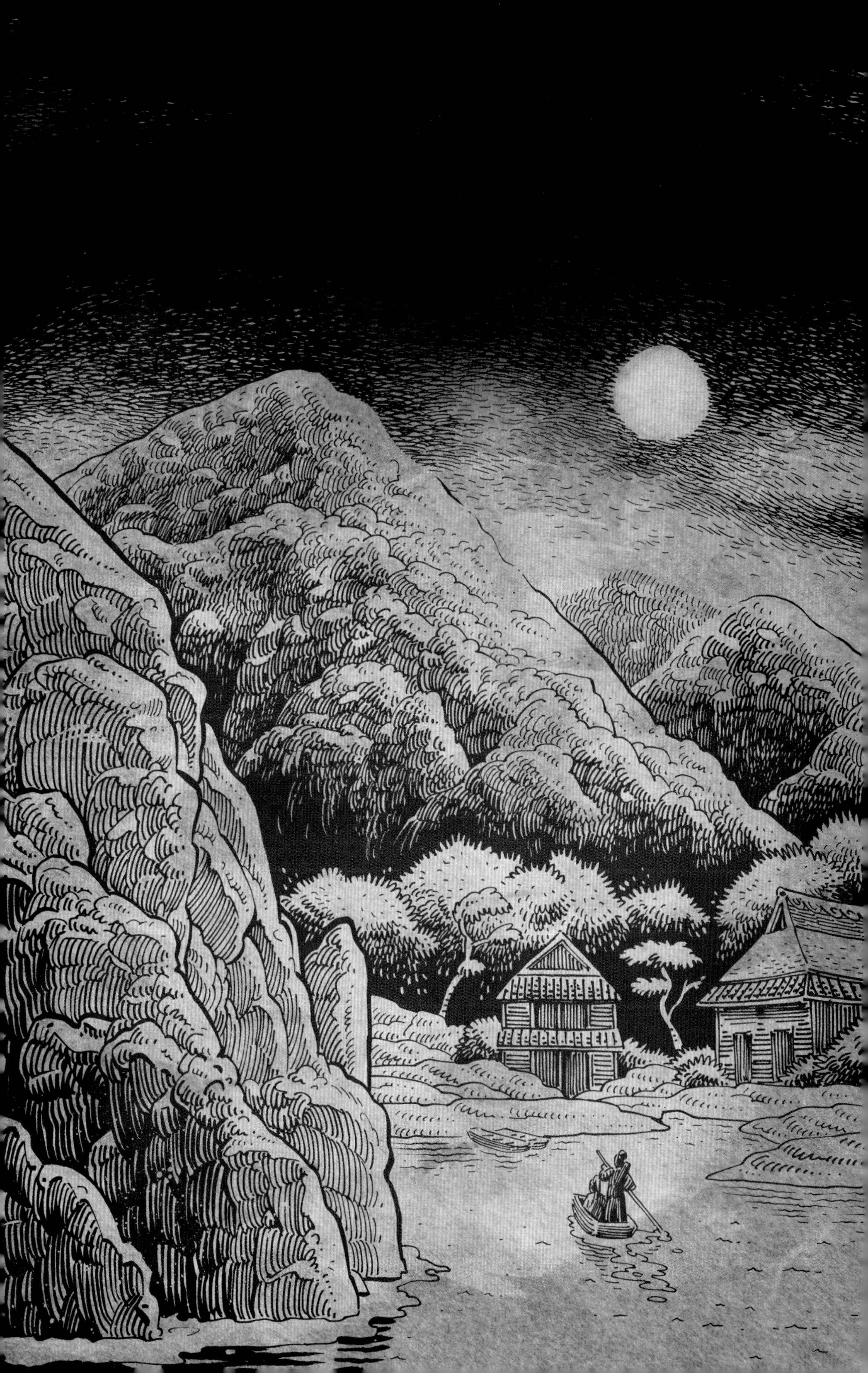

CHAPTER TWO

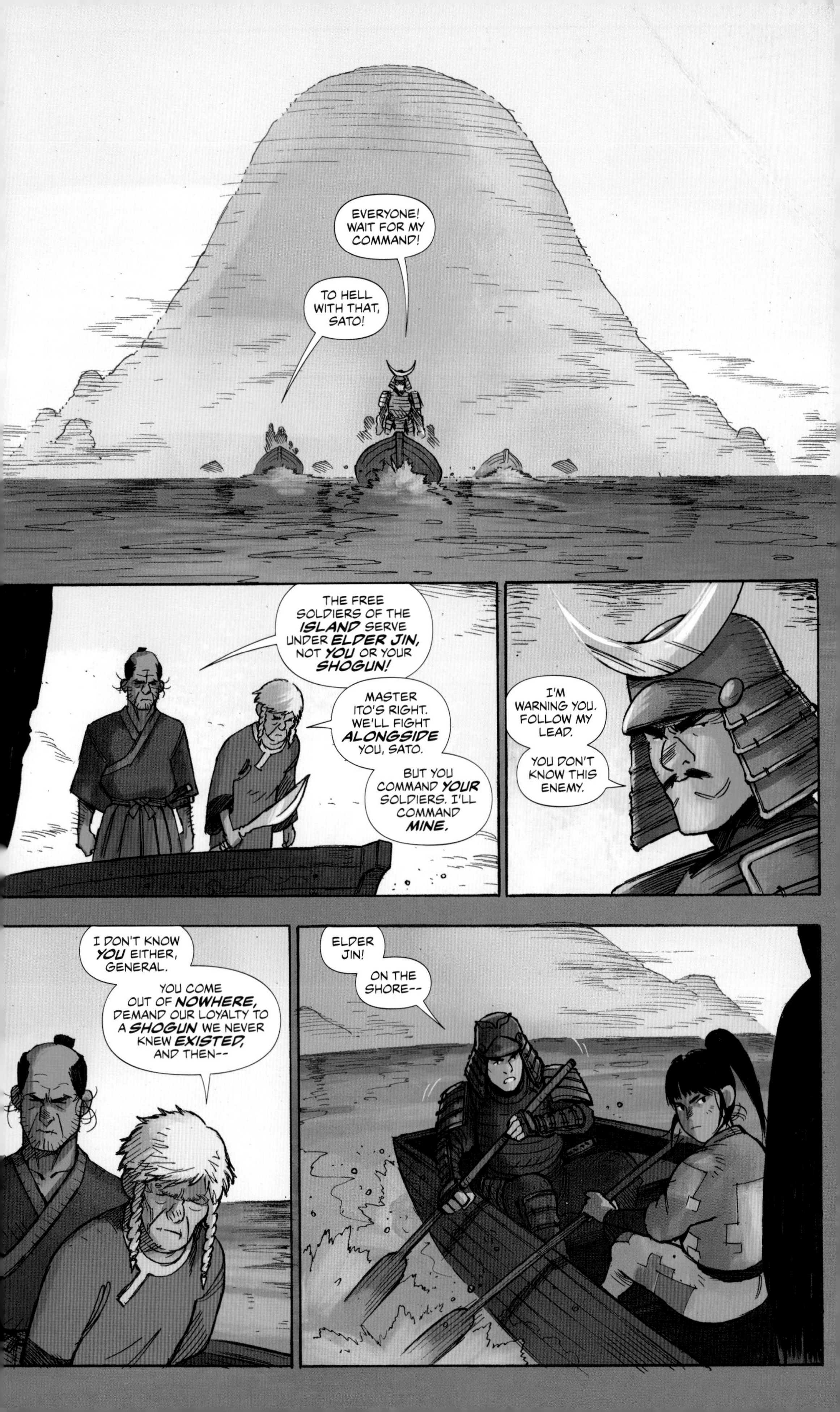
EVERYONE! WAIT FOR MY COMMAND!
TO HELL WITH THAT, SATO!
THE FREE SOLDIERS OF THE ISLAND SERVE UNDER ELDER JIN, NOT YOU OR YOUR SHOGUN!
MASTER ITO'S RIGHT. WE'LL FIGHT ALONGSIDE YOU, SATO.
BUT YOU COMMAND YOUR SOLDIERS. I'LL COMMAND MINE.
I'M WARNING YOU. FOLLOW MY LEAD.
YOU DON'T KNOW THIS ENEMY.
I DON'T KNOW YOU EITHER, GENERAL.
YOU COME OUT OF NOWHERE, DEMAND OUR LOYALTY TO A SHOGUN WE NEVER KNEW EXISTED, AND THEN--
ELDER JIN!
ON THE SHORE--

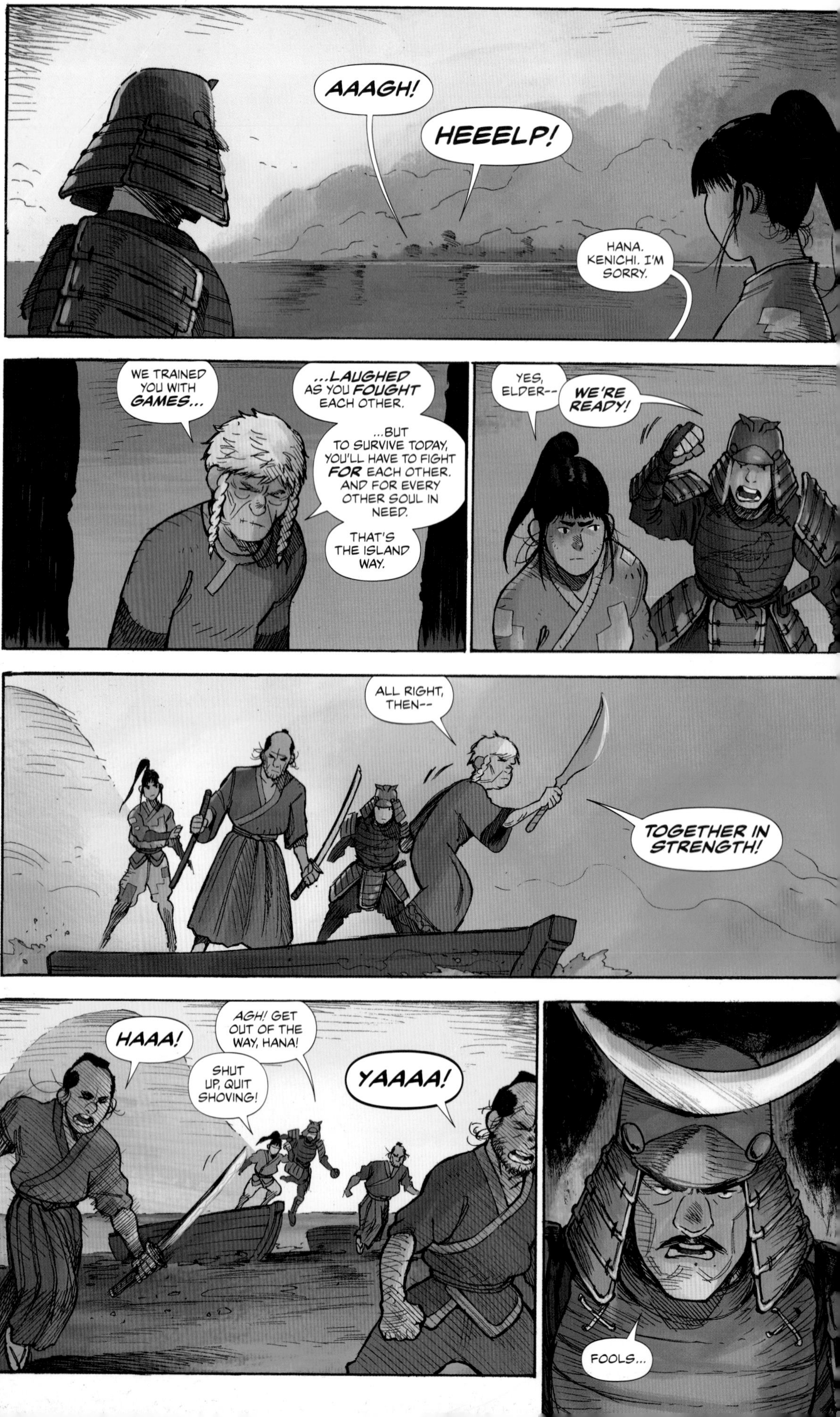

AAAGH!
HEEELP!
HANA. KENICHI. I'M SORRY.
WE TRAINED YOU WITH GAMES...
...LAUGHED AS YOU FOUGHT EACH OTHER.
...BUT TO SURVIVE TODAY, YOU'LL HAVE TO FIGHT FOR EACH OTHER. AND FOR EVERY OTHER SOUL IN NEED.
THAT'S THE ISLAND WAY.
YES, ELDER--
WE'RE READY!
ALL RIGHT, THEN--
TOGETHER IN STRENGTH!
HAAA!
AGH! GET OUT OF THE WAY, HANA!
SHUT UP, QUIT SHOVING!
YAAAA!
FOOLS...

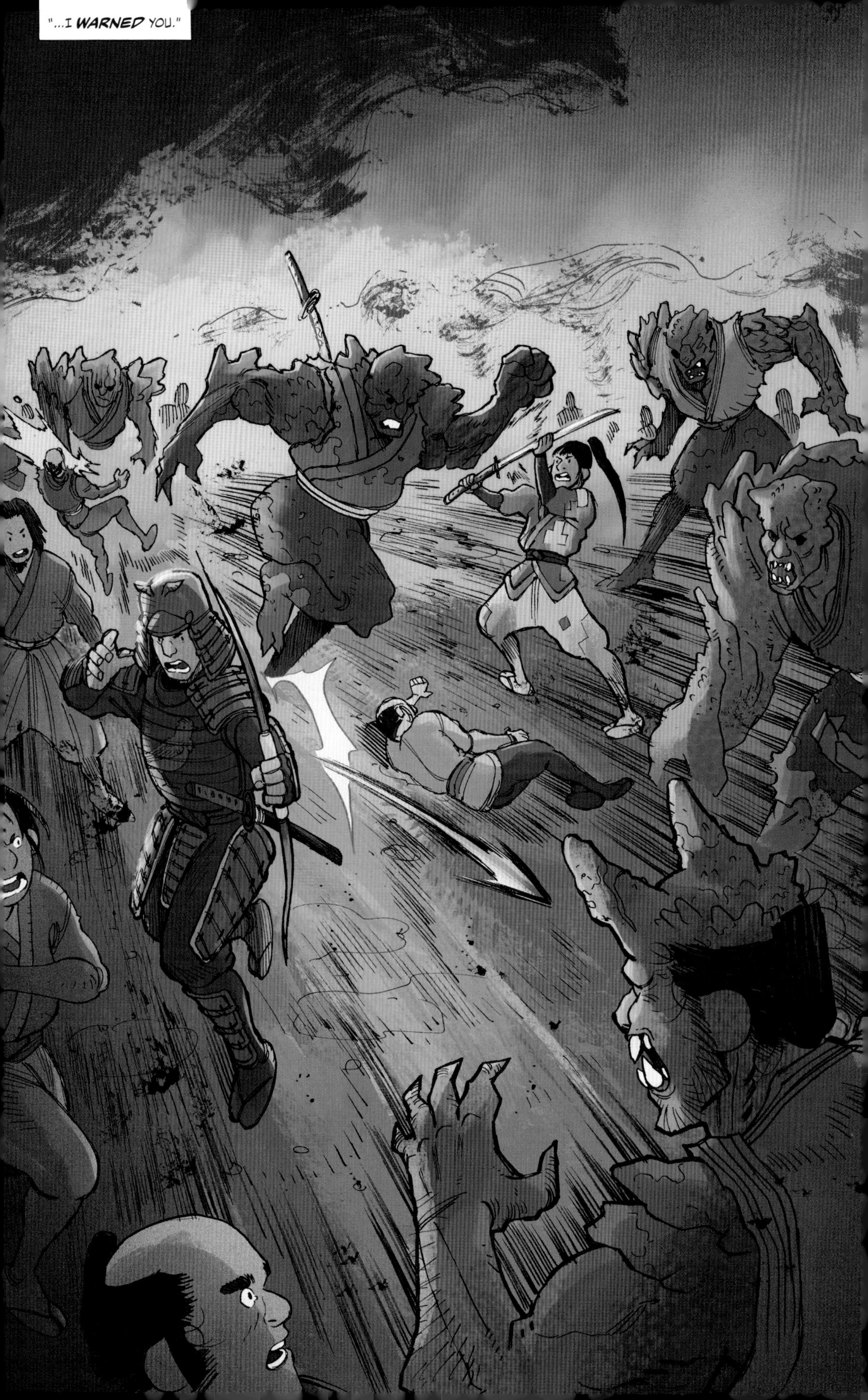
"...I WARNED YOU."

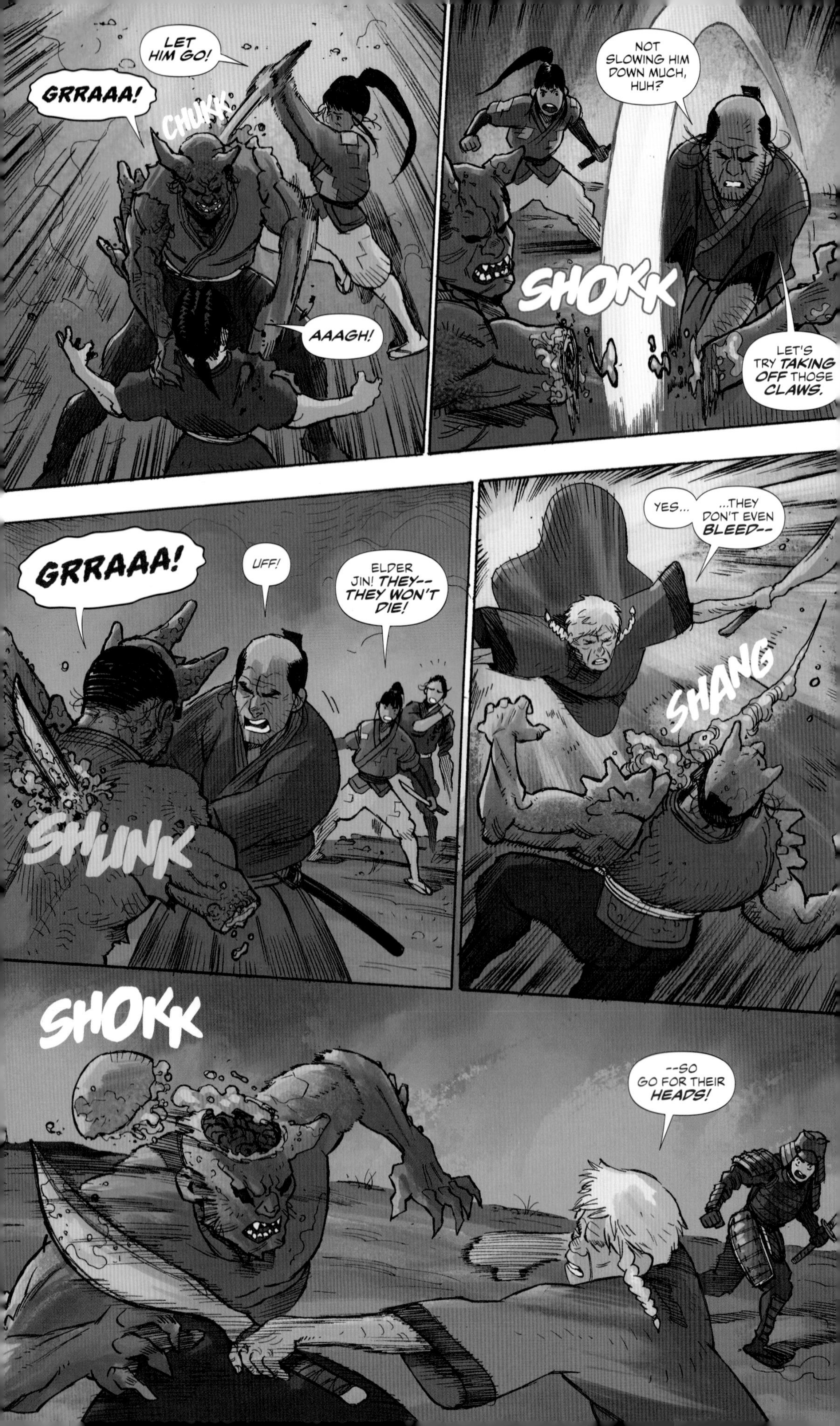
LET HIM GO!
GRRAAA!
CHUKK
AAAGH!
NOT SLOWING HIM DOWN MUCH, HUH?
SHOKK
LET'S TRY TAKING OFF THOSE CLAWS.
GRRAAA!
UFF!
ELDER JIN! THEY-- THEY WON'T DIE!
SHUNK
YES...
...THEY DON'T EVEN BLEED--
SHANG
SHOKK
--SO GO FOR THEIR HEADS!

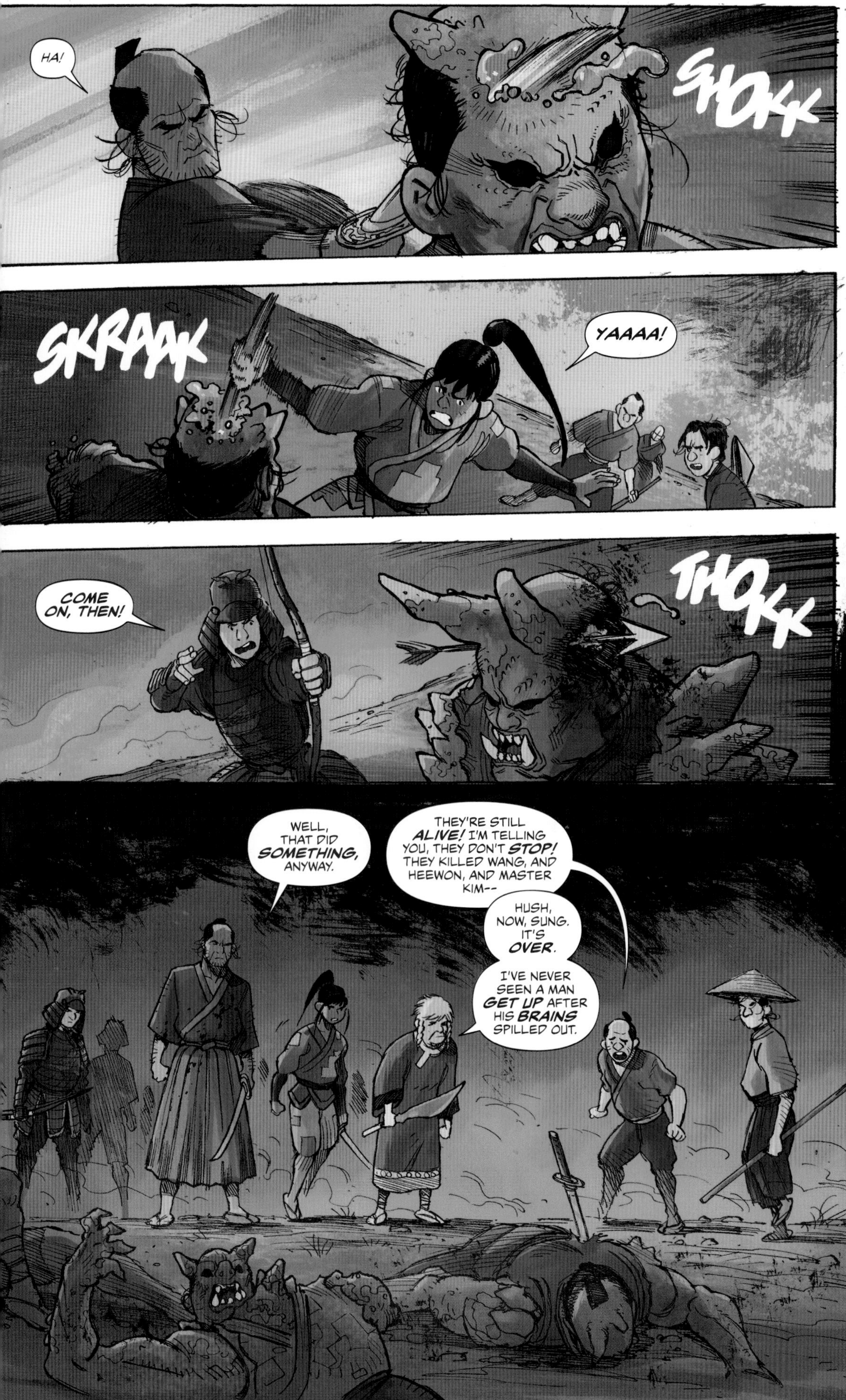
HA!
SHOKK
SKRAAK
YAAAA!
COME ON, THEN!
THOKK
WELL, THAT DID SOMETHING, ANYWAY.
THEY'RE STILL ALIVE! I'M TELLING YOU, THEY DON'T STOP! THEY KILLED WANG, AND HEEWON, AND MASTER KIM--
HUSH, NOW, SUNG. IT'S OVER.
I'VE NEVER SEEN A MAN GET UP AFTER HIS BRAINS SPILLED OUT.

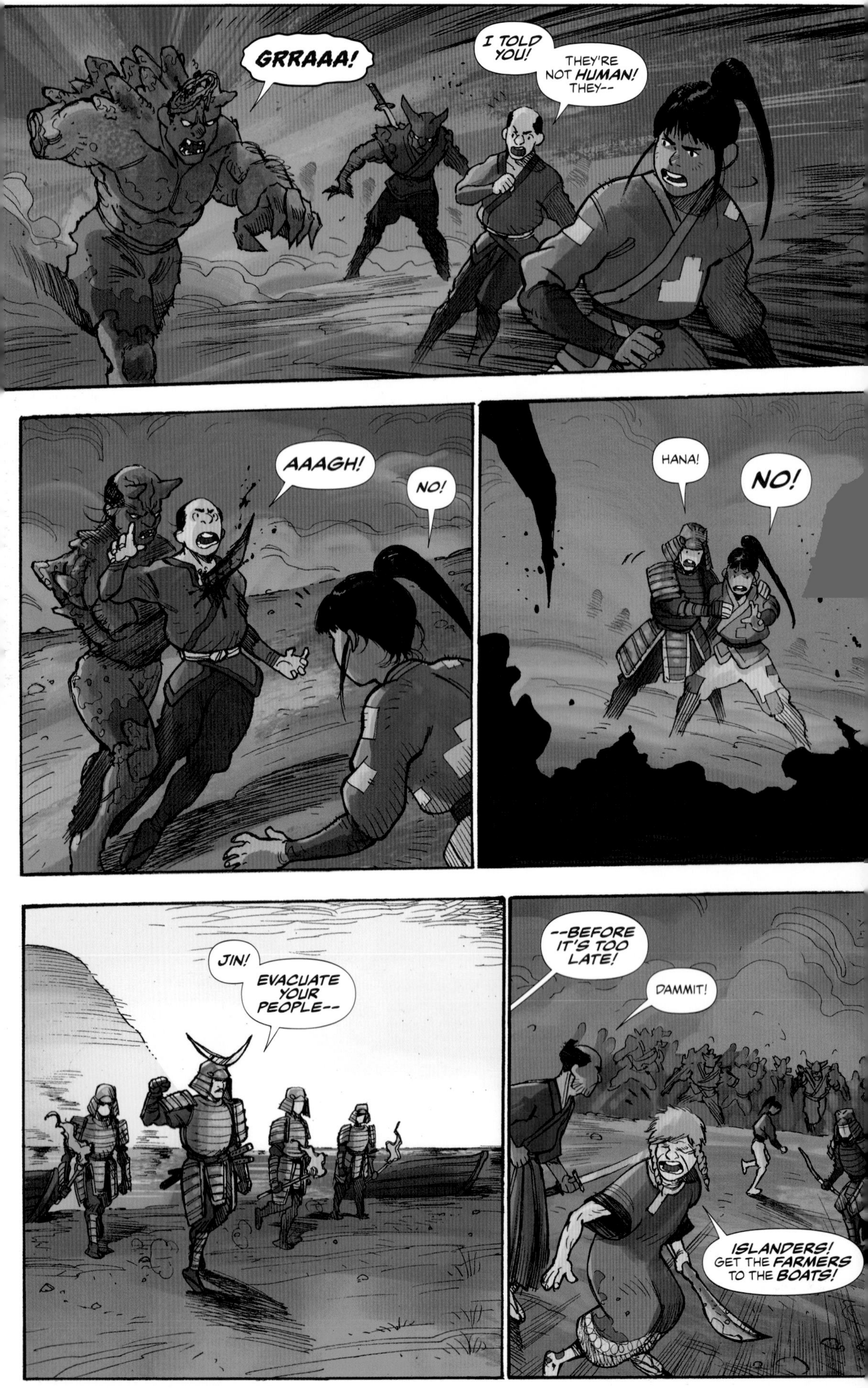
GRRAAA!
I TOLD YOU!
THEY'RE NOT HUMAN! THEY--
AAAGH!
NO!
HANA!
NO!
JIN!
EVACUATE YOUR PEOPLE--
--BEFORE IT'S TOO LATE!
DAMMIT!
ISLANDERS! GET THE FARMERS TO THE BOATS!

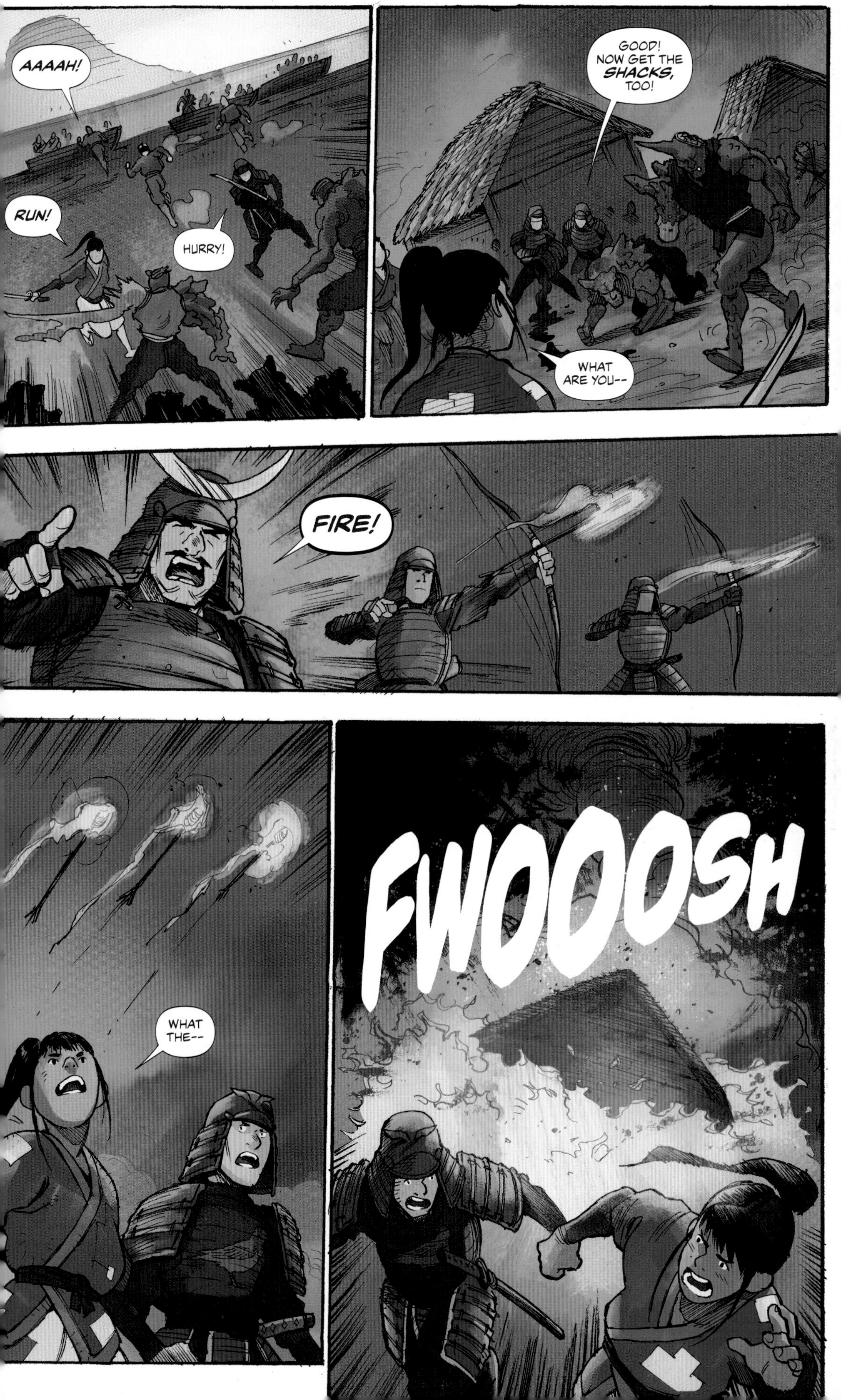
AAAAH!
RUN!
HURRY!
GOOD! NOW GET THE SHACKS, TOO!
WHAT ARE YOU--
FIRE!
WHAT THE--
FWOOOSH

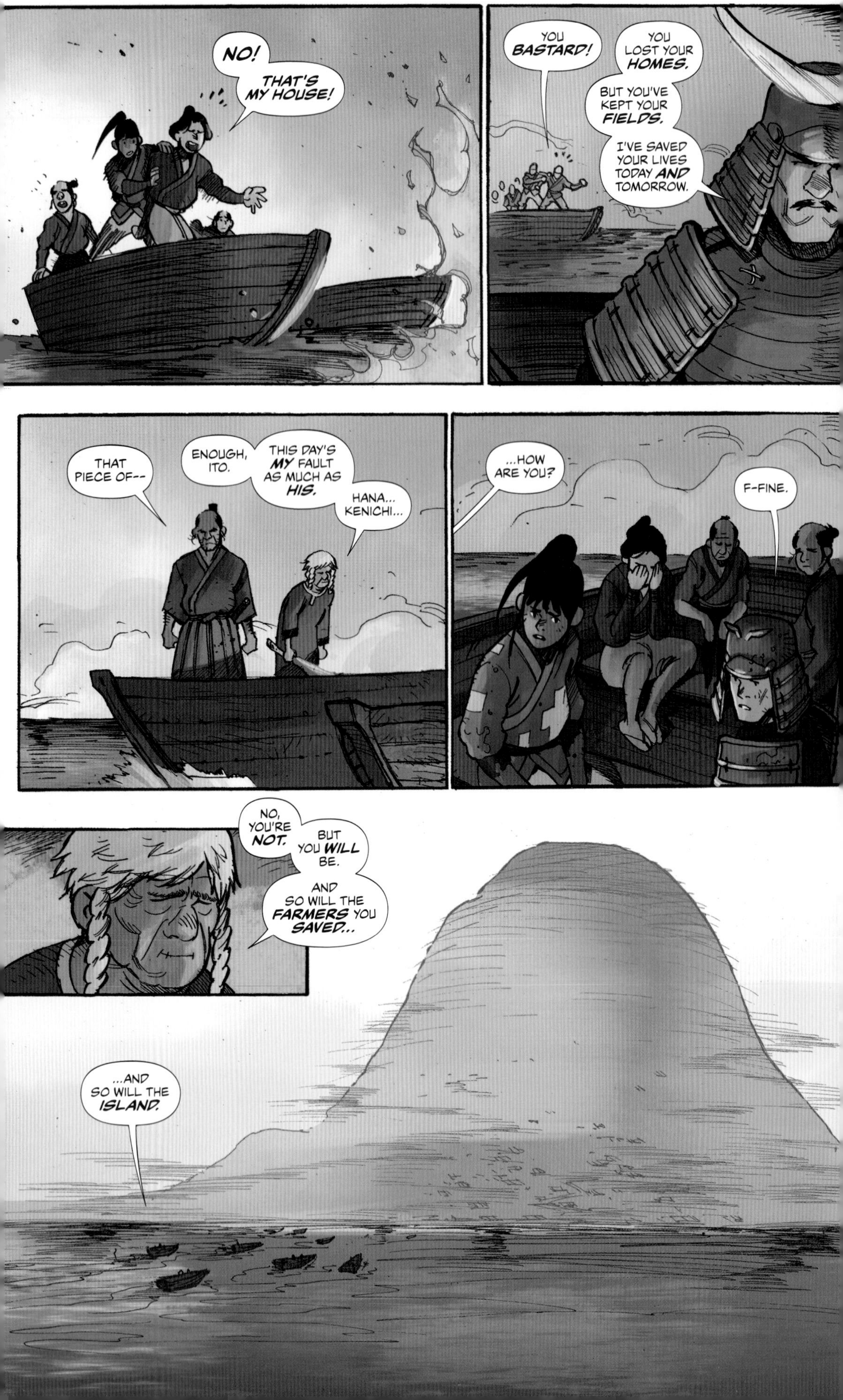
NO!
THAT'S MY HOUSE!
YOU BASTARD!
YOU LOST YOUR HOMES.
BUT YOU'VE KEPT YOUR FIELDS.
I'VE SAVED YOUR LIVES TODAY AND TOMORROW.
THAT PIECE OF--
ENOUGH, ITO.
THIS DAY'S MY FAULT AS MUCH AS HIS.
HANA... KENICHI...
...HOW ARE YOU?
F-FINE.
NO, YOU'RE NOT.
BUT YOU WILL BE.
AND SO WILL THE FARMERS YOU SAVED...
...AND SO WILL THE ISLAND.

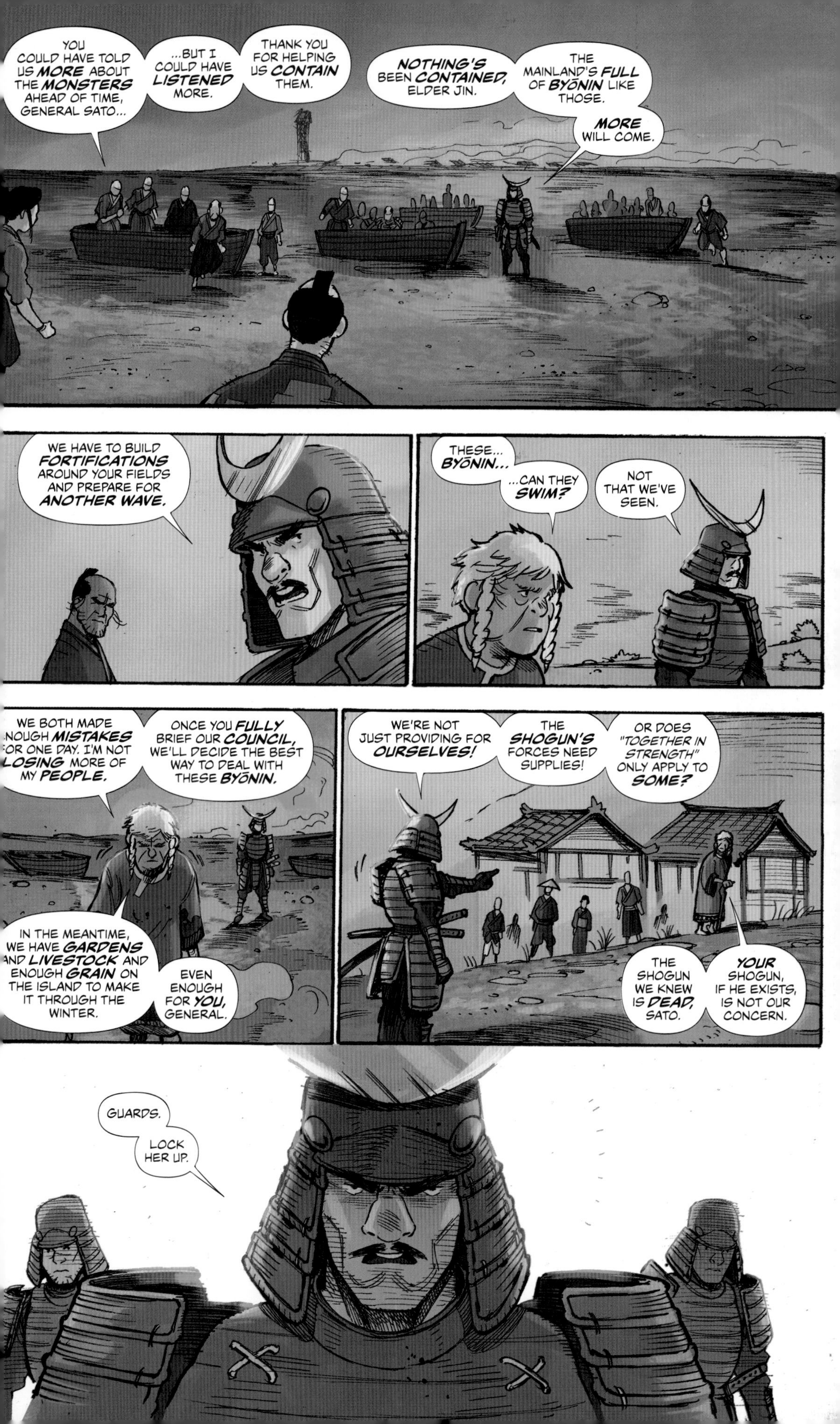

YOU COULD HAVE TOLD US MORE ABOUT THE MONSTERS AHEAD OF TIME, GENERAL SATO...
...BUT I COULD HAVE LISTENED MORE.
THANK YOU FOR HELPING US CONTAIN THEM.
NOTHING'S BEEN CONTAINED, ELDER JIN.
THE MAINLAND'S FULL OF BYŌNIN LIKE THOSE.
MORE WILL COME.
WE HAVE TO BUILD FORTIFICATIONS AROUND YOUR FIELDS AND PREPARE FOR ANOTHER WAVE.
THESE... BYŌNIN...
...CAN THEY SWIM?
NOT THAT WE'VE SEEN.
WE BOTH MADE ENOUGH MISTAKES FOR ONE DAY. I'M NOT LOSING MORE OF MY PEOPLE.
ONCE YOU FULLY BRIEF OUR COUNCIL, WE'LL DECIDE THE BEST WAY TO DEAL WITH THESE BYŌNIN.
IN THE MEANTIME, WE HAVE GARDENS AND LIVESTOCK AND ENOUGH GRAIN ON THE ISLAND TO MAKE IT THROUGH THE WINTER.
EVEN ENOUGH FOR YOU, GENERAL.
WE'RE NOT JUST PROVIDING FOR OURSELVES!
THE SHOGUN'S FORCES NEED SUPPLIES!
OR DOES "TOGETHER IN STRENGTH" ONLY APPLY TO SOME?
THE SHOGUN WE KNEW IS DEAD, SATO.
YOUR SHOGUN, IF HE EXISTS, IS NOT OUR CONCERN.
GUARDS.
LOCK HER UP.

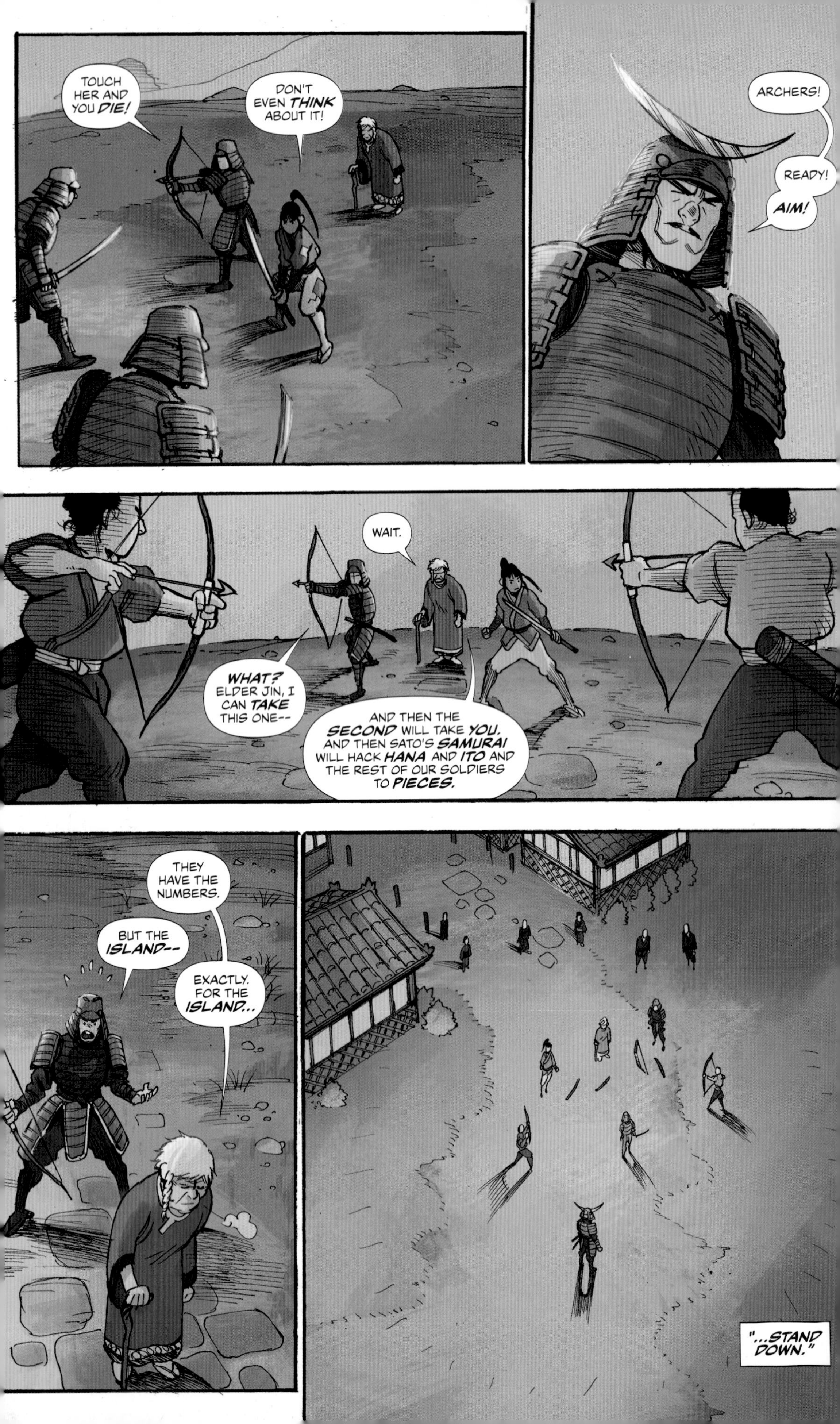
TOUCH HER AND YOU DIE!
DON'T EVEN THINK ABOUT IT!
ARCHERS!
READY!
AIM!
WAIT.
WHAT? ELDER JIN, I CAN TAKE THIS ONE--
AND THEN THE SECOND WILL TAKE YOU. AND THEN SATO'S SAMURAI WILL HACK HANA AND ITO AND THE REST OF OUR SOLDIERS TO PIECES.
THEY HAVE THE NUMBERS.
BUT THE ISLAND--
EXACTLY. FOR THE ISLAND...
"...STAND DOWN."

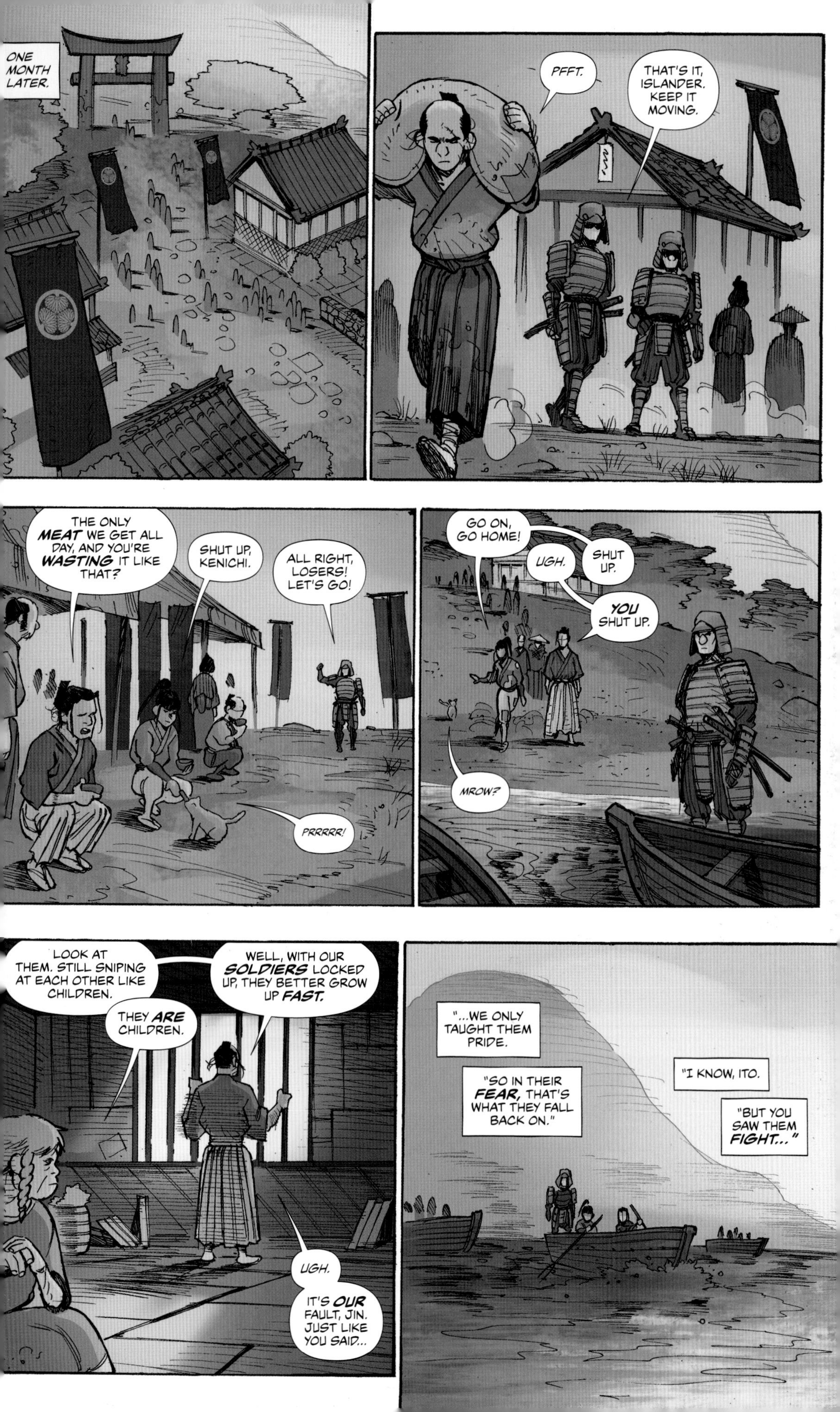
ONE MONTH LATER.
PFFT.
THAT'S IT, ISLANDER. KEEP IT MOVING.
THE ONLY MEAT WE GET ALL DAY, AND YOU'RE WASTING IT LIKE THAT?
SHUT UP, KENICHI.
ALL RIGHT, LOSERS! LET'S GO!
PRRRRR!
GO ON, GO HOME!
UGH.
SHUT UP.
YOU SHUT UP.
MROW?
LOOK AT THEM. STILL SNIPING AT EACH OTHER LIKE CHILDREN.
THEY ARE CHILDREN.
WELL, WITH OUR SOLDIERS LOCKED UP, THEY BETTER GROW UP FAST.
UGH.
IT'S OUR FAULT, JIN. JUST LIKE YOU SAID...
"...WE ONLY TAUGHT THEM PRIDE.
"SO IN THEIR FEAR, THAT'S WHAT THEY FALL BACK ON."
"I KNOW, ITO.
"BUT YOU SAW THEM FIGHT..."

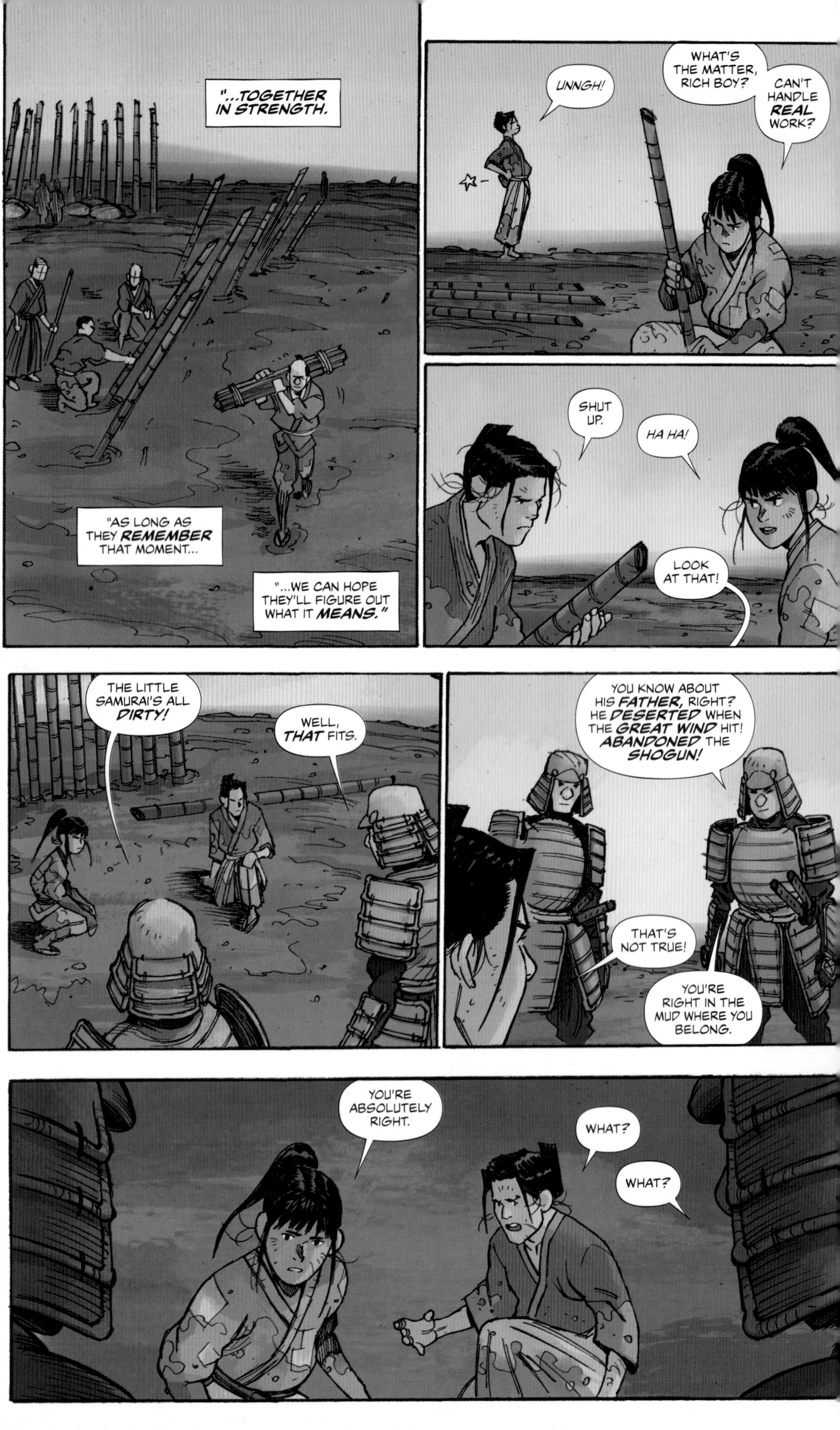

"...TOGETHER IN STRENGTH.
"AS LONG AS THEY REMEMBER THAT MOMENT...
"...WE CAN HOPE THEY'LL FIGURE OUT WHAT IT MEANS."
UNNGH!
WHAT'S THE MATTER, RICH BOY?
CAN'T HANDLE REAL WORK?
SHUT UP.
HA HA!
LOOK AT THAT!
THE LITTLE SAMURAI'S ALL DIRTY!
WELL, THAT FITS.
YOU KNOW ABOUT HIS FATHER, RIGHT? HE DESERTED WHEN THE GREAT WIND HIT! ABANDONED THE SHOGUN!
THAT'S NOT TRUE!
YOU'RE RIGHT IN THE MUD WHERE YOU BELONG.
YOU'RE ABSOLUTELY RIGHT.
WHAT?
WHAT?

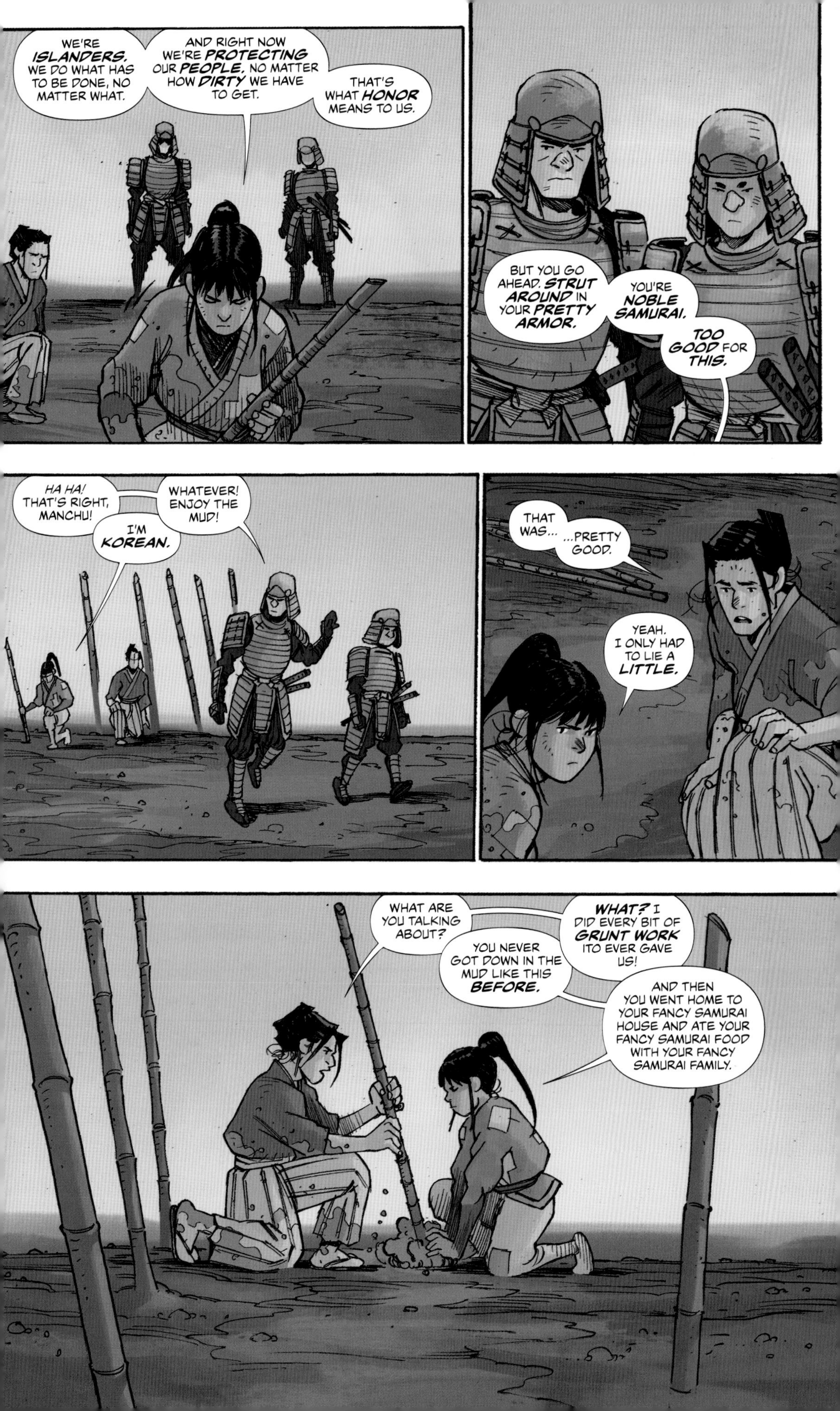

WE'RE ISLANDERS. WE DO WHAT HAS TO BE DONE, NO MATTER WHAT.
AND RIGHT NOW WE'RE PROTECTING OUR PEOPLE, NO MATTER HOW DIRTY WE HAVE TO GET.
THAT'S WHAT HONOR MEANS TO US.
BUT YOU GO AHEAD. STRUT AROUND IN YOUR PRETTY ARMOR.
YOU'RE NOBLE SAMURAI.
TOO GOOD FOR THIS.
HA HA! THAT'S RIGHT, MANCHU!
WHATEVER! ENJOY THE MUD!
I'M KOREAN.
THAT WAS...
...PRETTY GOOD.
YEAH. I ONLY HAD TO LIE A LITTLE.
WHAT ARE YOU TALKING ABOUT?
WHAT? I DID EVERY BIT OF GRUNT WORK ITO EVER GAVE US!
YOU NEVER GOT DOWN IN THE MUD LIKE THIS BEFORE.
AND THEN YOU WENT HOME TO YOUR FANCY SAMURAI HOUSE AND ATE YOUR FANCY SAMURAI FOOD WITH YOUR FANCY SAMURAI FAMILY.

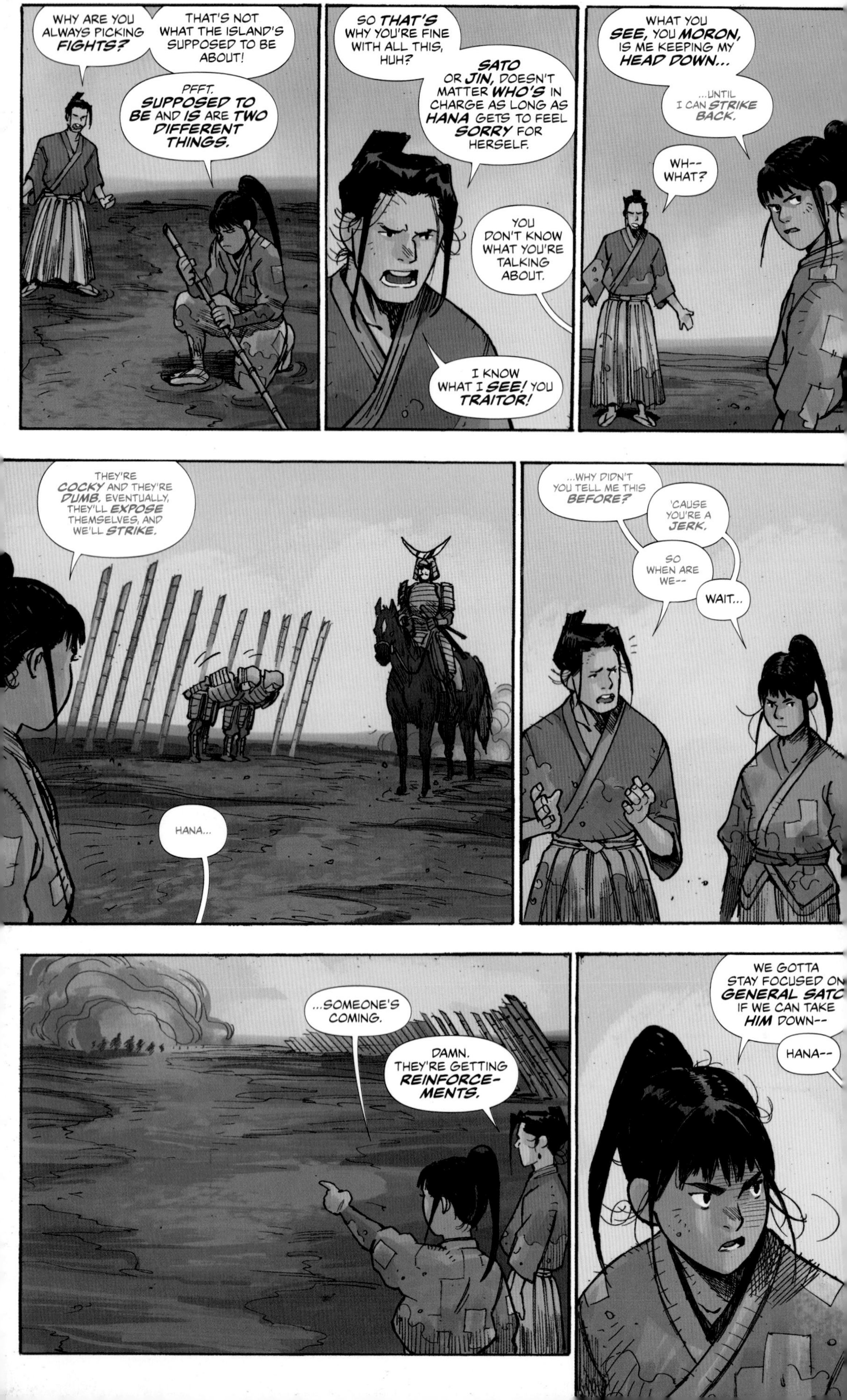

WHY ARE YOU ALWAYS PICKING FIGHTS?
THAT'S NOT WHAT THE ISLAND'S SUPPOSED TO BE ABOUT!
PFFT. SUPPOSED TO BE AND IS ARE TWO DIFFERENT THINGS.
SO THAT'S WHY YOU'RE FINE WITH ALL THIS, HUH?
SATO OR JIN, DOESN'T MATTER WHO'S IN CHARGE AS LONG AS HANA GETS TO FEEL SORRY FOR HERSELF.
YOU DON'T KNOW WHAT YOU'RE TALKING ABOUT.
I KNOW WHAT I SEE! YOU TRAITOR!
WHAT YOU SEE, YOU MORON, IS ME KEEPING MY HEAD DOWN...
...UNTIL I CAN STRIKE BACK.
WH-- WHAT?
THEY'RE COCKY AND THEY'RE DUMB. EVENTUALLY, THEY'LL EXPOSE THEMSELVES, AND WE'LL STRIKE.
HANA...
...WHY DIDN'T YOU TELL ME THIS BEFORE?
'CAUSE YOU'RE A JERK.
SO WHEN ARE WE--
WAIT...
...SOMEONE'S COMING.
DAMN. THEY'RE GETTING REINFORCE-MENTS.
WE GOTTA STAY FOCUSED ON GENERAL SATO. IF WE CAN TAKE HIM DOWN--
HANA--

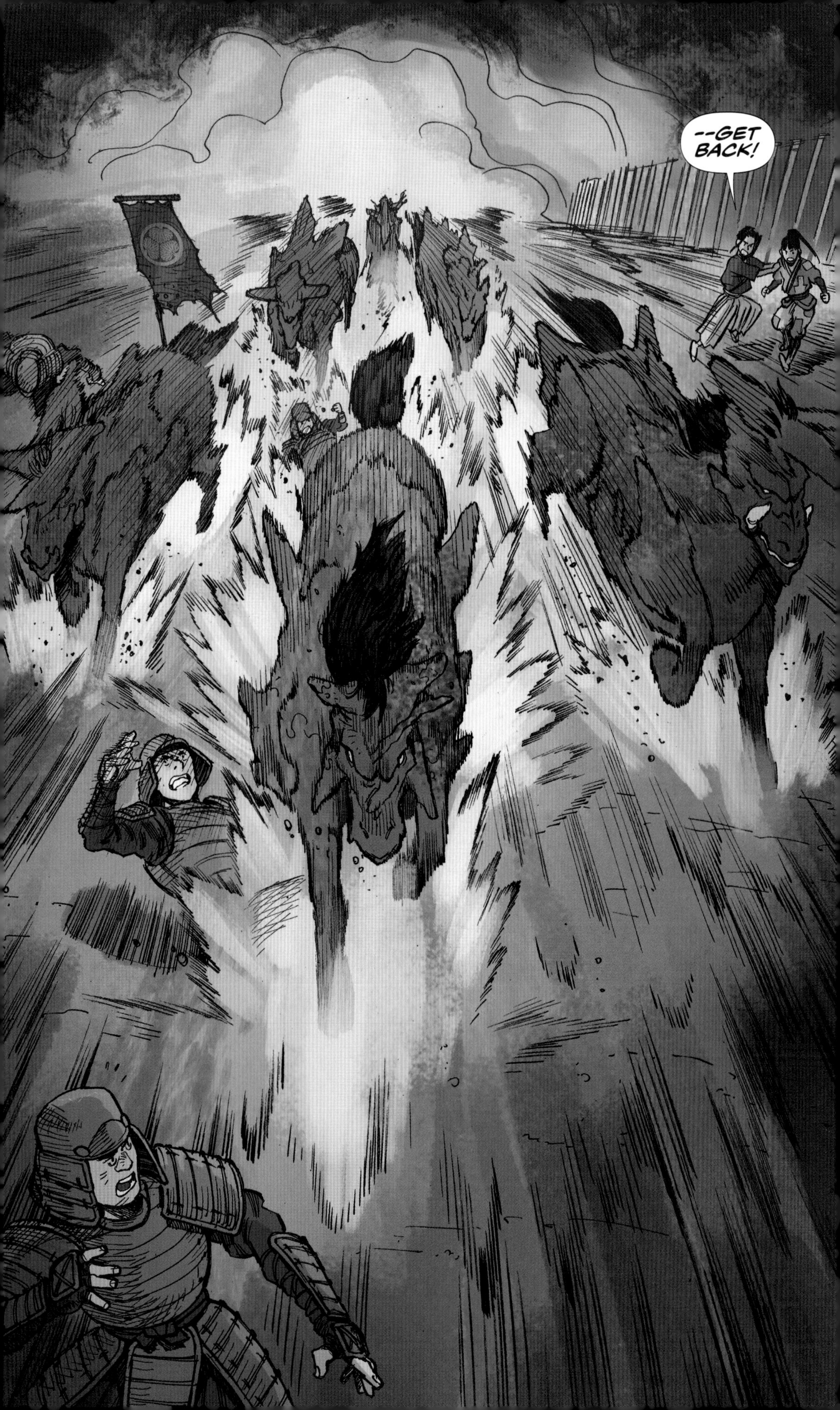
--GET BACK!

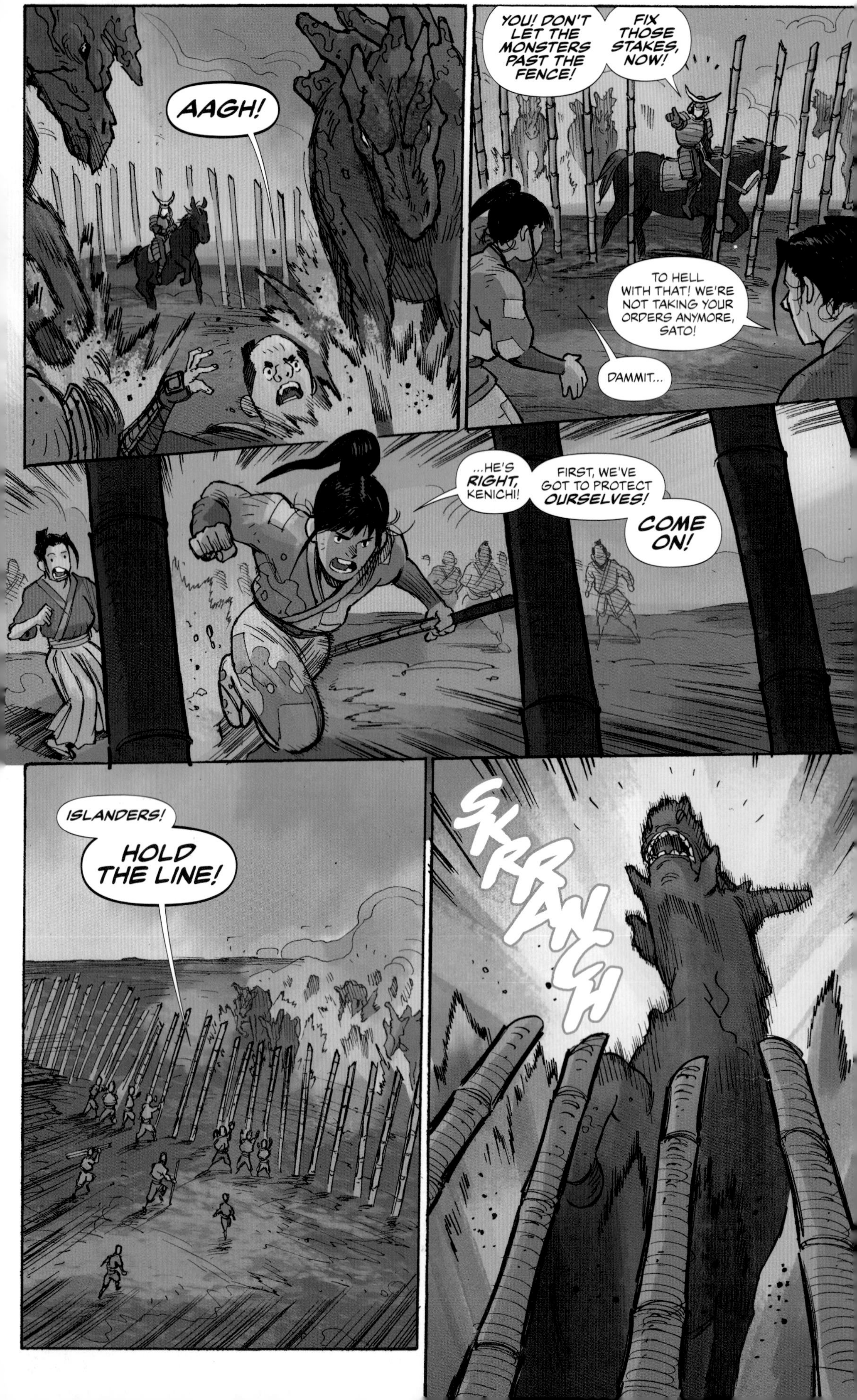
AAGH!
YOU! DON'T LET THE MONSTERS PAST THE FENCE!
FIX THOSE STAKES, NOW!
TO HELL WITH THAT! WE'RE NOT TAKING YOUR ORDERS ANYMORE, SATO!
DAMMIT...
...HE'S RIGHT, KENICHI!
FIRST, WE'VE GOT TO PROTECT OURSELVES!
COME ON!
ISLANDERS!
HOLD THE LINE!
SKRRANCH

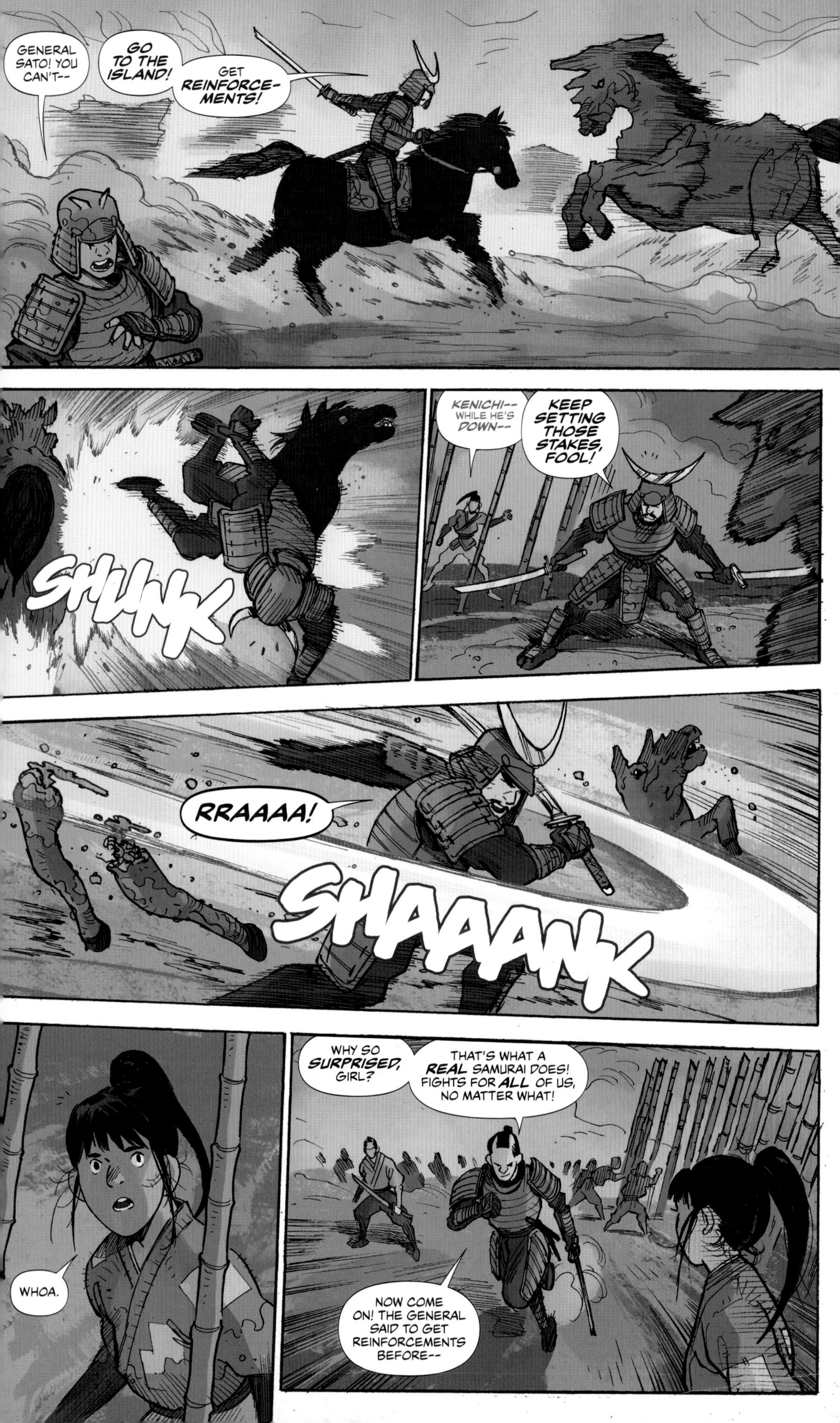
GENERAL SATO! YOU CAN'T--
GO TO THE ISLAND!
GET REINFORCEMENTS!
SHUNK
KENICHI-- WHILE HE'S DOWN--
KEEP SETTING THOSE STAKES, FOOL!
RRAAAA!
SHAAAANK
WHOA.
WHY SO SURPRISED, GIRL?
THAT'S WHAT A REAL SAMURAI DOES! FIGHTS FOR ALL OF US, NO MATTER WHAT!
NOW COME ON! THE GENERAL SAID TO GET REINFORCEMENTS BEFORE--

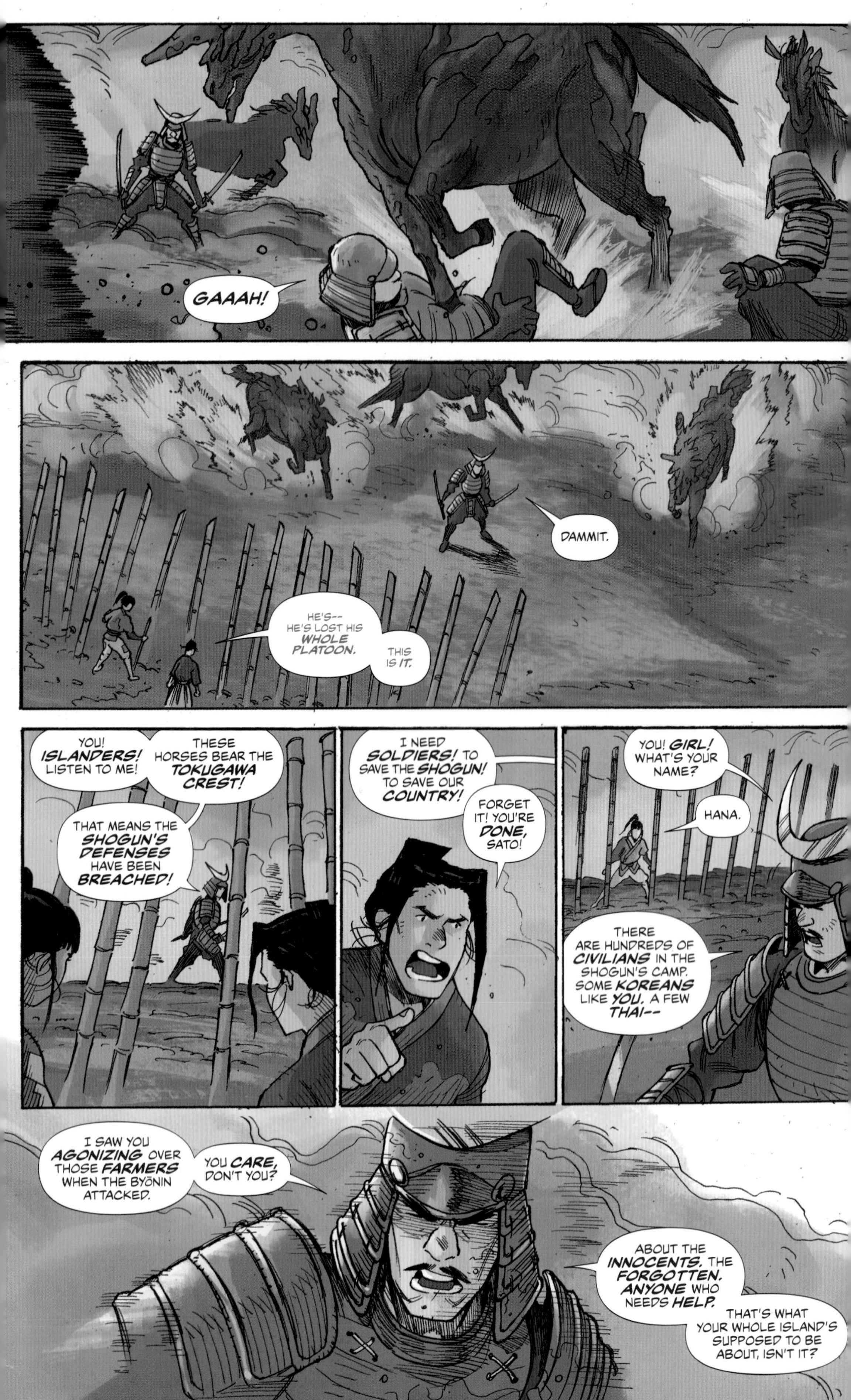
GAAAH!
DAMMIT.
HE'S-- HE'S LOST HIS WHOLE PLATOON.
THIS IS IT.
YOU! ISLANDERS! LISTEN TO ME!
THESE HORSES BEAR THE TOKUGAWA CREST!
THAT MEANS THE SHOGUN'S DEFENSES HAVE BEEN BREACHED!
I NEED SOLDIERS! TO SAVE THE SHOGUN! TO SAVE OUR COUNTRY!
FORGET IT! YOU'RE DONE, SATO!
YOU! GIRL! WHAT'S YOUR NAME?
HANA.
THERE ARE HUNDREDS OF CIVILIANS IN THE SHOGUN'S CAMP. SOME KOREANS LIKE YOU. A FEW THAI--
I SAW YOU AGONIZING OVER THOSE FARMERS WHEN THE BYŌNIN ATTACKED.
YOU CARE, DON'T YOU?
ABOUT THE INNOCENTS. THE FORGOTTEN. ANYONE WHO NEEDS HELP.
THAT'S WHAT YOUR WHOLE ISLAND'S SUPPOSED TO BE ABOUT, ISN'T IT?

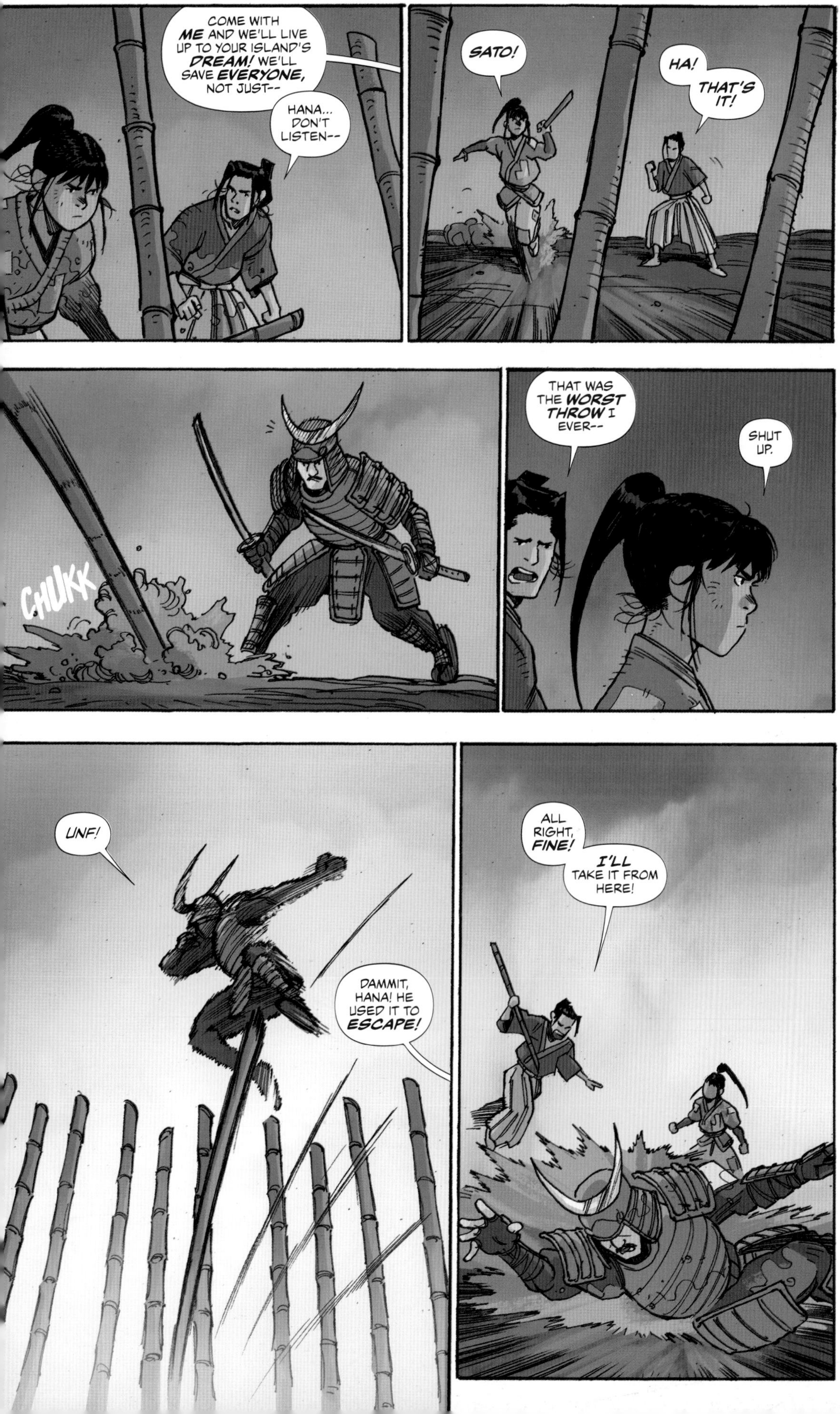
COME WITH ME AND WE'LL LIVE UP TO YOUR ISLAND'S DREAM! WE'LL SAVE EVERYONE, NOT JUST--
HANA... DON'T LISTEN--
SATO!
HA!
THAT'S IT!
CHUKK
THAT WAS THE WORST THROW I EVER--
SHUT UP.
UNF!
DAMMIT, HANA! HE USED IT TO ESCAPE!
ALL RIGHT, FINE!
I'LL TAKE IT FROM HERE!

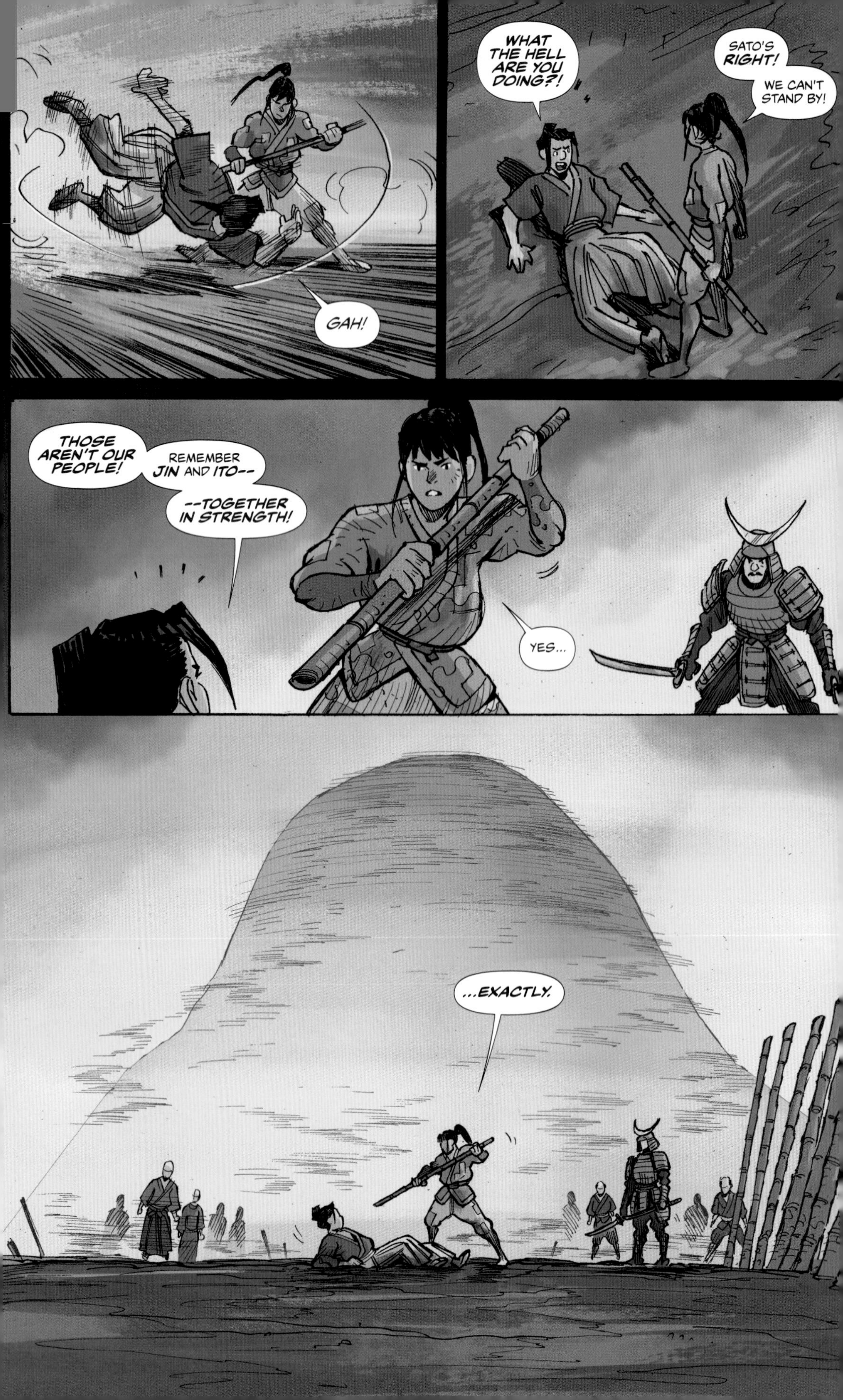
GAH!
WHAT THE HELL ARE YOU DOING?!
SATO'S RIGHT!
WE CAN'T STAND BY!
THOSE AREN'T OUR PEOPLE!
REMEMBER JIN AND ITO--
--TOGETHER IN STRENGTH!
YES...
...EXACTLY.

Issue Two Cover by **Ethan Young**

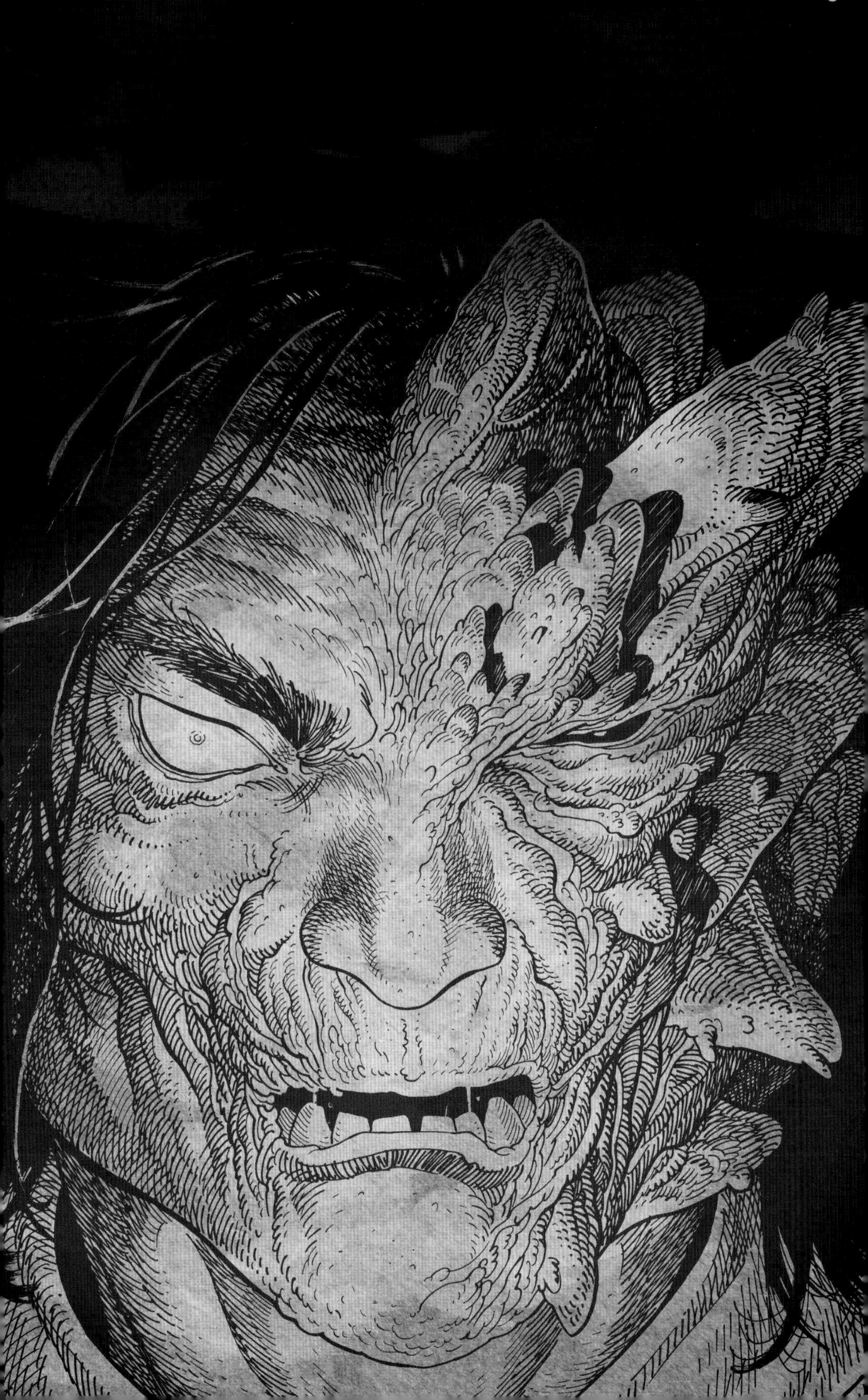

CHAPTER THREE

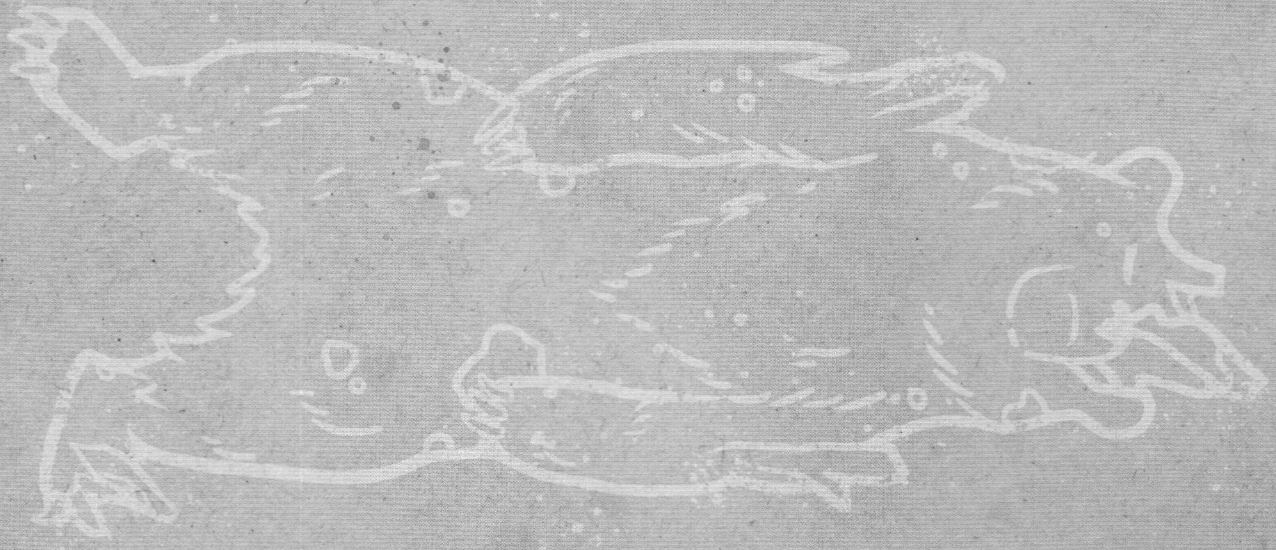

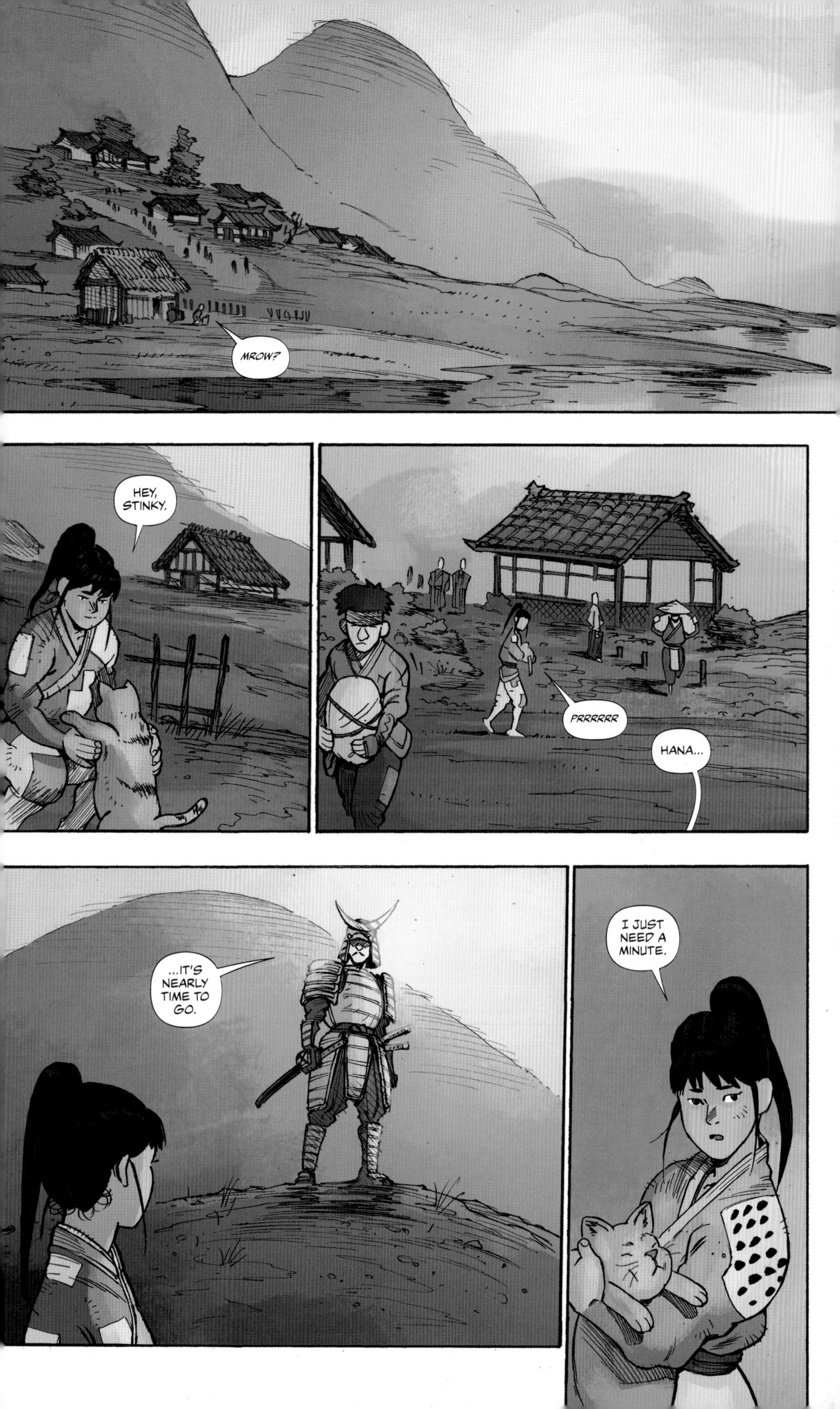
MROW?
HEY, STINKY.
PRRRRRR
HANA...
...IT'S NEARLY TIME TO GO.
I JUST NEED A MINUTE.

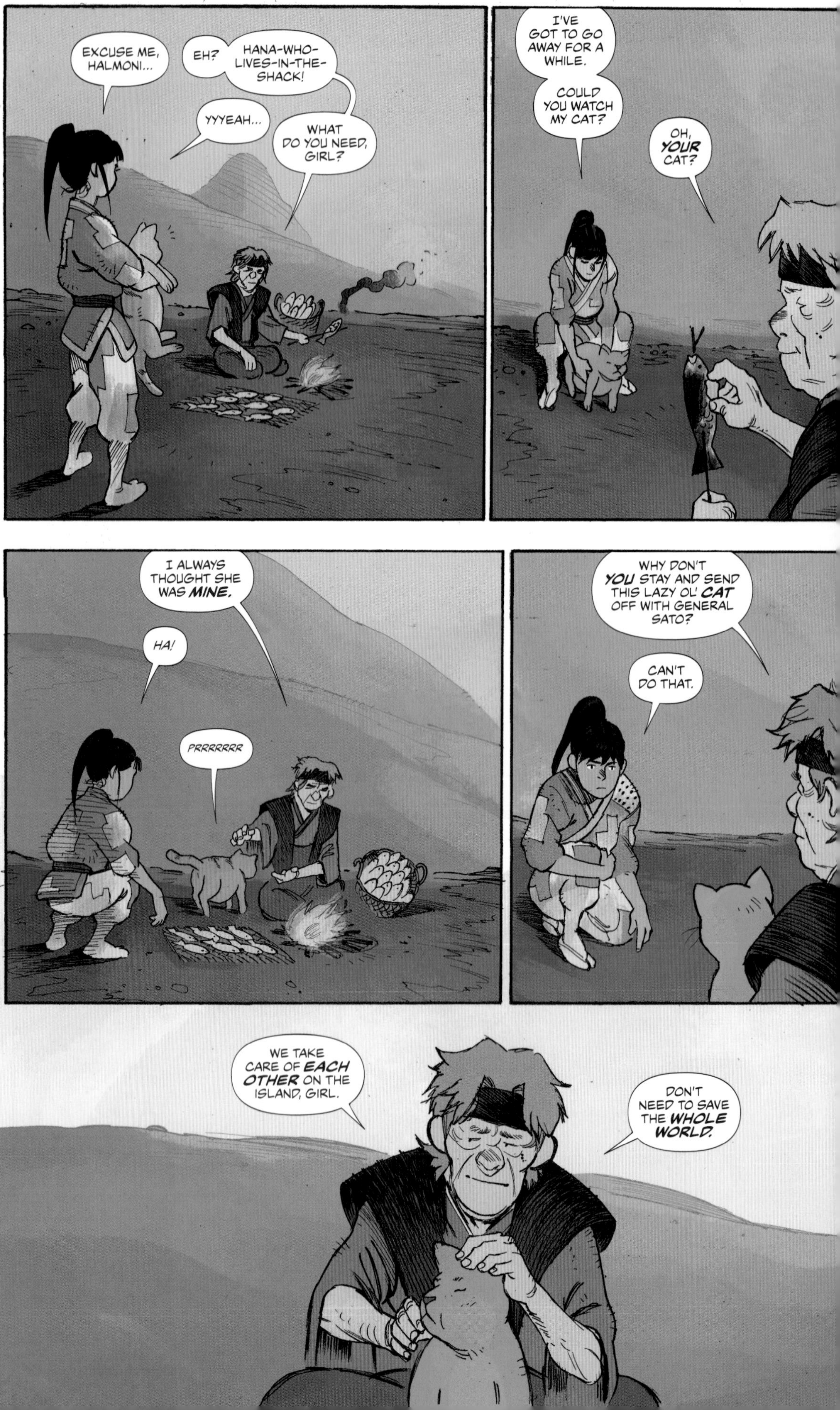
EXCUSE ME, HALMONI...
EH?
HANA-WHO-LIVES-IN-THE-SHACK!
YYYEAH...
WHAT DO YOU NEED, GIRL?
I'VE GOT TO GO AWAY FOR A WHILE.
COULD YOU WATCH MY CAT?
OH, YOUR CAT?
I ALWAYS THOUGHT SHE WAS MINE.
HA!
PRRRRRRR
WHY DON'T YOU STAY AND SEND THIS LAZY OL' CAT OFF WITH GENERAL SATO?
CAN'T DO THAT.
WE TAKE CARE OF EACH OTHER ON THE ISLAND, GIRL.
DON'T NEED TO SAVE THE WHOLE WORLD.

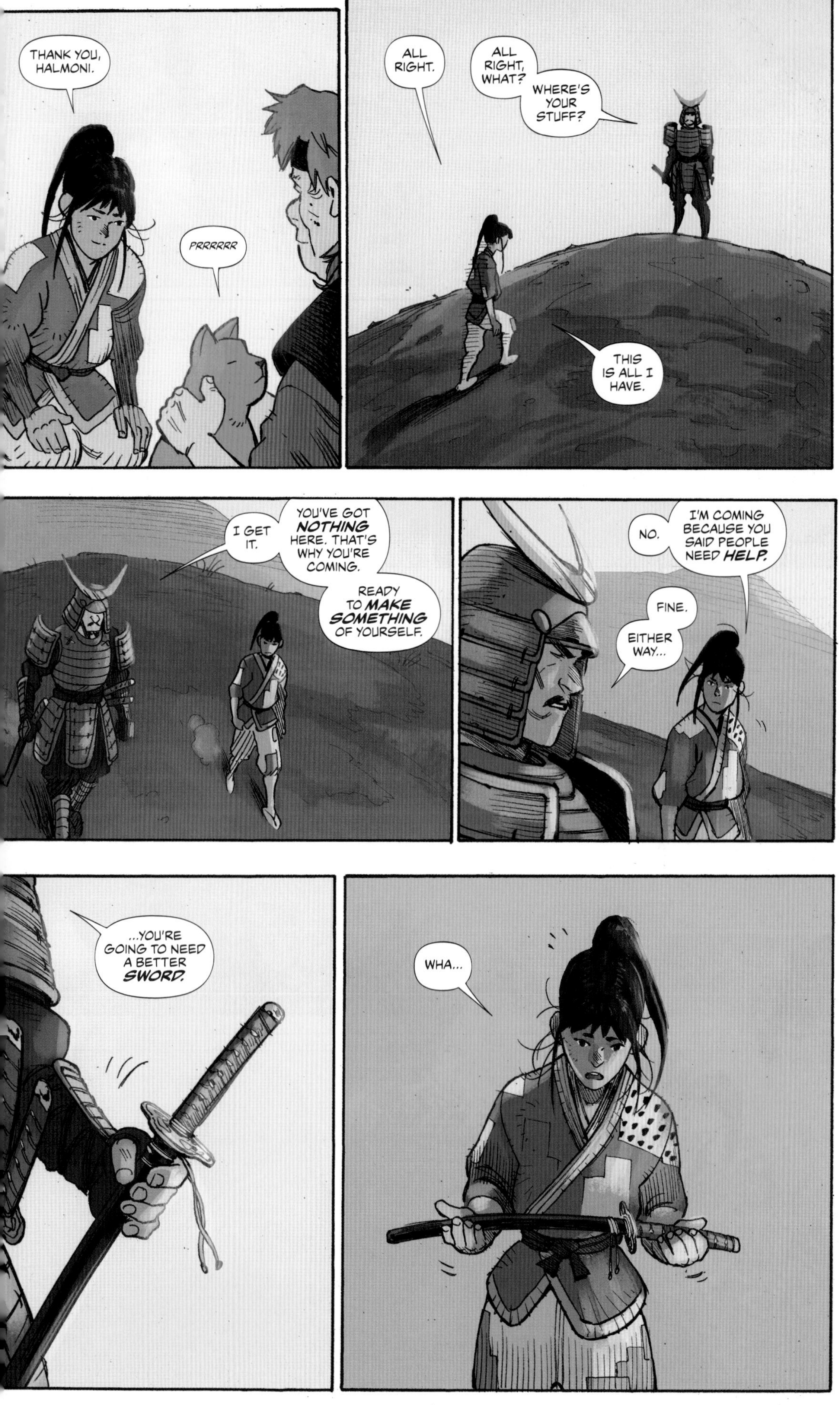
THANK YOU, HALMONI.
PRRRRRR
ALL RIGHT.
ALL RIGHT, WHAT?
WHERE'S YOUR STUFF?
THIS IS ALL I HAVE.
I GET IT.
YOU'VE GOT NOTHING HERE. THAT'S WHY YOU'RE COMING.
READY TO MAKE SOMETHING OF YOURSELF.
NO.
I'M COMING BECAUSE YOU SAID PEOPLE NEED HELP.
FINE.
EITHER WAY...
...YOU'RE GOING TO NEED A BETTER SWORD.
WHA...

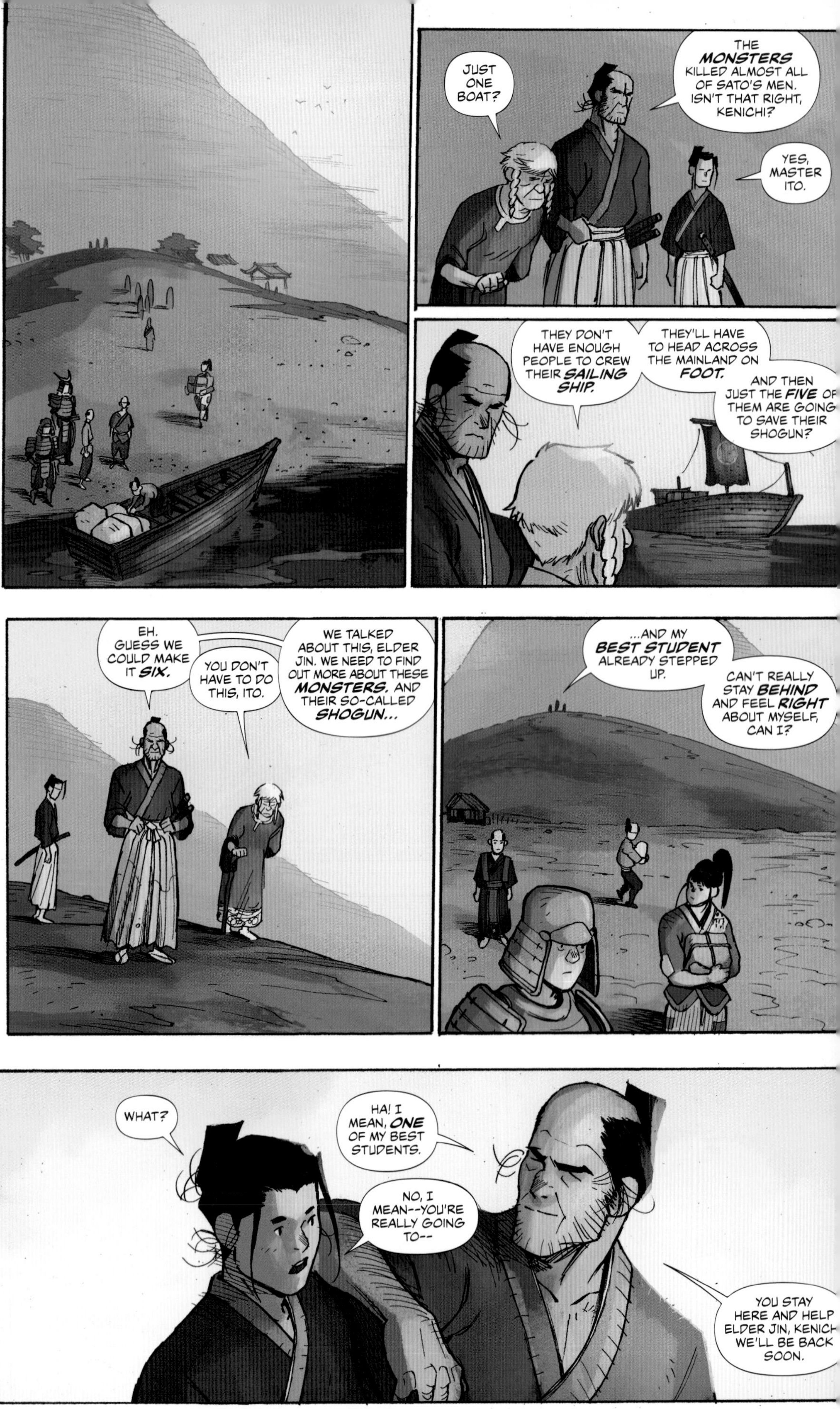
JUST ONE BOAT?
THE MONSTERS KILLED ALMOST ALL OF SATO'S MEN. ISN'T THAT RIGHT, KENICHI?
YES, MASTER ITO.
THEY DON'T HAVE ENOUGH PEOPLE TO CREW THEIR SAILING SHIP.
THEY'LL HAVE TO HEAD ACROSS THE MAINLAND ON FOOT.
AND THEN JUST THE FIVE OF THEM ARE GOING TO SAVE THEIR SHOGUN?
EH. GUESS WE COULD MAKE IT SIX.
YOU DON'T HAVE TO DO THIS, ITO.
WE TALKED ABOUT THIS, ELDER JIN. WE NEED TO FIND OUT MORE ABOUT THESE MONSTERS. AND THEIR SO-CALLED SHOGUN...
...AND MY BEST STUDENT ALREADY STEPPED UP.
CAN'T REALLY STAY BEHIND AND FEEL RIGHT ABOUT MYSELF, CAN I?
WHAT?
HA! I MEAN, ONE OF MY BEST STUDENTS.
NO, I MEAN--YOU'RE REALLY GOING TO--
YOU STAY HERE AND HELP ELDER JIN, KENICH
WE'LL BE BACK SOON.

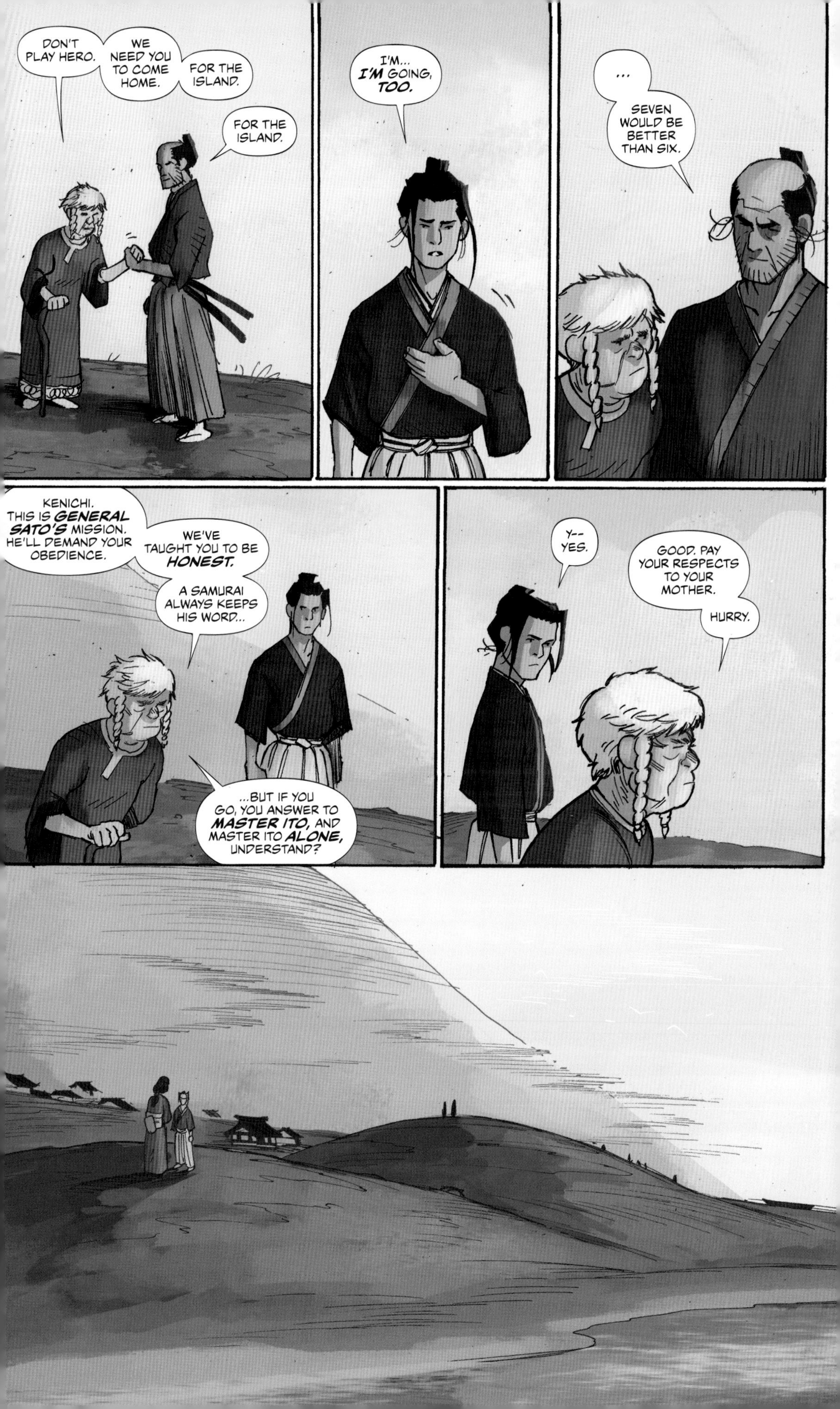
DON'T PLAY HERO.
WE NEED YOU TO COME HOME.
FOR THE ISLAND.
FOR THE ISLAND.
I'M... I'M GOING, TOO.
...
SEVEN WOULD BE BETTER THAN SIX.
KENICHI. THIS IS GENERAL SATO'S MISSION. HE'LL DEMAND YOUR OBEDIENCE.
WE'VE TAUGHT YOU TO BE HONEST.
A SAMURAI ALWAYS KEEPS HIS WORD...
...BUT IF YOU GO, YOU ANSWER TO MASTER ITO, AND MASTER ITO ALONE, UNDERSTAND?
Y-- YES.
GOOD. PAY YOUR RESPECTS TO YOUR MOTHER.
HURRY.

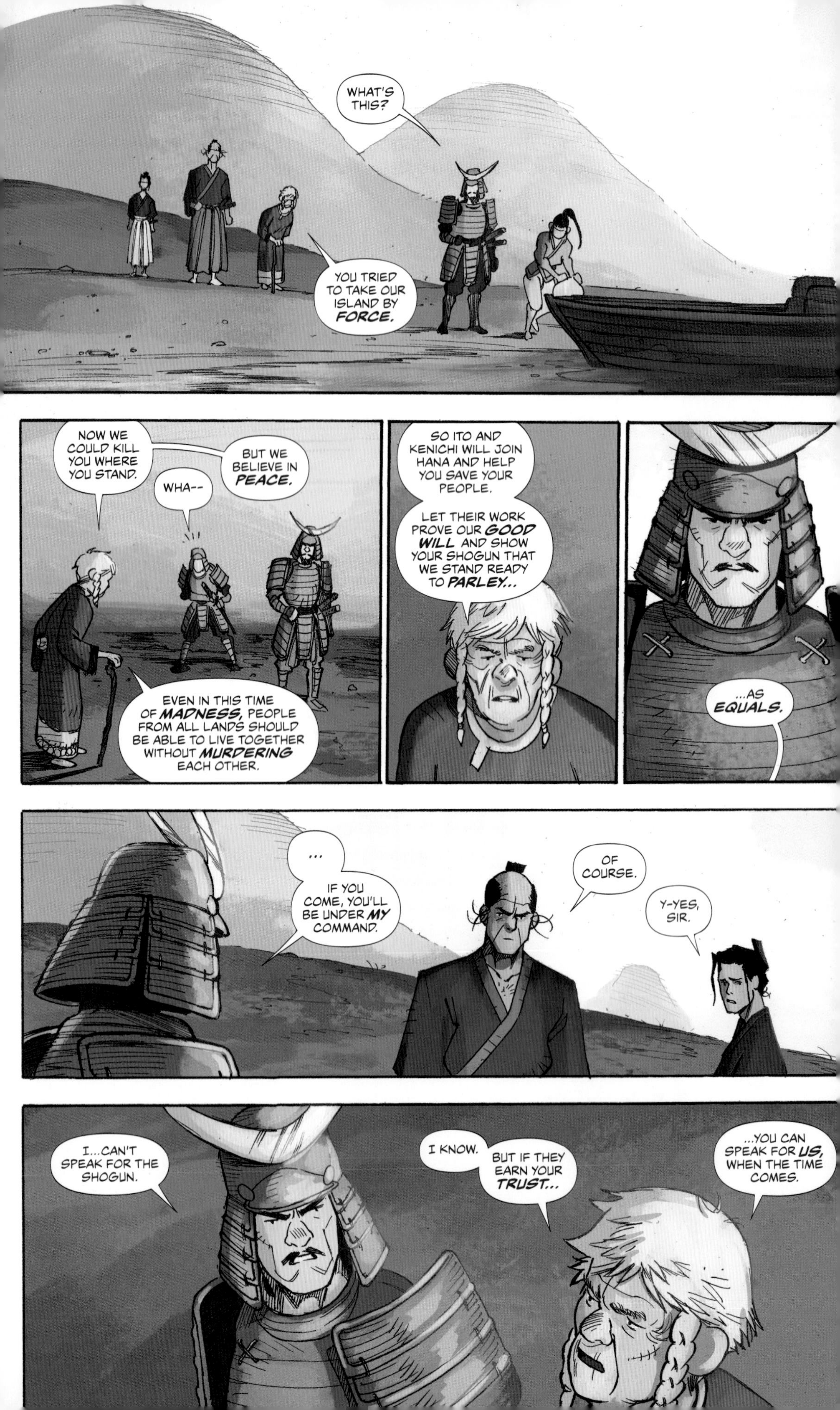
WHAT'S THIS?
YOU TRIED TO TAKE OUR ISLAND BY FORCE.
NOW WE COULD KILL YOU WHERE YOU STAND.
BUT WE BELIEVE IN PEACE.
WHA--
EVEN IN THIS TIME OF MADNESS, PEOPLE FROM ALL LANDS SHOULD BE ABLE TO LIVE TOGETHER WITHOUT MURDERING EACH OTHER.
SO ITO AND KENICHI WILL JOIN HANA AND HELP YOU SAVE YOUR PEOPLE.
LET THEIR WORK PROVE OUR GOOD WILL AND SHOW YOUR SHOGUN THAT WE STAND READY TO PARLEY...
...AS EQUALS.
...
IF YOU COME, YOU'LL BE UNDER MY COMMAND.
OF COURSE.
Y-YES, SIR.
I...CAN'T SPEAK FOR THE SHOGUN.
I KNOW.
BUT IF THEY EARN YOUR TRUST...
...YOU CAN SPEAK FOR US, WHEN THE TIME COMES.

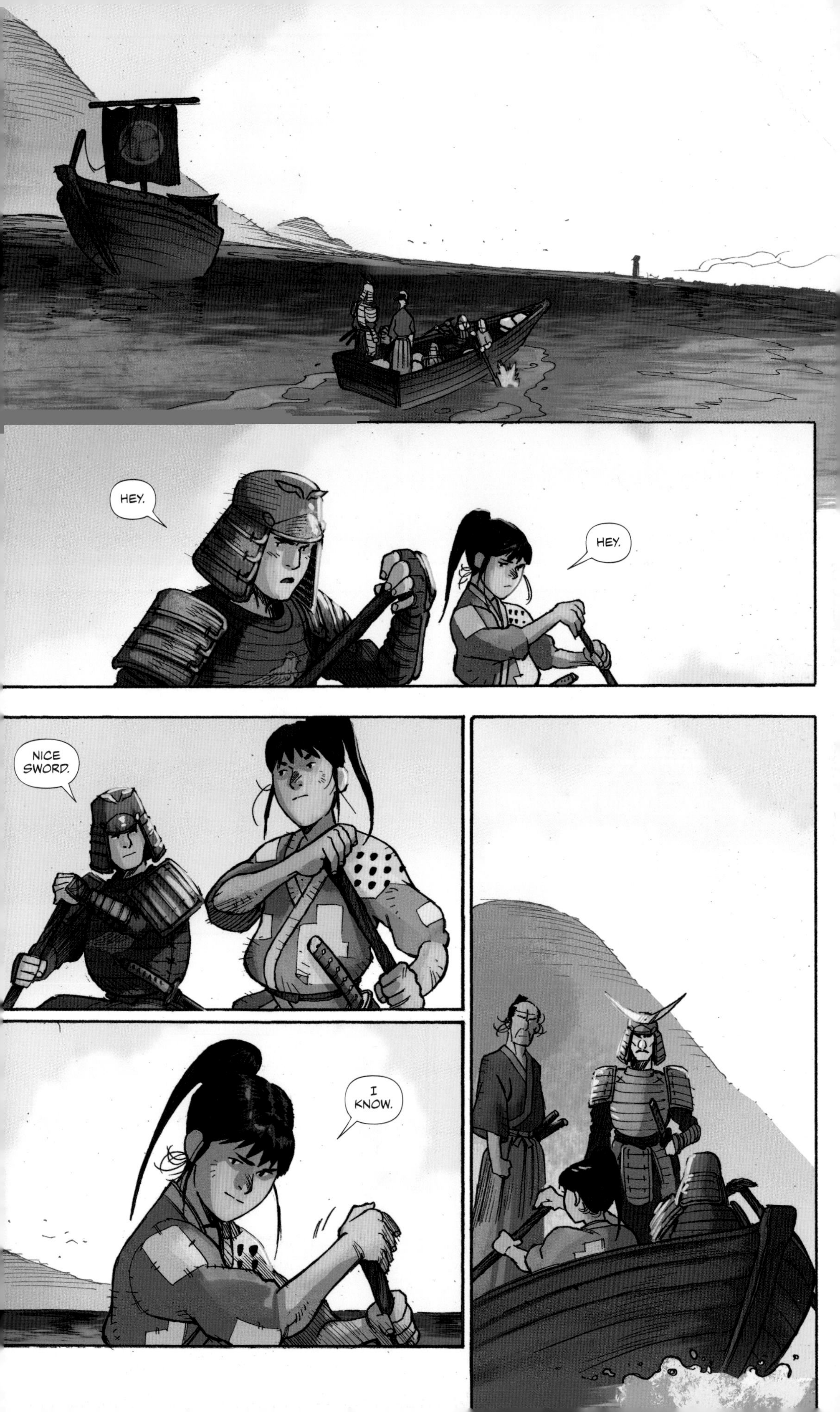
HEY.
HEY.
NICE SWORD.
I KNOW.

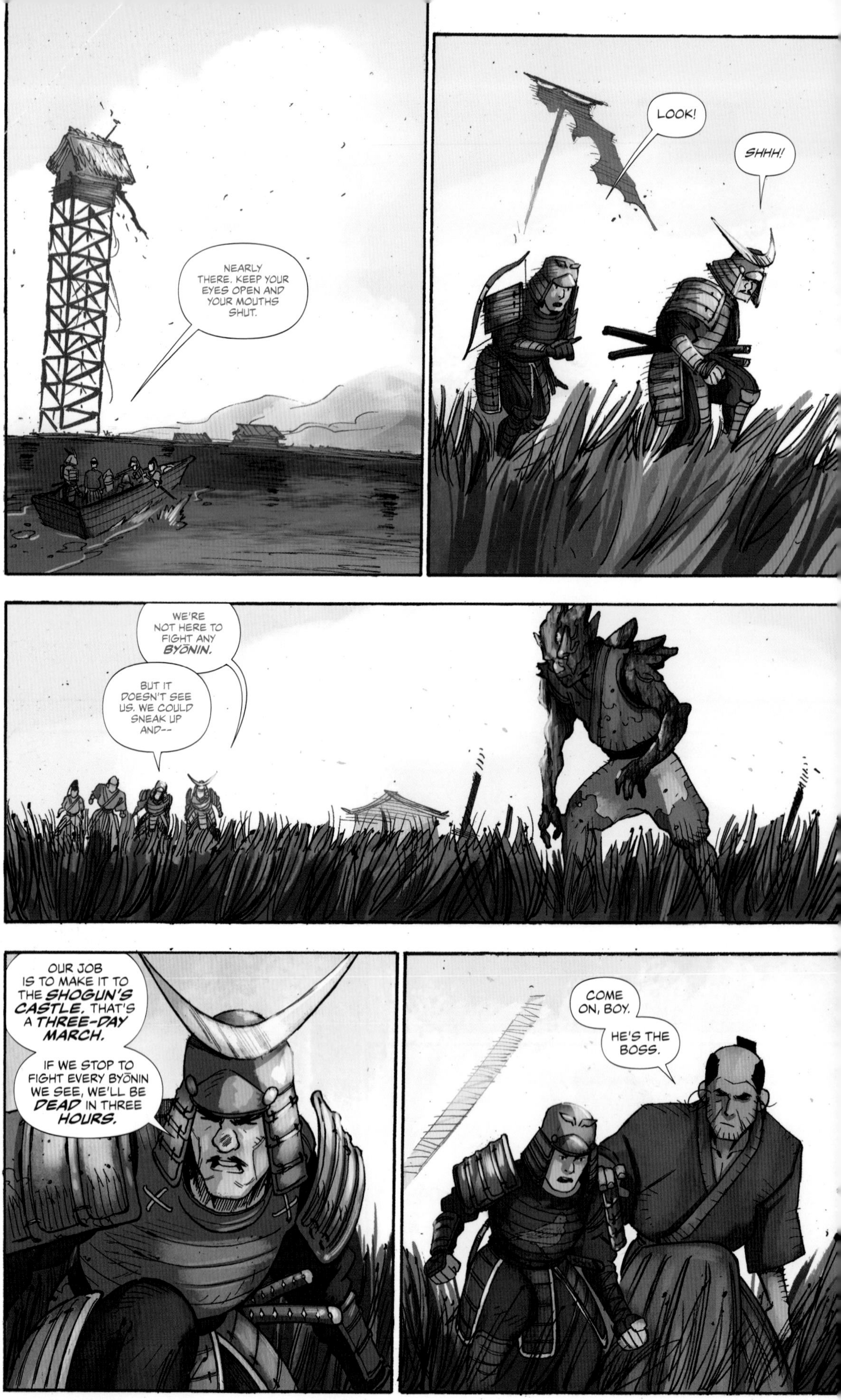

NEARLY THERE. KEEP YOUR EYES OPEN AND YOUR MOUTHS SHUT.
LOOK!
SHHH!
WE'RE NOT HERE TO FIGHT ANY BYŌNIN.
BUT IT DOESN'T SEE US. WE COULD SNEAK UP AND--
OUR JOB IS TO MAKE IT TO THE SHOGUN'S CASTLE. THAT'S A THREE-DAY MARCH.
IF WE STOP TO FIGHT EVERY BYŌNIN WE SEE, WE'LL BE DEAD IN THREE HOURS.
COME ON, BOY.
HE'S THE BOSS.

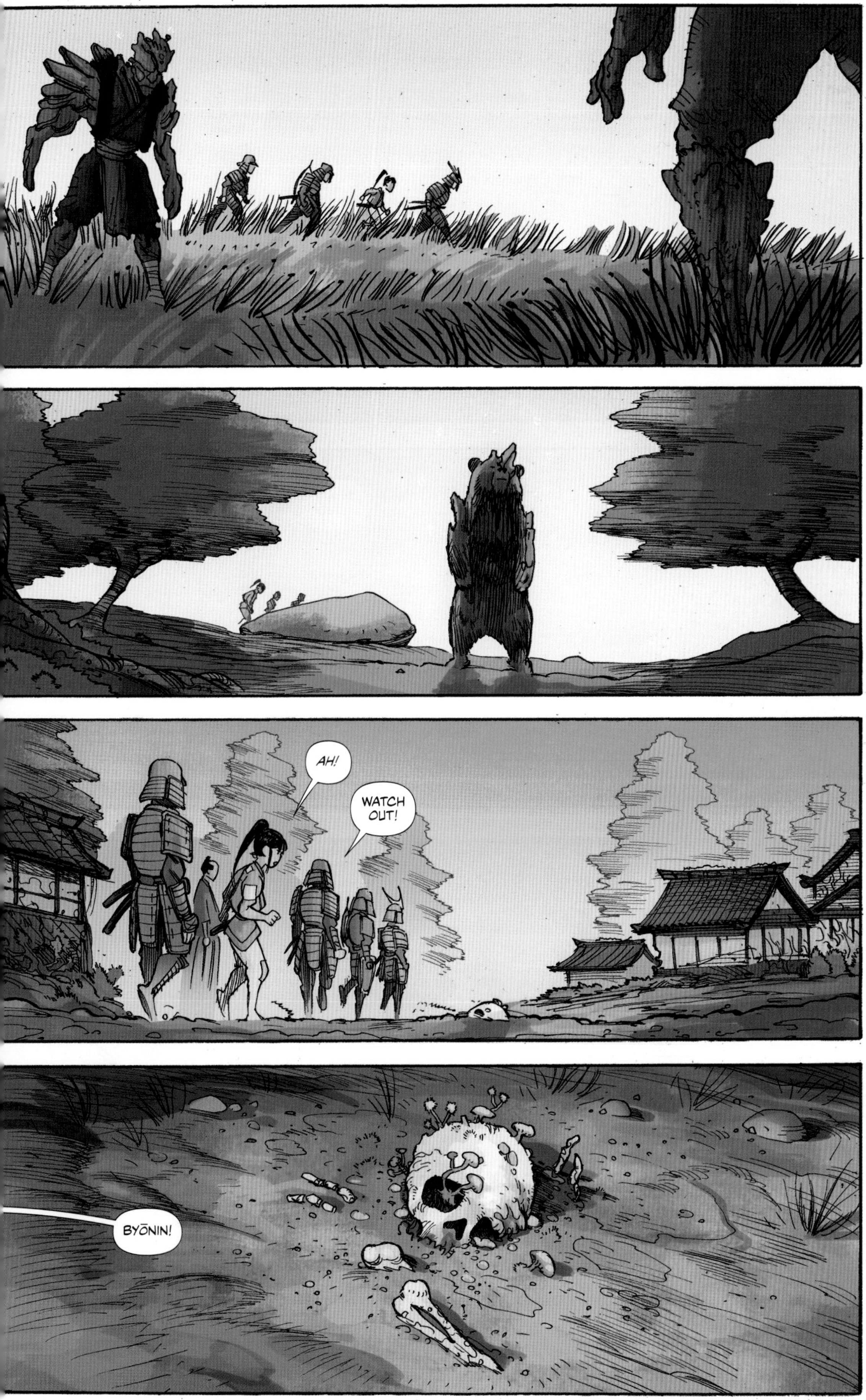
AH!
WATCH OUT!
BYŌNIN!

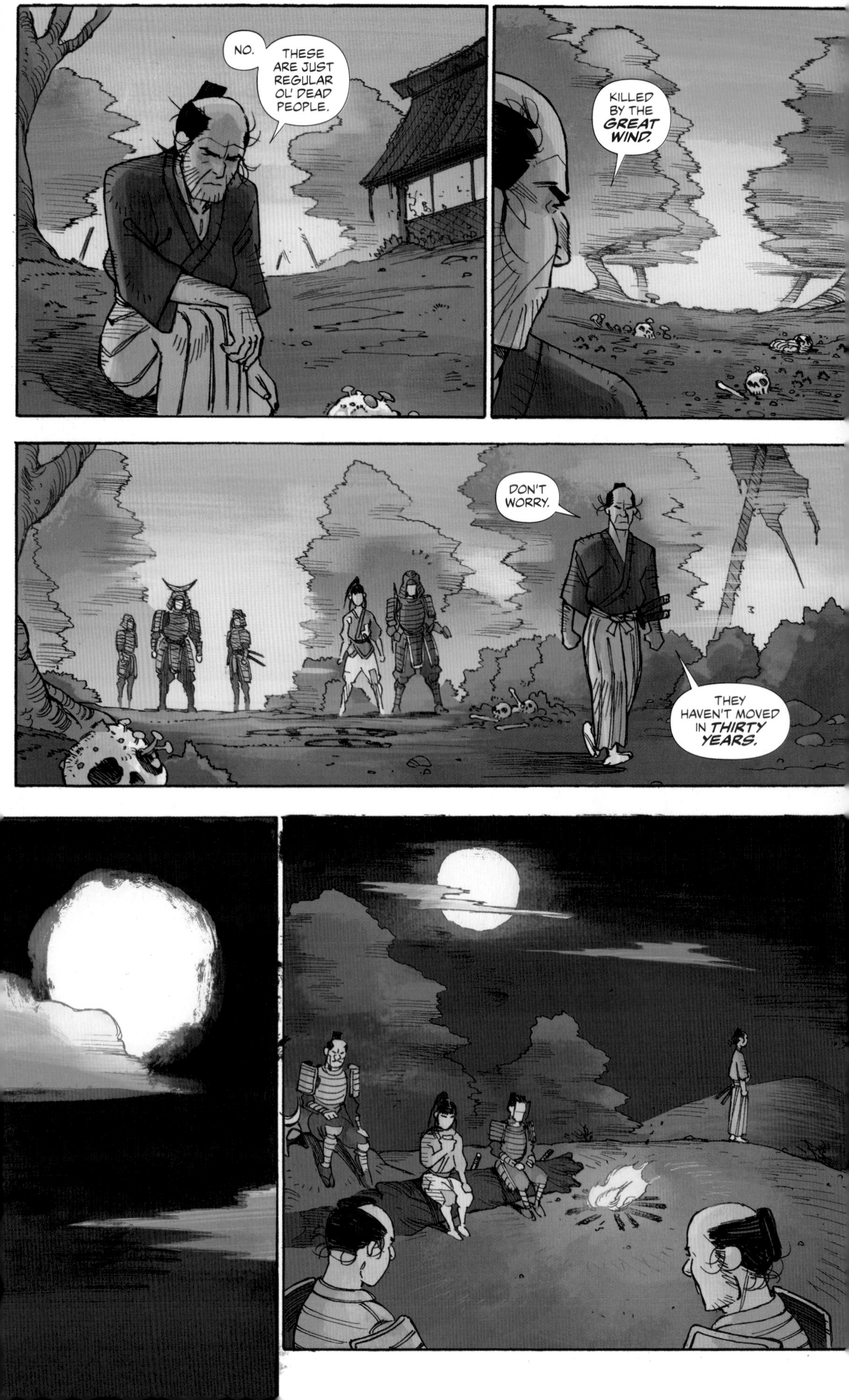
NO.
THESE ARE JUST REGULAR OL' DEAD PEOPLE.
KILLED BY THE GREAT WIND.
DON'T WORRY.
THEY HAVEN'T MOVED IN THIRTY YEARS.

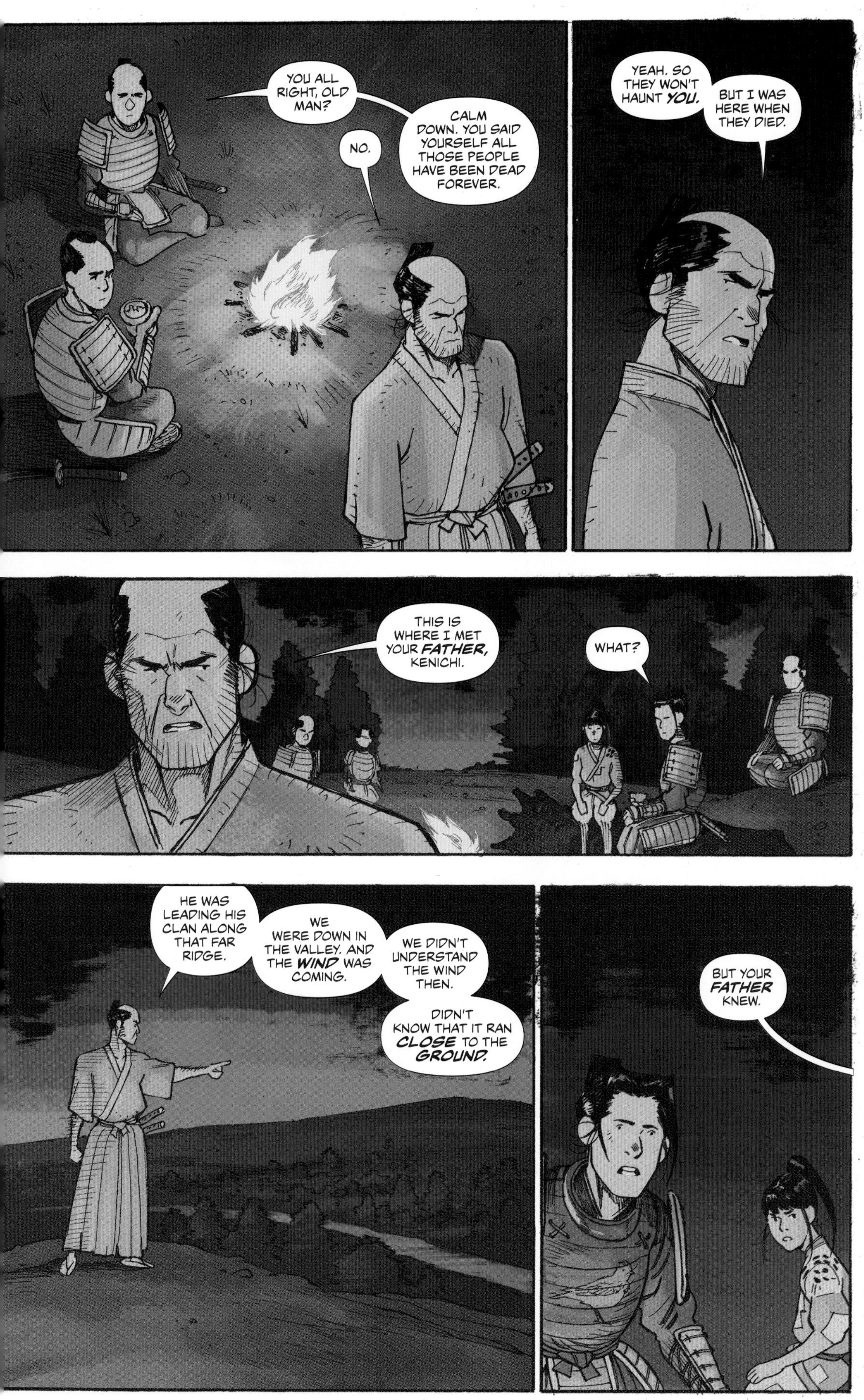
YOU ALL RIGHT, OLD MAN?
NO.
CALM DOWN. YOU SAID YOURSELF ALL THOSE PEOPLE HAVE BEEN DEAD FOREVER.
YEAH. SO THEY WON'T HAUNT YOU.
BUT I WAS HERE WHEN THEY DIED.
THIS IS WHERE I MET YOUR FATHER, KENICHI.
WHAT?
HE WAS LEADING HIS CLAN ALONG THAT FAR RIDGE.
WE WERE DOWN IN THE VALLEY. AND THE WIND WAS COMING.
WE DIDN'T UNDERSTAND THE WIND THEN.
DIDN'T KNOW THAT IT RAN CLOSE TO THE GROUND.
BUT YOUR FATHER KNEW.

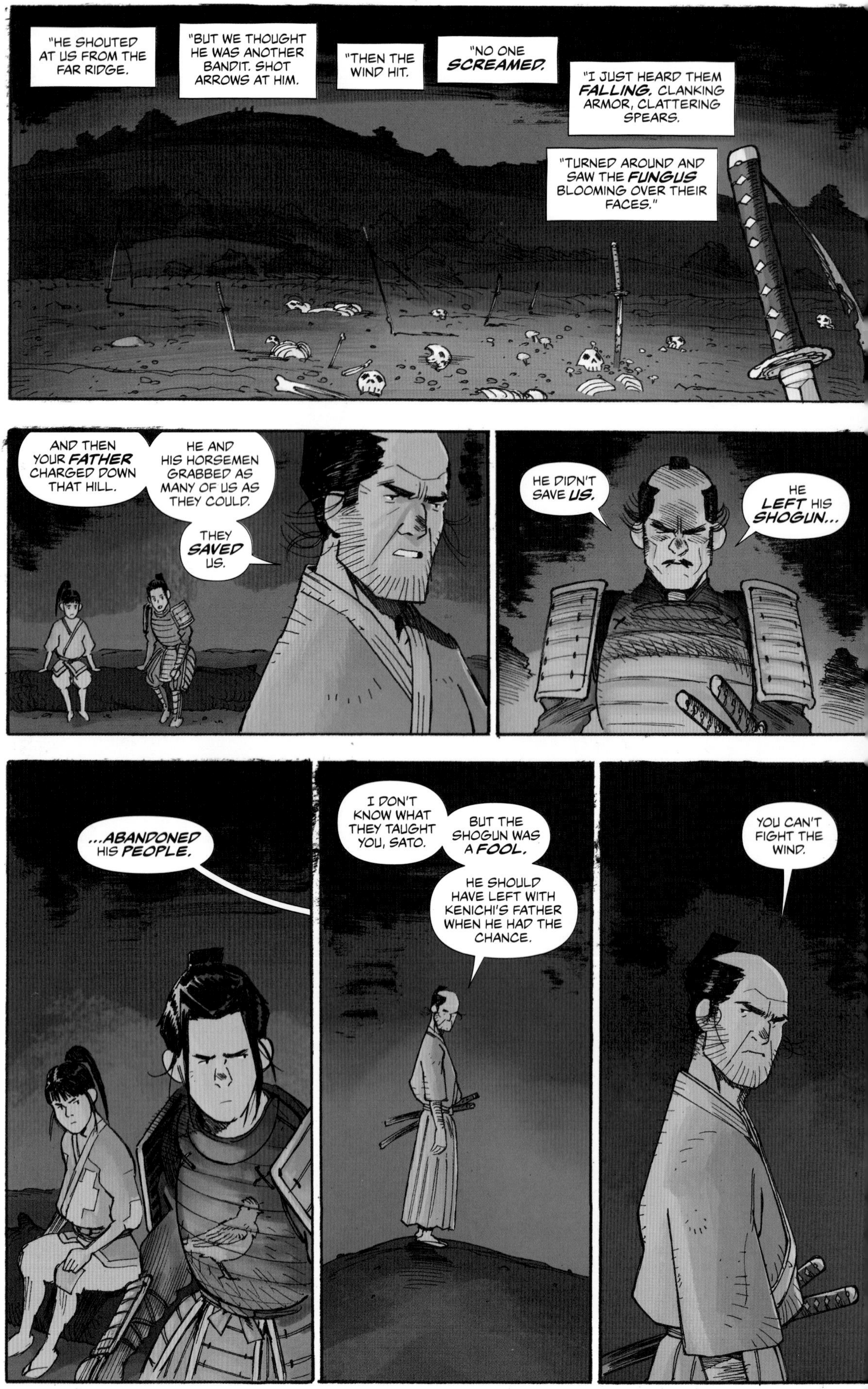
"HE SHOUTED AT US FROM THE FAR RIDGE.
"BUT WE THOUGHT HE WAS ANOTHER BANDIT. SHOT ARROWS AT HIM.
"THEN THE WIND HIT.
"NO ONE SCREAMED.
"I JUST HEARD THEM FALLING. CLANKING ARMOR, CLATTERING SPEARS.
"TURNED AROUND AND SAW THE FUNGUS BLOOMING OVER THEIR FACES."
AND THEN YOUR FATHER CHARGED DOWN THAT HILL.
HE AND HIS HORSEMEN GRABBED AS MANY OF US AS THEY COULD.
THEY SAVED US.
HE DIDN'T SAVE US.
HE LEFT HIS SHOGUN...
...ABANDONED HIS PEOPLE.
I DON'T KNOW WHAT THEY TAUGHT YOU, SATO.
BUT THE SHOGUN WAS A FOOL.
HE SHOULD HAVE LEFT WITH KENICHI'S FATHER WHEN HE HAD THE CHANCE.
YOU CAN'T FIGHT THE WIND.

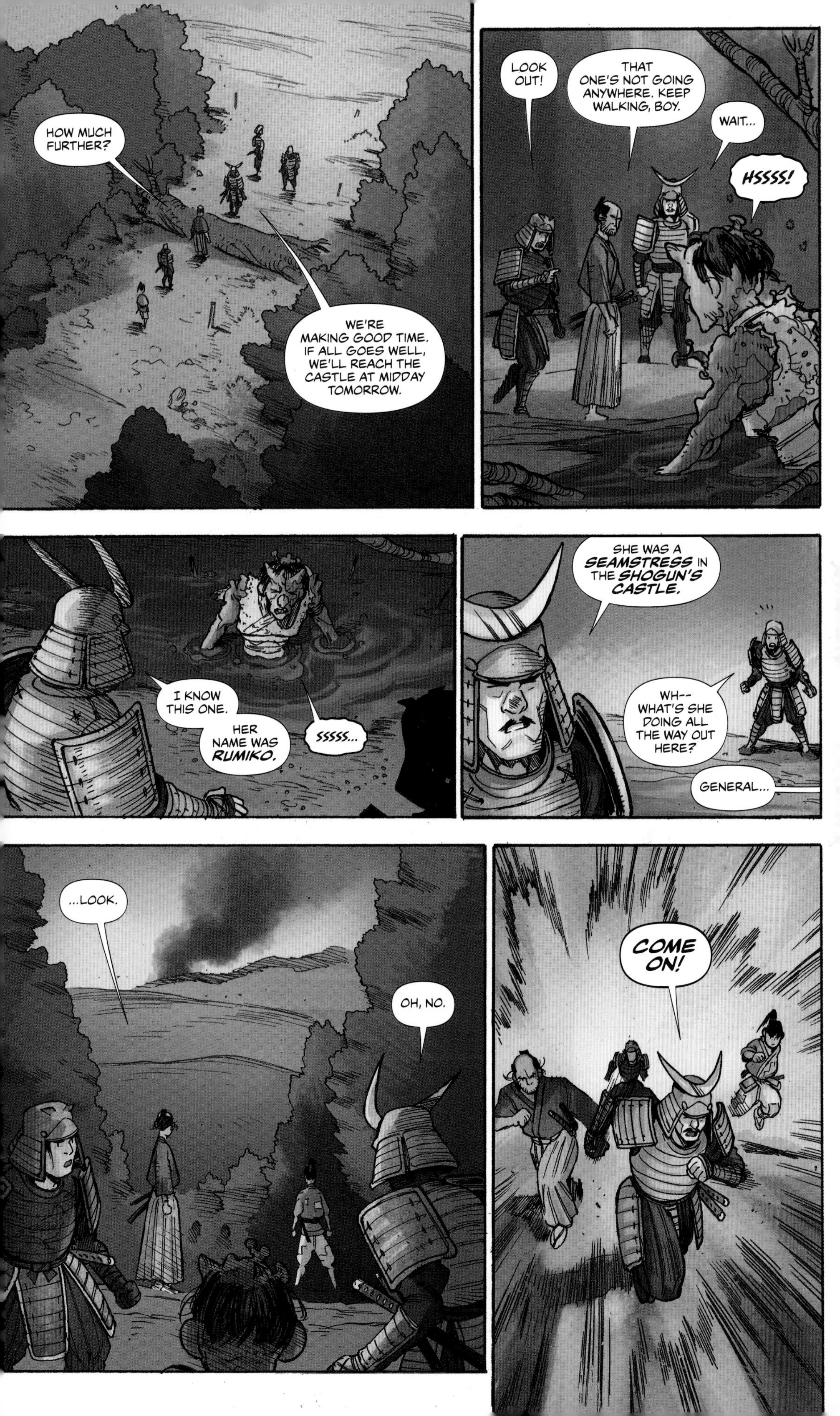
HOW MUCH FURTHER?
WE'RE MAKING GOOD TIME. IF ALL GOES WELL, WE'LL REACH THE CASTLE AT MIDDAY TOMORROW.
LOOK OUT!
THAT ONE'S NOT GOING ANYWHERE. KEEP WALKING, BOY.
WAIT...
HSSSS!
I KNOW THIS ONE.
HER NAME WAS RUMIKO.
SSSSS...
SHE WAS A SEAMSTRESS IN THE SHOGUN'S CASTLE.
WH-- WHAT'S SHE DOING ALL THE WAY OUT HERE?
GENERAL...
...LOOK.
OH, NO.
COME ON!

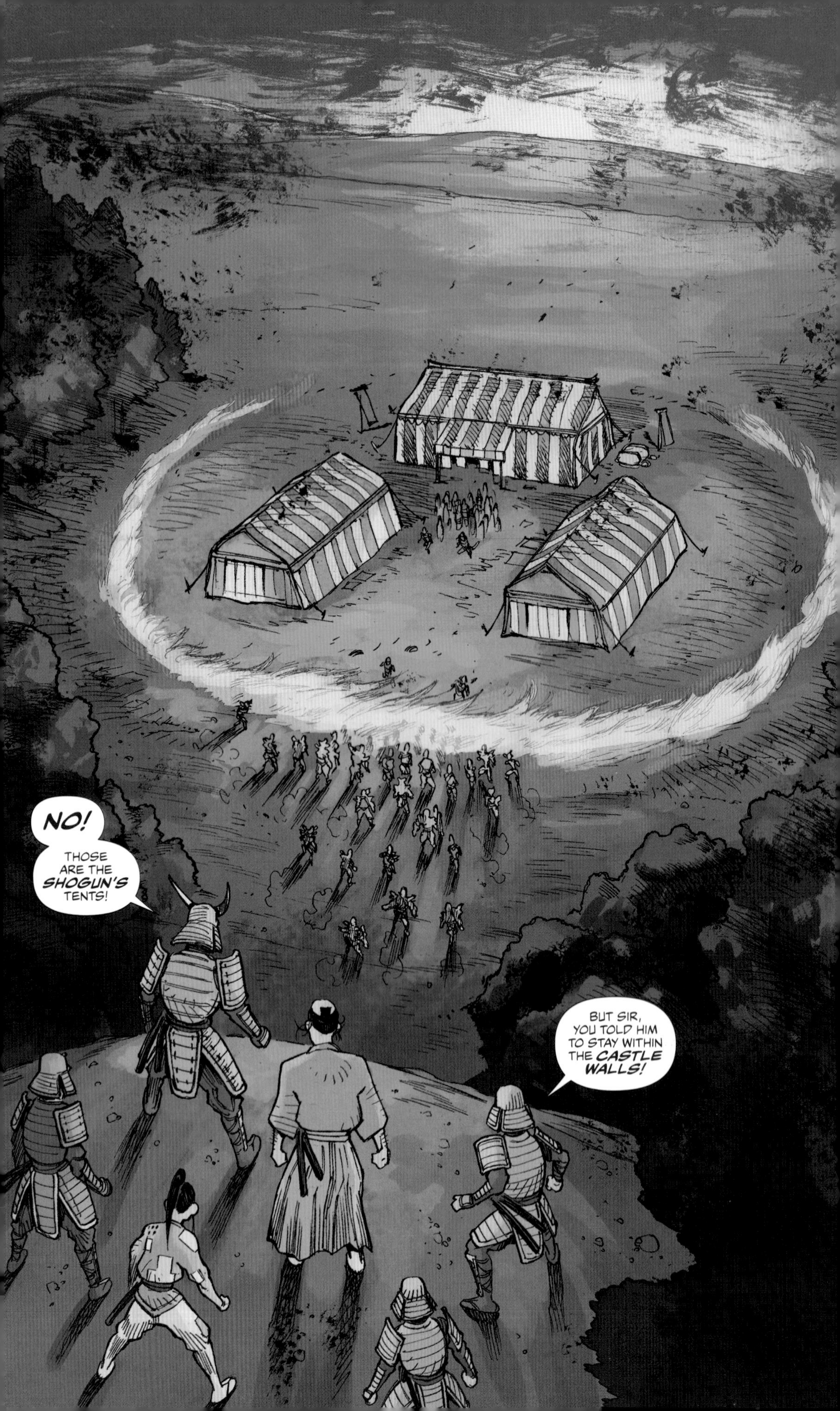
NO!
THOSE ARE THE SHOGUN'S TENTS!
BUT SIR, YOU TOLD HIM TO STAY WITHIN THE CASTLE WALLS!

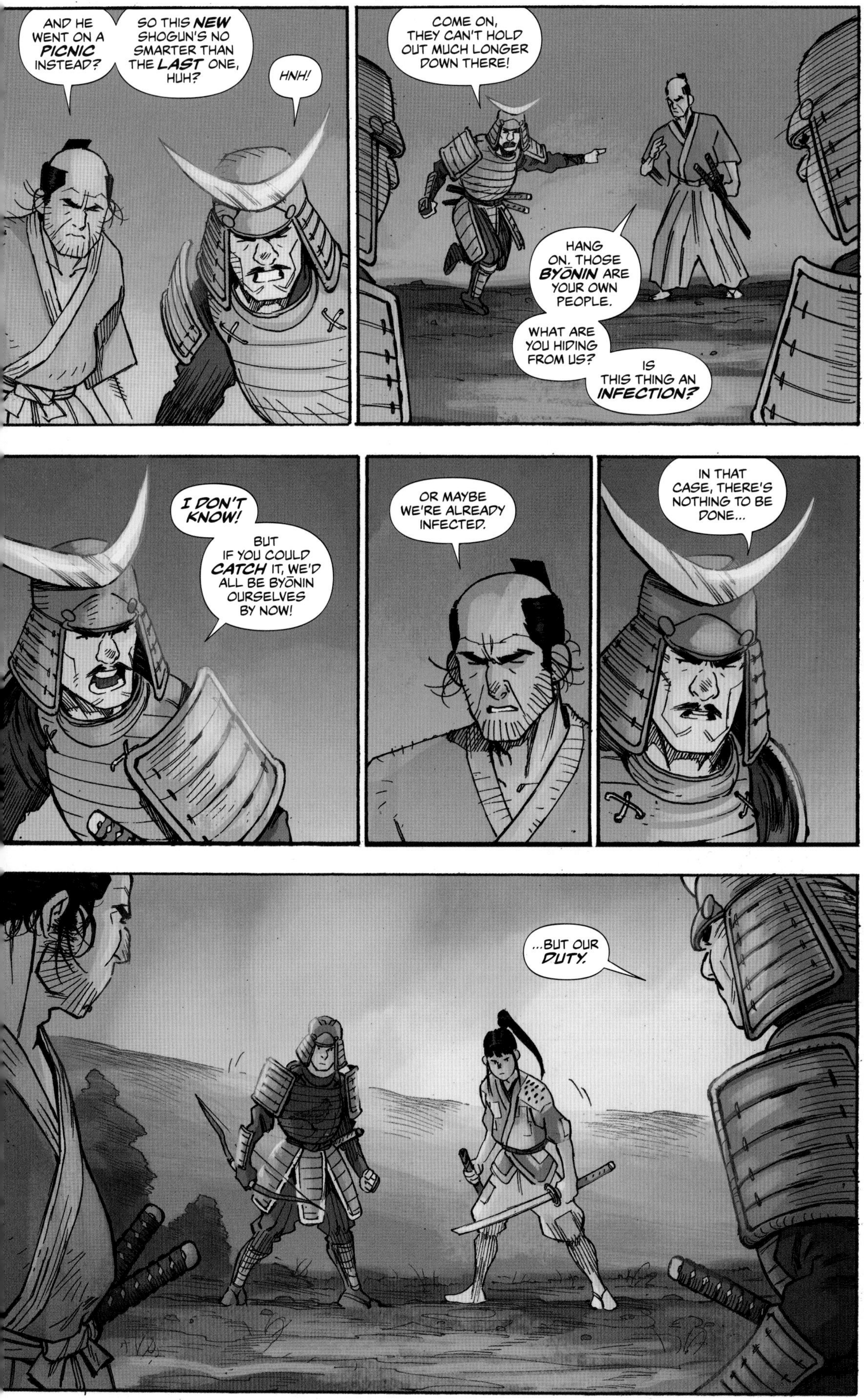

AND HE WENT ON A PICNIC INSTEAD?
SO THIS NEW SHOGUN'S NO SMARTER THAN THE LAST ONE, HUH?
HNH!
COME ON, THEY CAN'T HOLD OUT MUCH LONGER DOWN THERE!
HANG ON. THOSE BYŌNIN ARE YOUR OWN PEOPLE.
WHAT ARE YOU HIDING FROM US?
IS THIS THING AN INFECTION?
I DON'T KNOW!
BUT IF YOU COULD CATCH IT, WE'D ALL BE BYŌNIN OURSELVES BY NOW!
OR MAYBE WE'RE ALREADY INFECTED.
IN THAT CASE, THERE'S NOTHING TO BE DONE...
...BUT OUR DUTY.

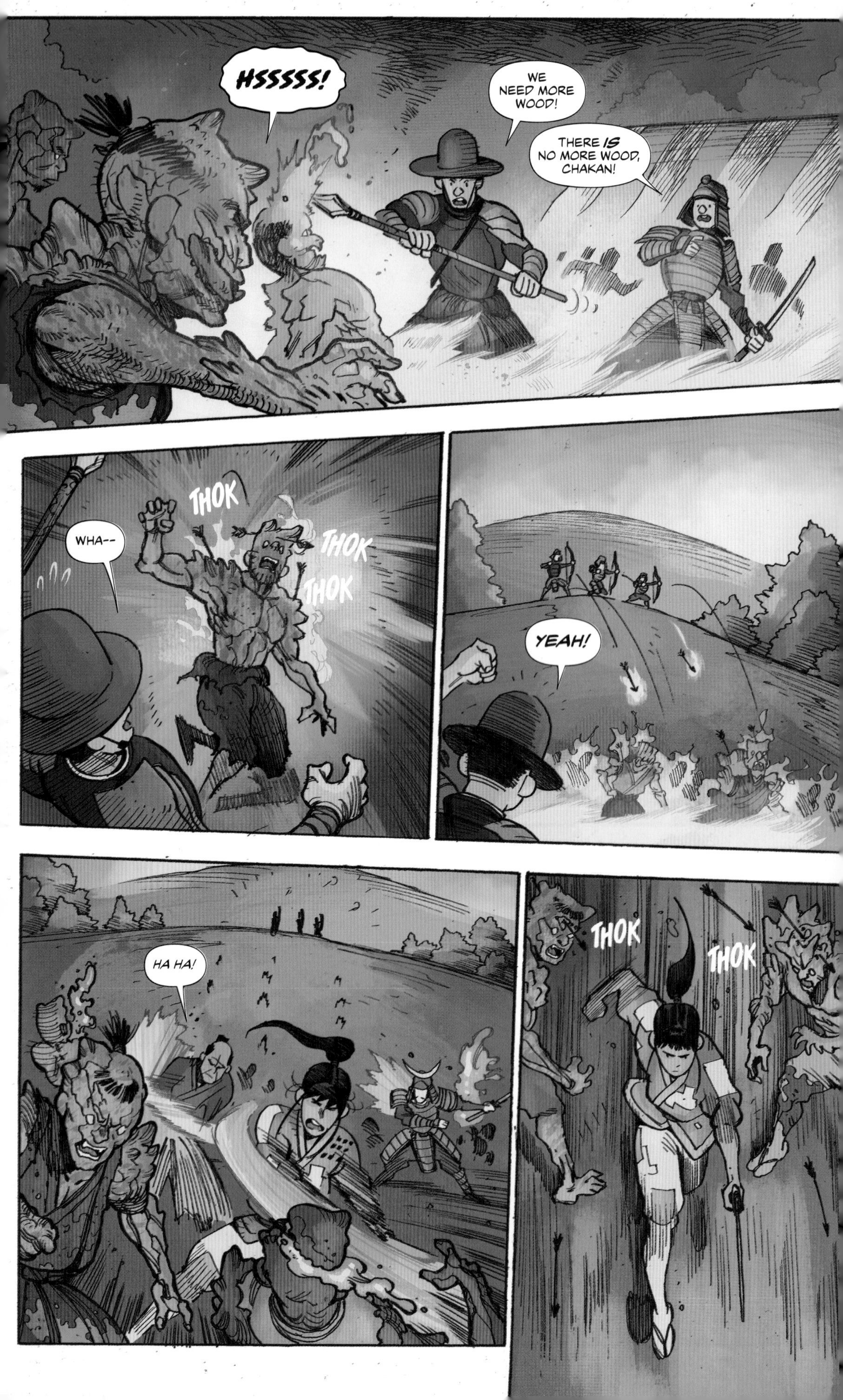
HSSSSS!
WE NEED MORE WOOD!
THERE IS NO MORE WOOD, CHAKAN!
WHA--
THOK
THOK
THOK
YEAH!
HA HA!
THOK
THOK

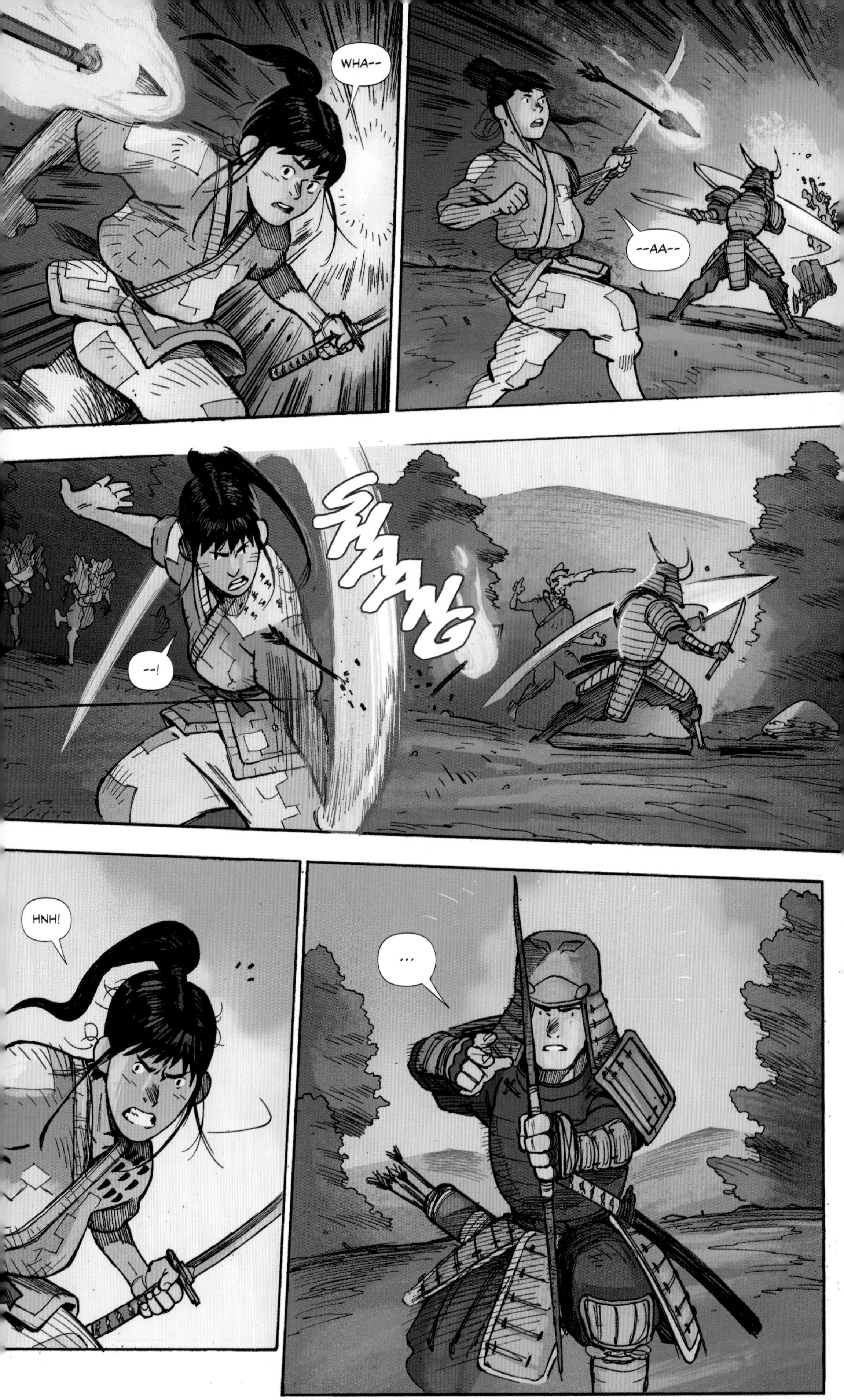
WHA--
--AA--
SHAANG
--!
HNH!
...

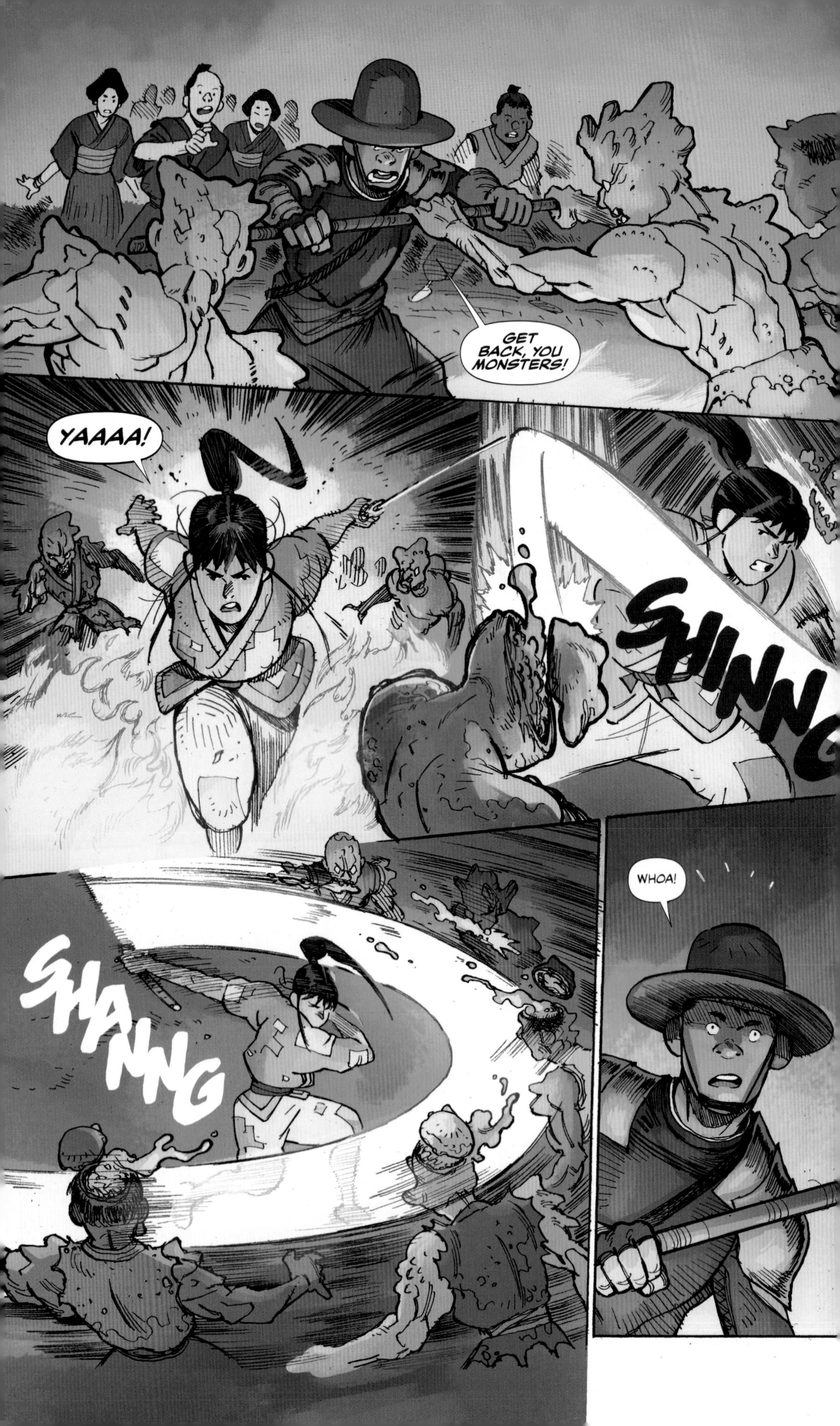
GET BACK, YOU MONSTERS!
YAAAA!
SHINNG
SHANNG
WHOA!

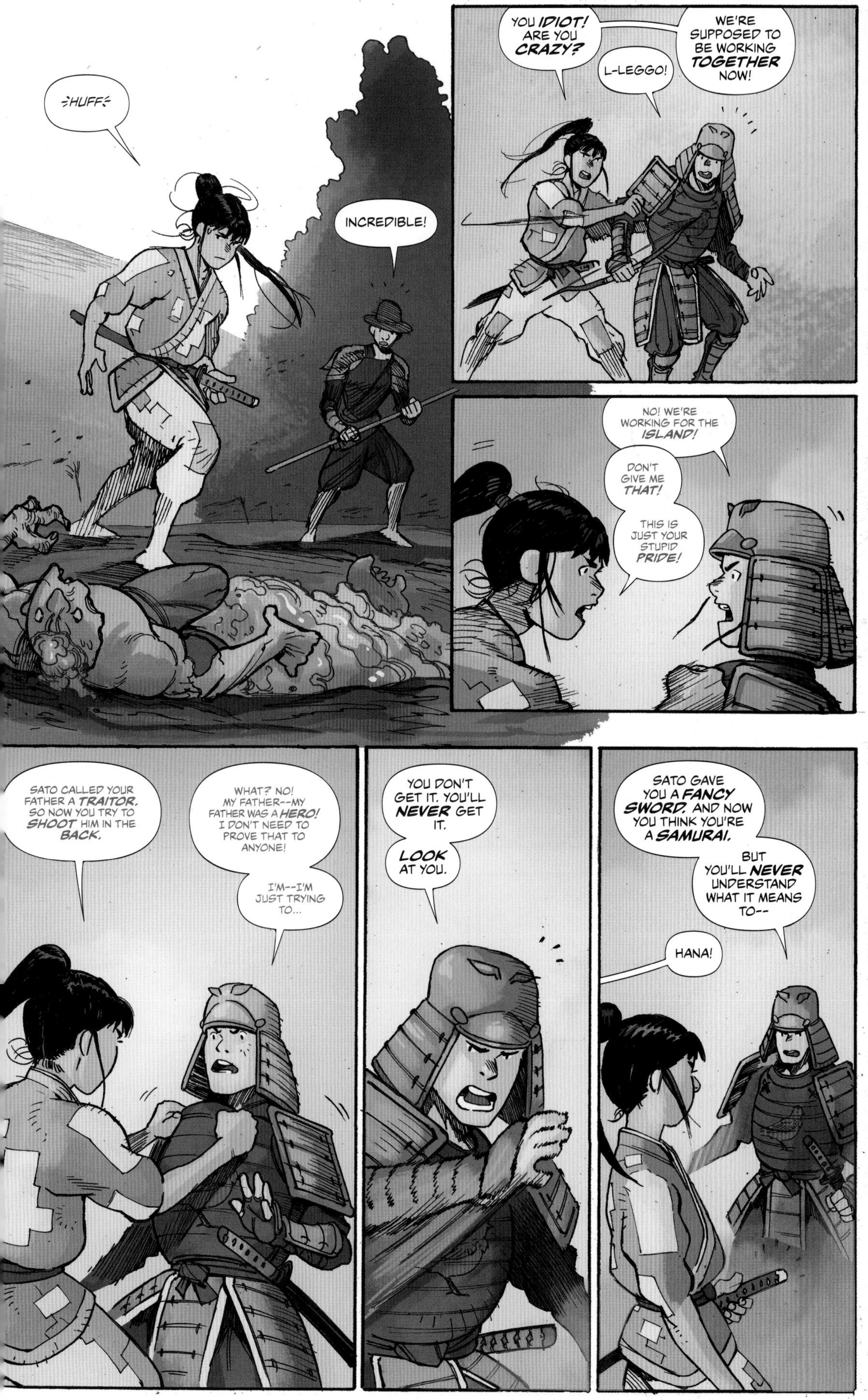
HUFF
INCREDIBLE!
YOU IDIOT! ARE YOU CRAZY?
L-LEGGO!
WE'RE SUPPOSED TO BE WORKING TOGETHER NOW!
NO! WE'RE WORKING FOR THE ISLAND!
DON'T GIVE ME THAT!
THIS IS JUST YOUR STUPID PRIDE!
SATO CALLED YOUR FATHER A TRAITOR, SO NOW YOU TRY TO SHOOT HIM IN THE BACK.
WHAT? NO! MY FATHER--MY FATHER WAS A HERO! I DON'T NEED TO PROVE THAT TO ANYONE!
I'M--I'M JUST TRYING TO...
YOU DON'T GET IT. YOU'LL NEVER GET IT.
LOOK AT YOU.
SATO GAVE YOU A FANCY SWORD, AND NOW YOU THINK YOU'RE A SAMURAI.
BUT YOU'LL NEVER UNDERSTAND WHAT IT MEANS TO--
HANA!

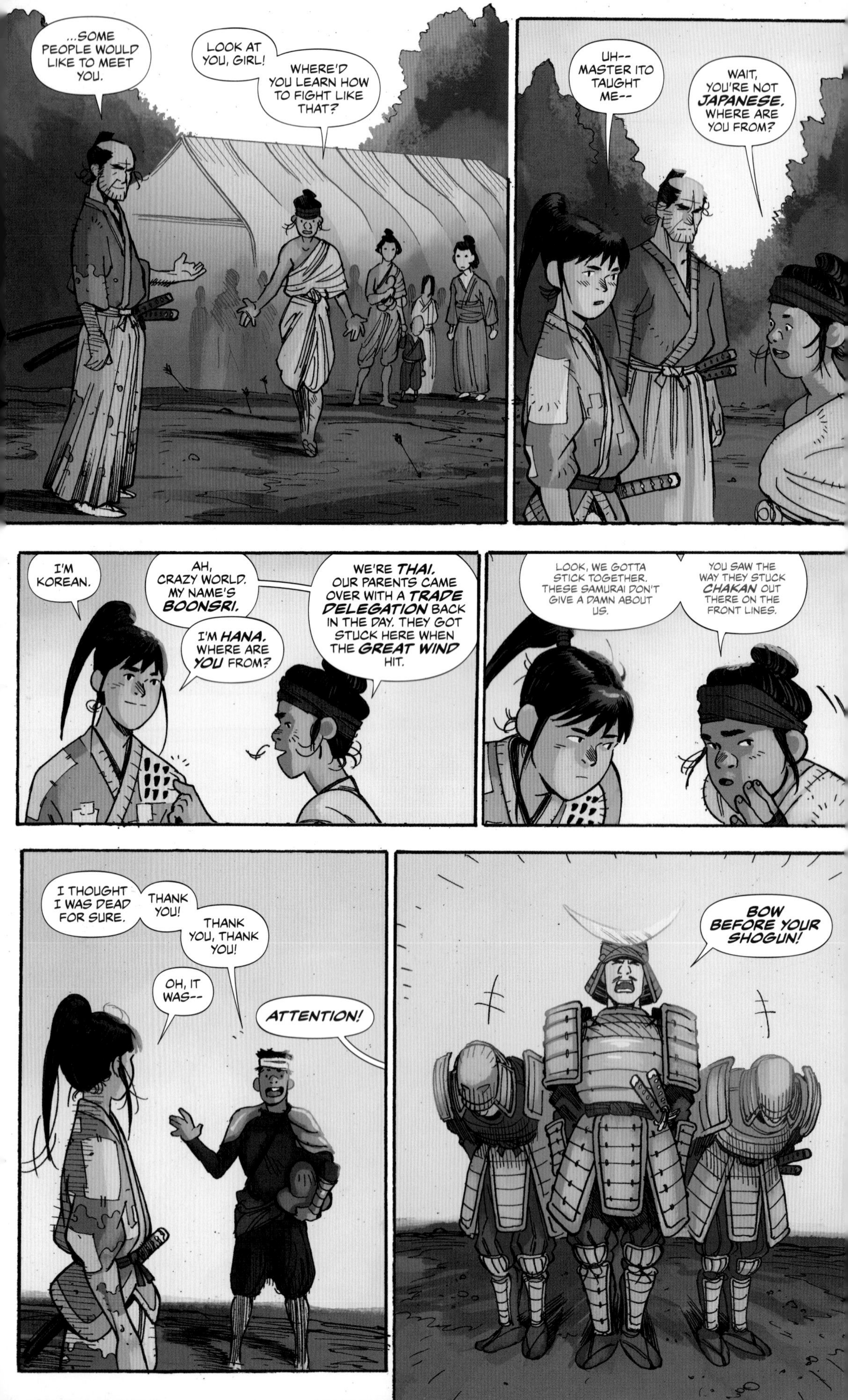
...SOME PEOPLE WOULD LIKE TO MEET YOU.
LOOK AT YOU, GIRL!
WHERE'D YOU LEARN HOW TO FIGHT LIKE THAT?
UH-- MASTER ITO TAUGHT ME--
WAIT, YOU'RE NOT JAPANESE. WHERE ARE YOU FROM?
I'M KOREAN.
AH, CRAZY WORLD. MY NAME'S BOONSRI.
I'M HANA. WHERE ARE YOU FROM?
WE'RE THAI. OUR PARENTS CAME OVER WITH A TRADE DELEGATION BACK IN THE DAY. THEY GOT STUCK HERE WHEN THE GREAT WIND HIT.
LOOK, WE GOTTA STICK TOGETHER. THESE SAMURAI DON'T GIVE A DAMN ABOUT US.
YOU SAW THE WAY THEY STUCK CHAKAN OUT THERE ON THE FRONT LINES.
I THOUGHT I WAS DEAD FOR SURE.
THANK YOU!
THANK YOU, THANK YOU!
OH, IT WAS--
ATTENTION!
BOW BEFORE YOUR SHOGUN!

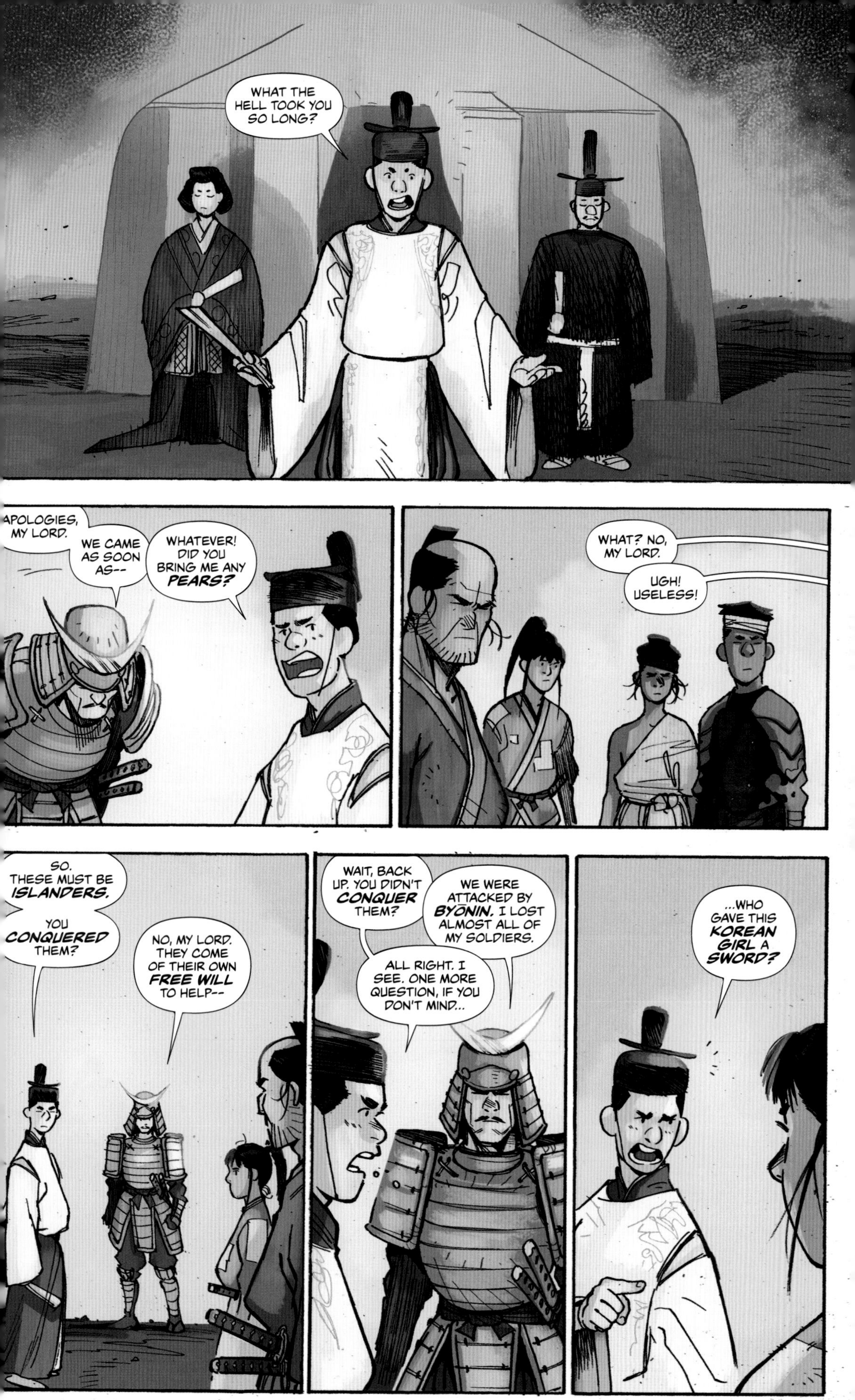
WHAT THE HELL TOOK YOU SO LONG?
APOLOGIES, MY LORD.
WE CAME AS SOON AS--
WHATEVER! DID YOU BRING ME ANY PEARS?
WHAT? NO, MY LORD.
UGH! USELESS!
SO. THESE MUST BE ISLANDERS.
YOU CONQUERED THEM?
NO, MY LORD. THEY COME OF THEIR OWN FREE WILL TO HELP--
WAIT, BACK UP. YOU DIDN'T CONQUER THEM?
WE WERE ATTACKED BY BYŌNIN. I LOST ALMOST ALL OF MY SOLDIERS.
ALL RIGHT. I SEE. ONE MORE QUESTION, IF YOU DON'T MIND...
...WHO GAVE THIS KOREAN GIRL A SWORD?

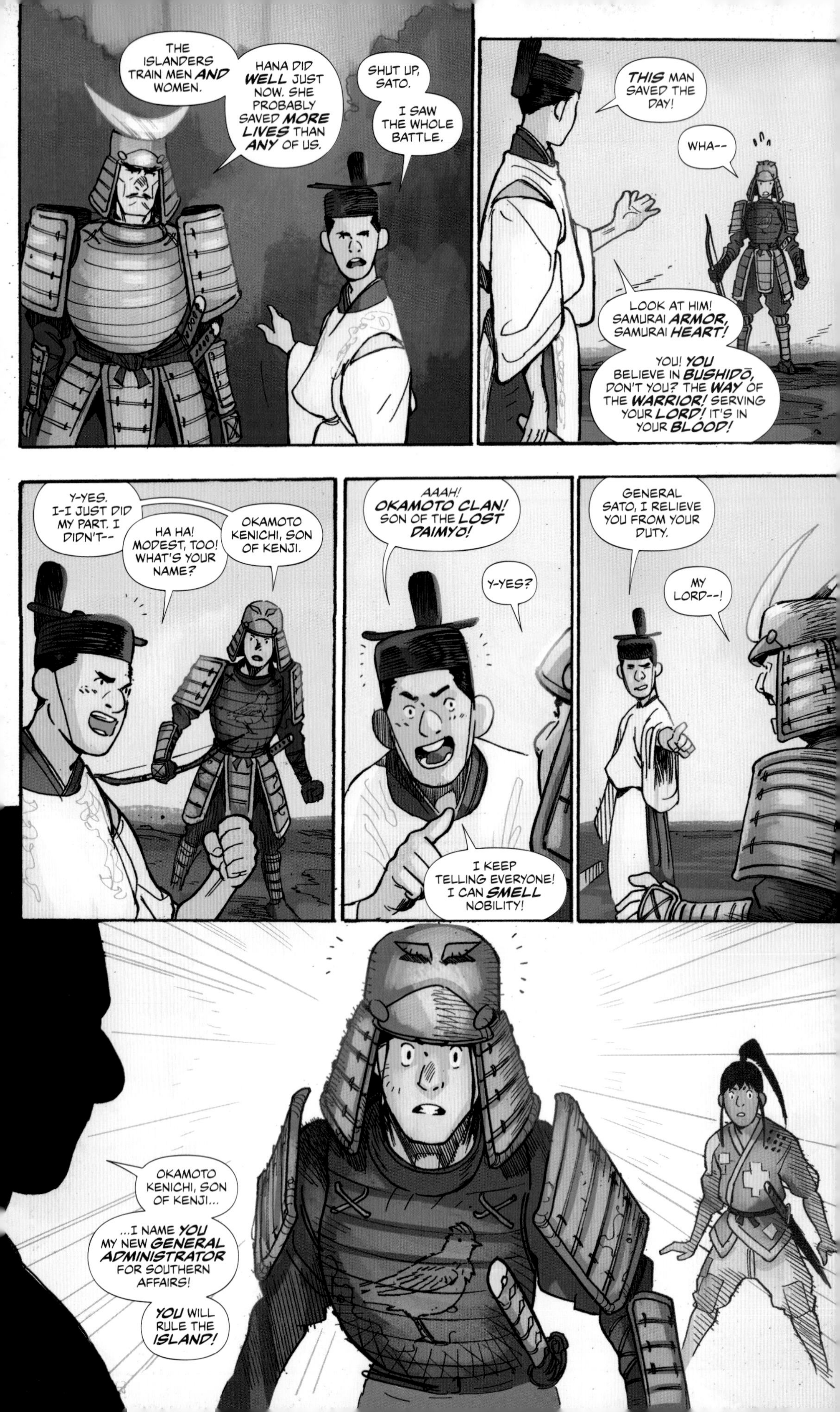
THE ISLANDERS TRAIN MEN AND WOMEN.
HANA DID WELL JUST NOW. SHE PROBABLY SAVED MORE LIVES THAN ANY OF US.
SHUT UP, SATO.
I SAW THE WHOLE BATTLE.
THIS MAN SAVED THE DAY!
WHA--
LOOK AT HIM! SAMURAI ARMOR, SAMURAI HEART!
YOU! YOU BELIEVE IN BUSHIDŌ, DON'T YOU? THE WAY OF THE WARRIOR! SERVING YOUR LORD! IT'S IN YOUR BLOOD!
Y-YES. I-I JUST DID MY PART. I DIDN'T--
HA HA! MODEST, TOO! WHAT'S YOUR NAME?
OKAMOTO KENICHI, SON OF KENJI.
AAAH! OKAMOTO CLAN! SON OF THE LOST DAIMYO!
Y-YES?
I KEEP TELLING EVERYONE! I CAN SMELL NOBILITY!
GENERAL SATO, I RELIEVE YOU FROM YOUR DUTY.
MY LORD--!
OKAMOTO KENICHI, SON OF KENJI...
...I NAME YOU MY NEW GENERAL ADMINISTRATOR FOR SOUTHERN AFFAIRS!
YOU WILL RULE THE ISLAND!

Issue Three Cover by **Ethan Young**

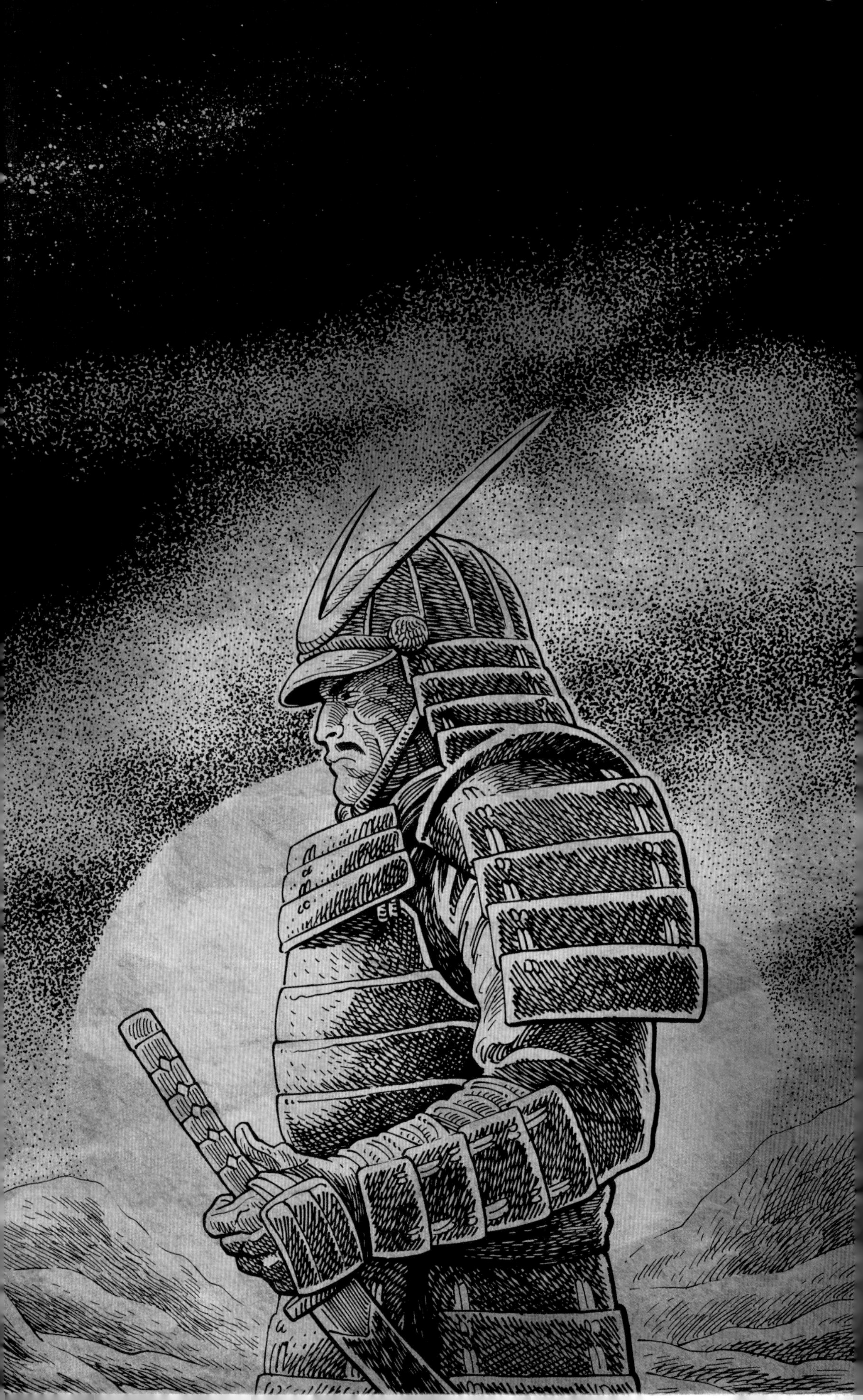

CHAPTER FOUR

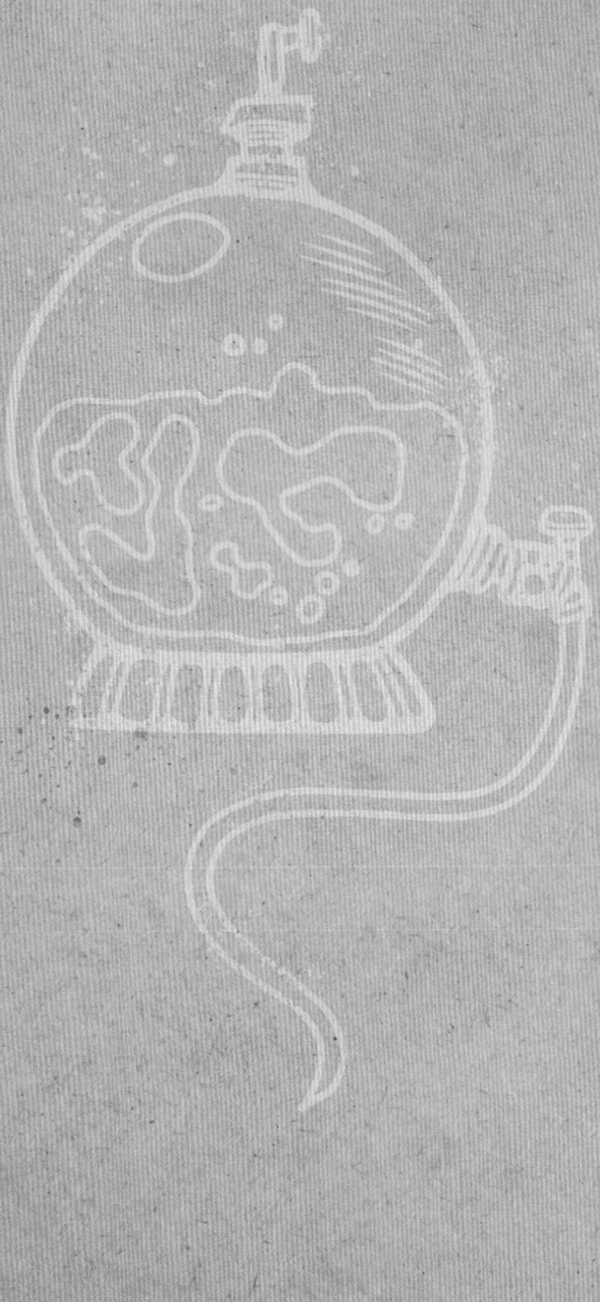

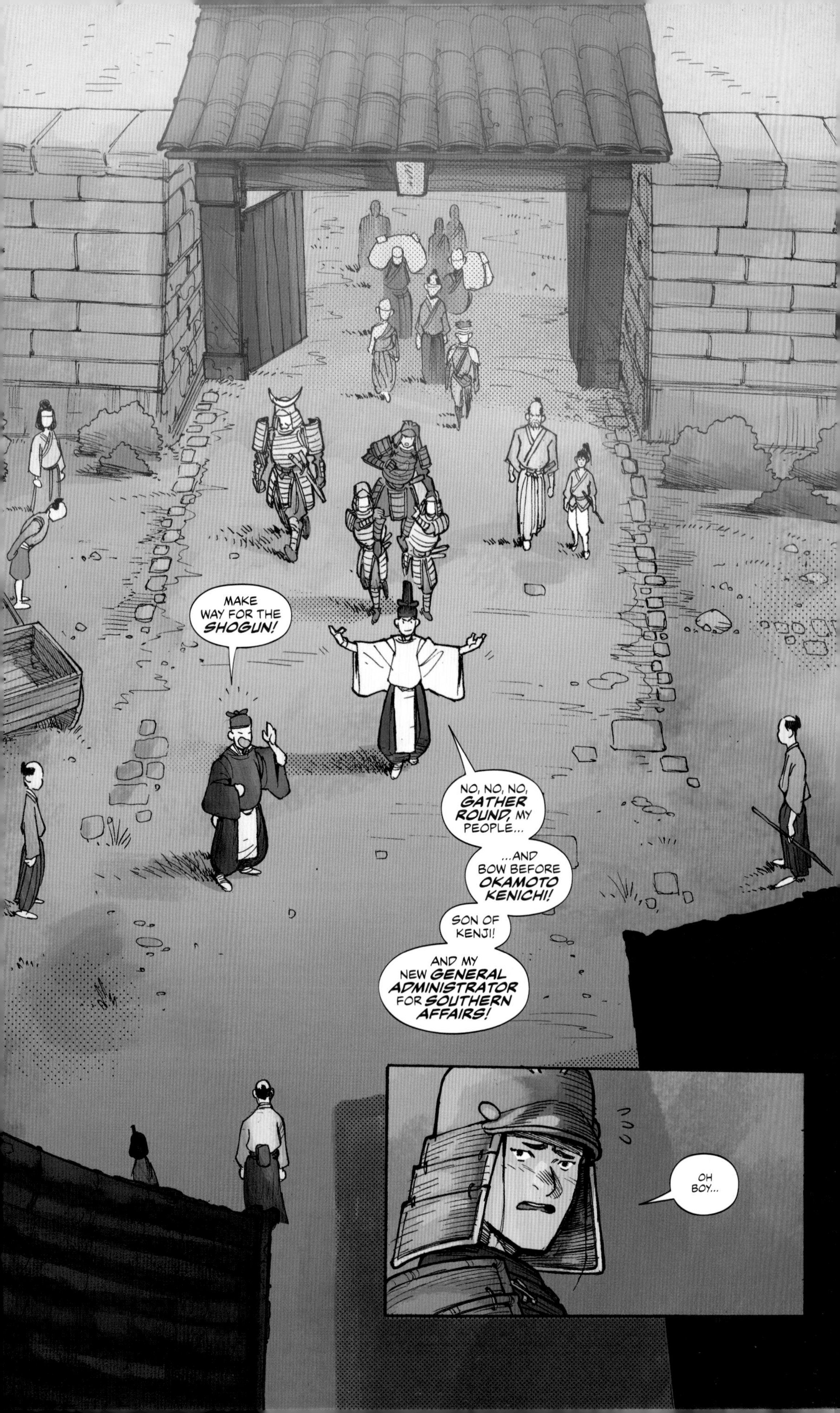
MAKE WAY FOR THE SHOGUN!
NO, NO, NO, GATHER ROUND, MY PEOPLE...
...AND BOW BEFORE OKAMOTO KENICHI!
SON OF KENJI!
AND MY NEW GENERAL ADMINISTRATOR FOR SOUTHERN AFFAIRS!
OH BOY...

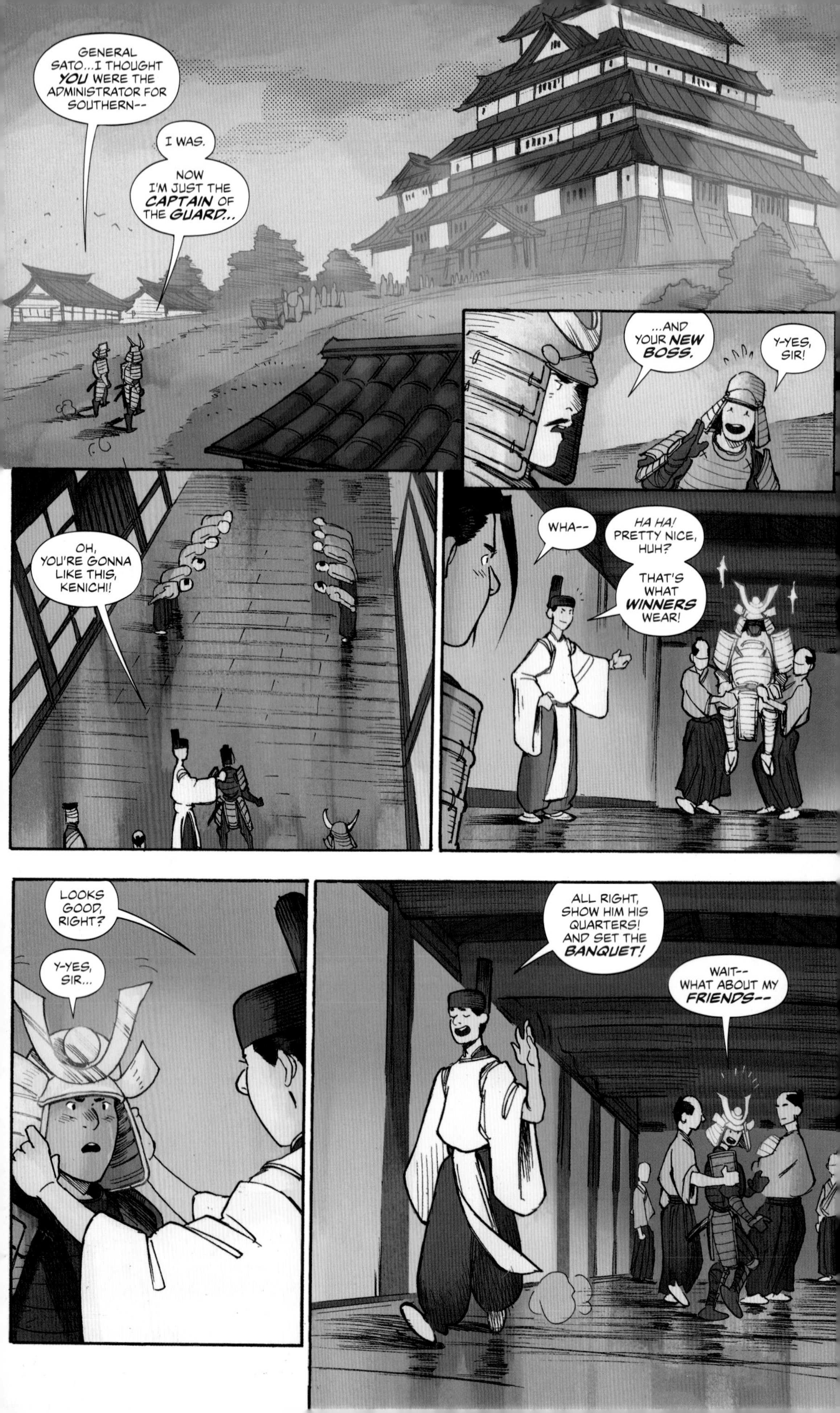
GENERAL SATO...I THOUGHT YOU WERE THE ADMINISTRATOR FOR SOUTHERN--
I WAS.
NOW I'M JUST THE CAPTAIN OF THE GUARD...
...AND YOUR NEW BOSS.
Y-YES, SIR!
OH, YOU'RE GONNA LIKE THIS, KENICHI!
WHA--
HA HA! PRETTY NICE, HUH?
THAT'S WHAT WINNERS WEAR!
LOOKS GOOD, RIGHT?
Y-YES, SIR...
ALL RIGHT, SHOW HIM HIS QUARTERS! AND SET THE BANQUET!
WAIT-- WHAT ABOUT MY FRIENDS--

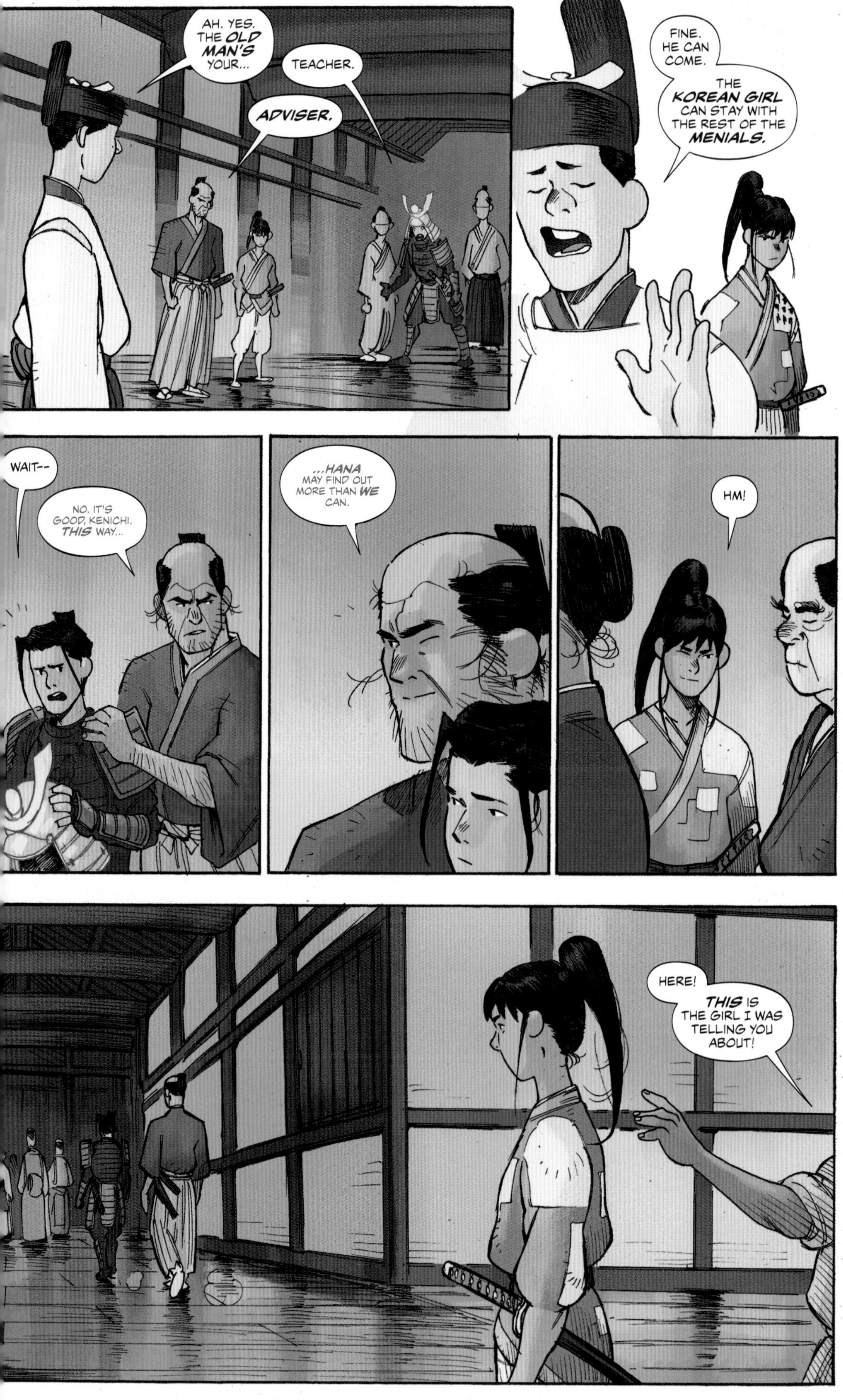
AH. YES. THE OLD MAN'S YOUR...
TEACHER.
ADVISER.
FINE. HE CAN COME.
THE KOREAN GIRL CAN STAY WITH THE REST OF THE MENIALS.
WAIT--
NO. IT'S GOOD, KENICHI. THIS WAY...
...HANA MAY FIND OUT MORE THAN WE CAN.
HM!
HERE!
THIS IS THE GIRL I WAS TELLING YOU ABOUT!

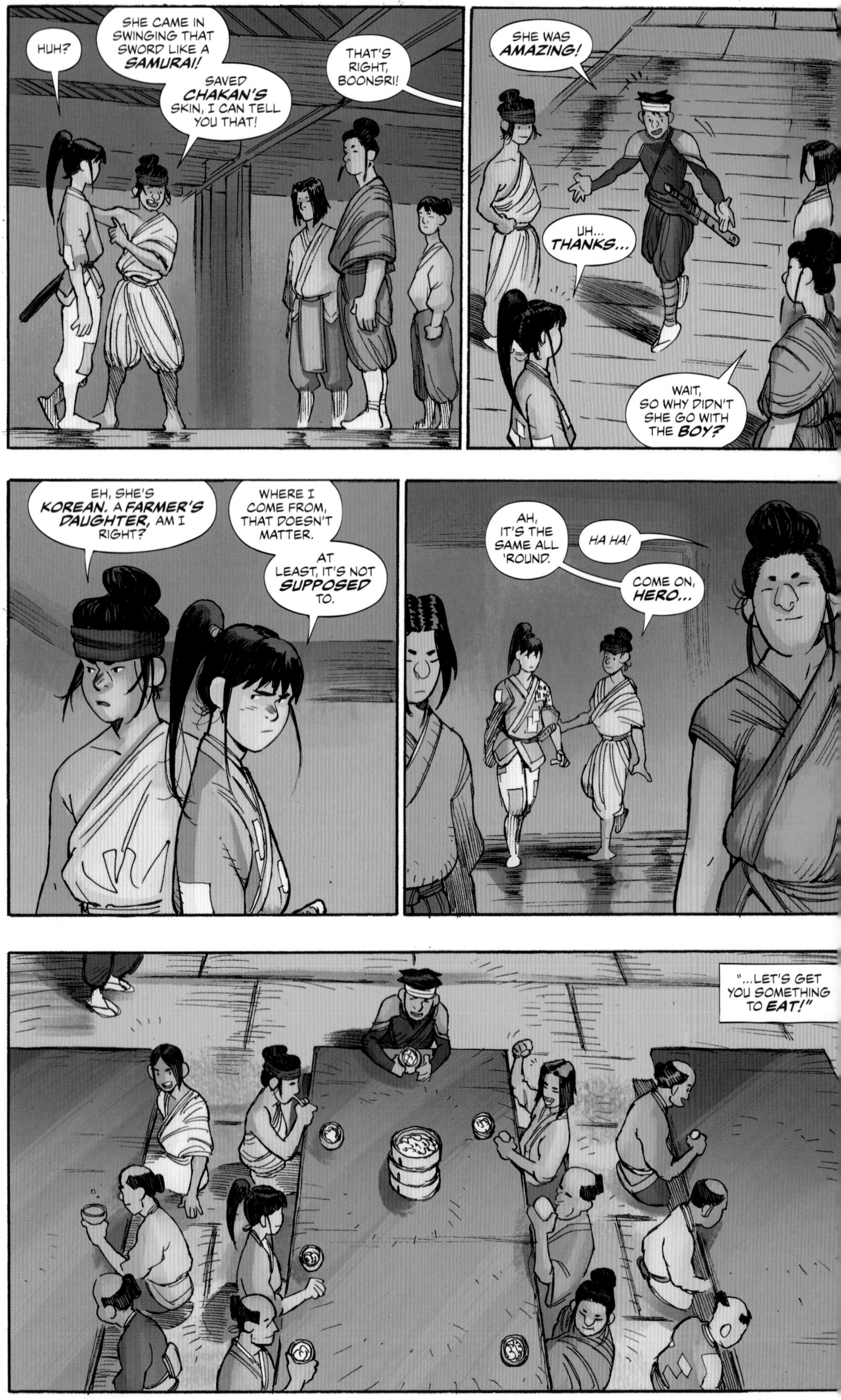
HUH?
SHE CAME IN SWINGING THAT SWORD LIKE A SAMURAI!
SAVED CHAKAN'S SKIN, I CAN TELL YOU THAT!
THAT'S RIGHT, BOONSRI!
SHE WAS AMAZING!
UH... THANKS...
WAIT, SO WHY DIDN'T SHE GO WITH THE BOY?
EH, SHE'S KOREAN. A FARMER'S DAUGHTER, AM I RIGHT?
WHERE I COME FROM, THAT DOESN'T MATTER.
AT LEAST, IT'S NOT SUPPOSED TO.
AH, IT'S THE SAME ALL 'ROUND.
HA HA!
COME ON, HERO...
"...LET'S GET YOU SOMETHING TO EAT!"

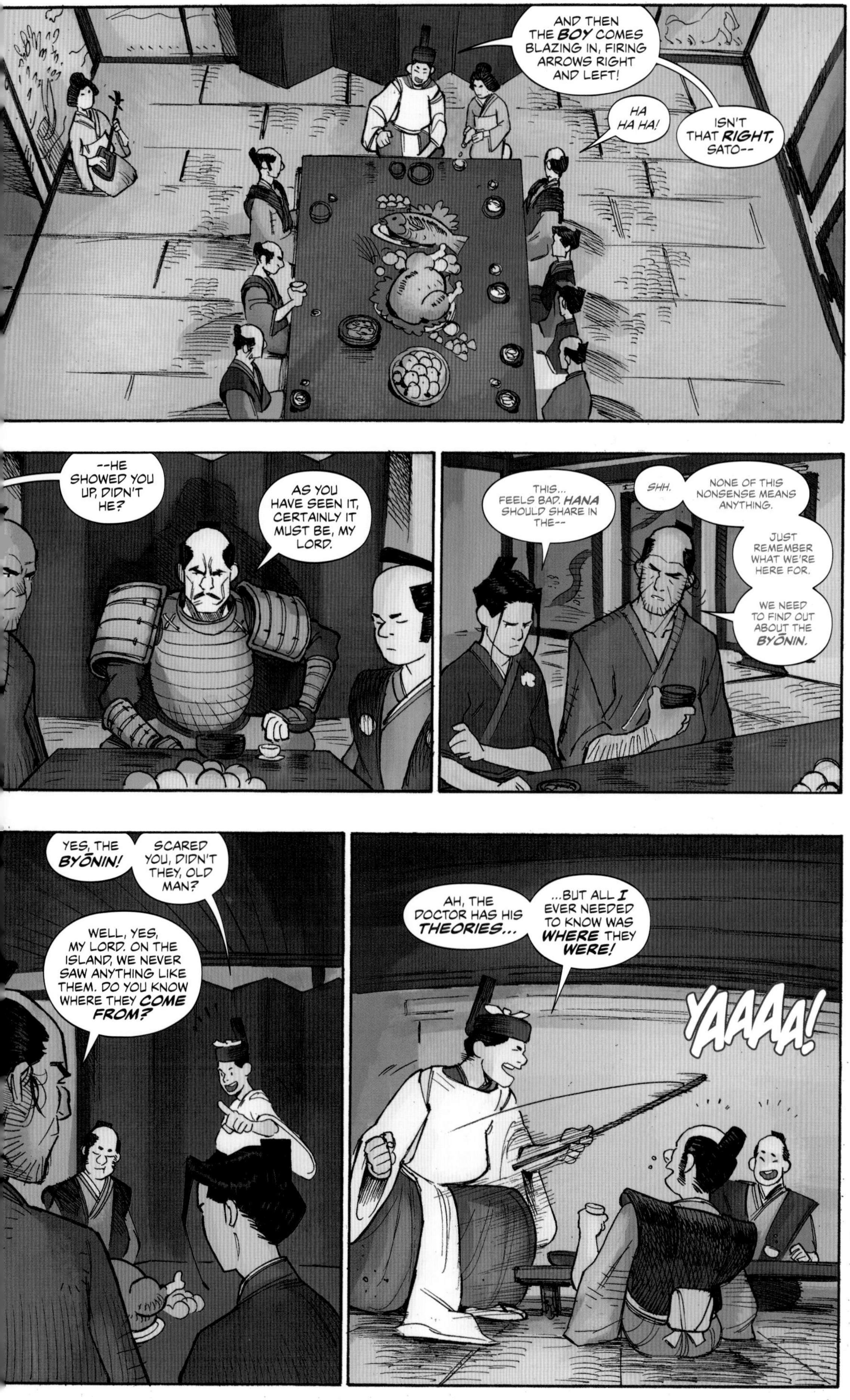

AND THEN THE BOY COMES BLAZING IN, FIRING ARROWS RIGHT AND LEFT!
HA HA HA!
ISN'T THAT RIGHT, SATO--
--HE SHOWED YOU UP, DIDN'T HE?
AS YOU HAVE SEEN IT, CERTAINLY IT MUST BE, MY LORD.
THIS... FEELS BAD. HANA SHOULD SHARE IN THE--
SHH.
NONE OF THIS NONSENSE MEANS ANYTHING.
JUST REMEMBER WHAT WE'RE HERE FOR.
WE NEED TO FIND OUT ABOUT THE BYŌNIN.
YES, THE BYŌNIN!
SCARED YOU, DIDN'T THEY, OLD MAN?
WELL, YES, MY LORD. ON THE ISLAND, WE NEVER SAW ANYTHING LIKE THEM. DO YOU KNOW WHERE THEY COME FROM?
AH, THE DOCTOR HAS HIS THEORIES...
...BUT ALL I EVER NEEDED TO KNOW WAS WHERE THEY WERE!
YAAAA!

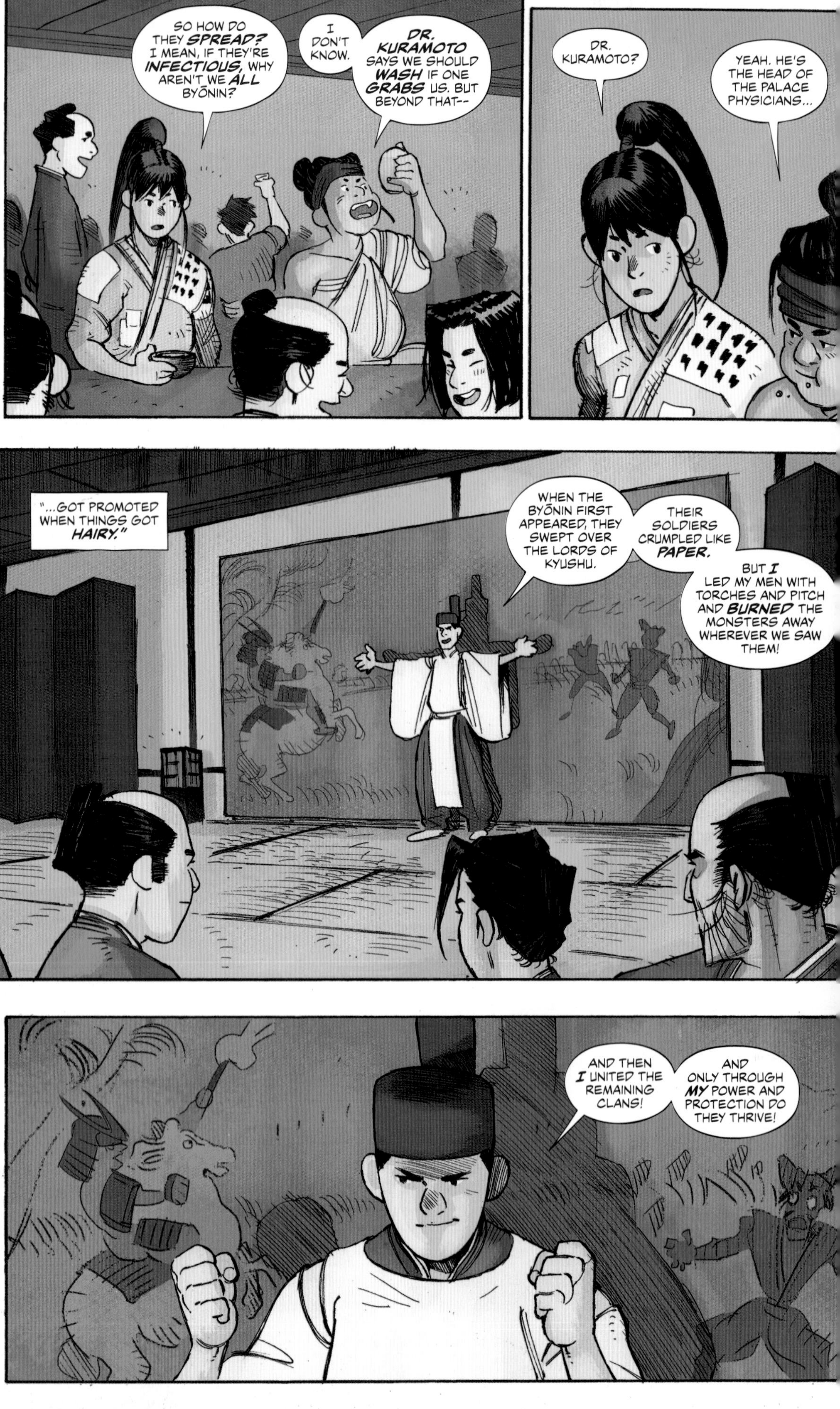
SO HOW DO THEY SPREAD? I MEAN, IF THEY'RE INFECTIOUS, WHY AREN'T WE ALL BYŌNIN?
I DON'T KNOW.
DR. KURAMOTO SAYS WE SHOULD WASH IF ONE GRABS US. BUT BEYOND THAT--
DR. KURAMOTO?
YEAH. HE'S THE HEAD OF THE PALACE PHYSICIANS...
"...GOT PROMOTED WHEN THINGS GOT HAIRY."
WHEN THE BYŌNIN FIRST APPEARED, THEY SWEPT OVER THE LORDS OF KYUSHU.
THEIR SOLDIERS CRUMPLED LIKE PAPER.
BUT I LED MY MEN WITH TORCHES AND PITCH AND BURNED THE MONSTERS AWAY WHEREVER WE SAW THEM!
AND THEN I UNITED THE REMAINING CLANS!
AND ONLY THROUGH MY POWER AND PROTECTION DO THEY THRIVE!

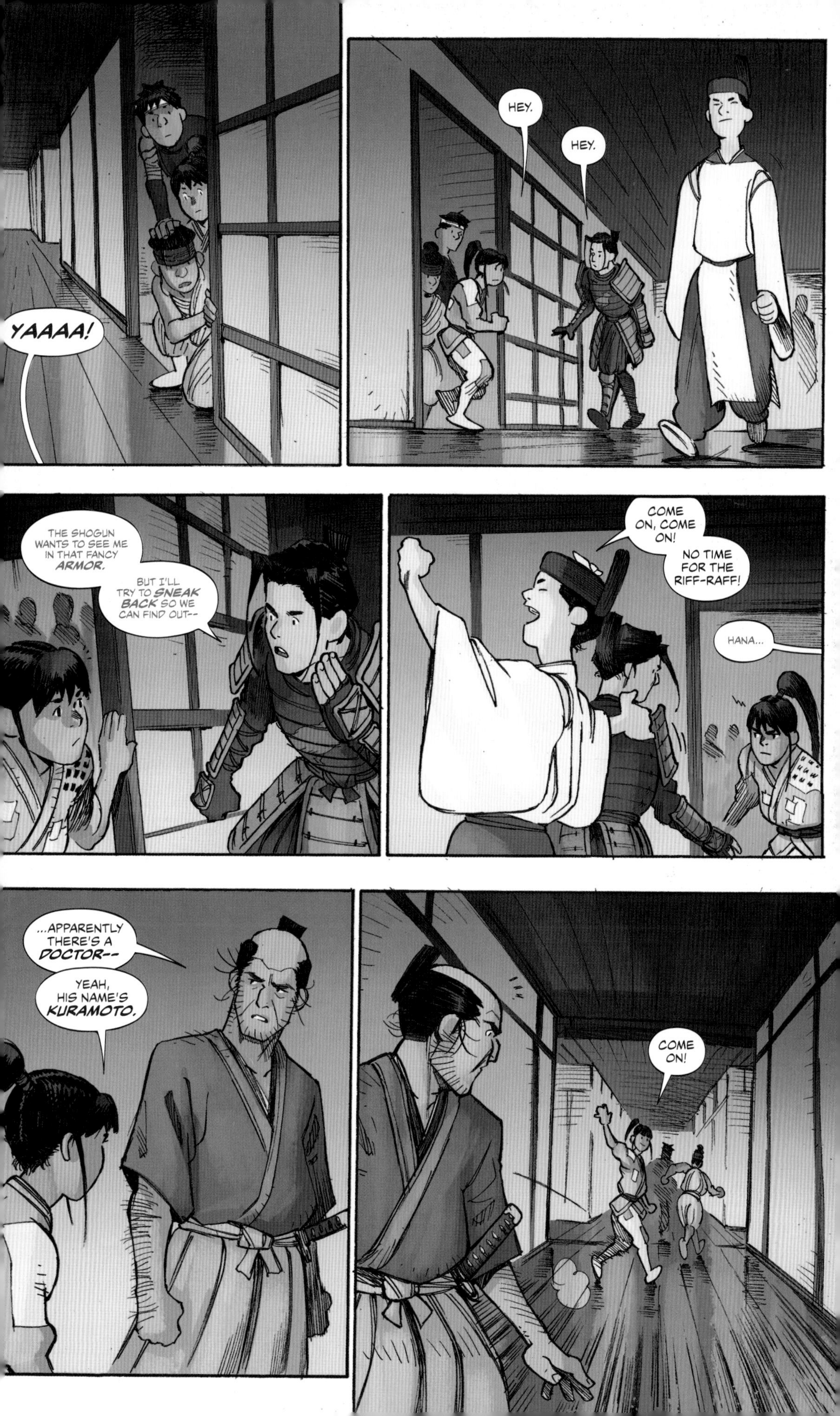
YAAAA!
HEY.
HEY.
THE SHOGUN WANTS TO SEE ME IN THAT FANCY ARMOR.
BUT I'LL TRY TO SNEAK BACK SO WE CAN FIND OUT--
COME ON, COME ON!
NO TIME FOR THE RIFF-RAFF!
HANA...
...APPARENTLY THERE'S A DOCTOR--
YEAH, HIS NAME'S KURAMOTO.
COME ON!

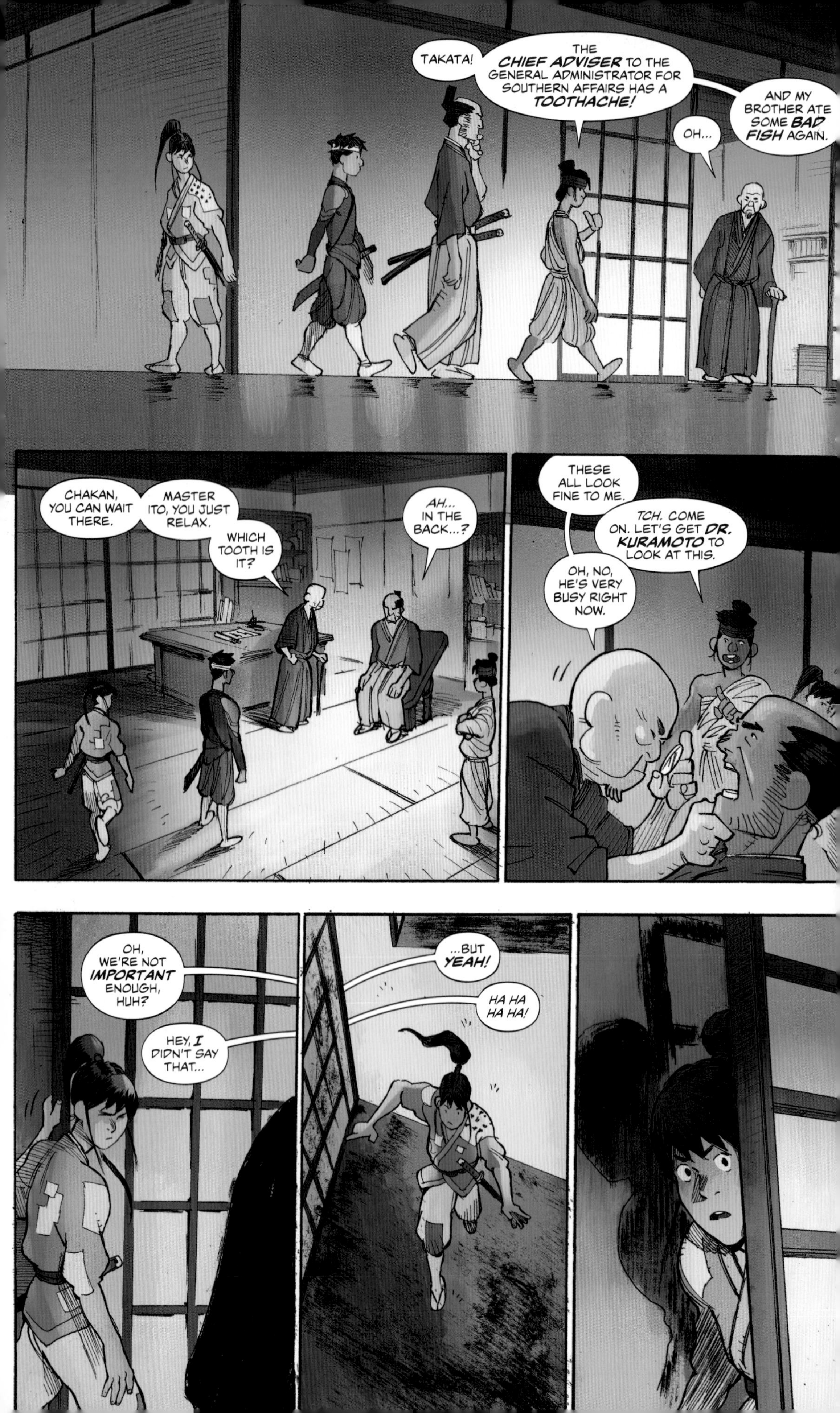
TAKATA!
THE CHIEF ADVISER TO THE GENERAL ADMINISTRATOR FOR SOUTHERN AFFAIRS HAS A TOOTHACHE!
AND MY BROTHER ATE SOME BAD FISH AGAIN.
OH...
CHAKAN, YOU CAN WAIT THERE.
MASTER ITO, YOU JUST RELAX.
WHICH TOOTH IS IT?
AH... IN THE BACK...?
THESE ALL LOOK FINE TO ME.
TCH. COME ON. LET'S GET DR. KURAMOTO TO LOOK AT THIS.
OH, NO, HE'S VERY BUSY RIGHT NOW.
OH, WE'RE NOT IMPORTANT ENOUGH, HUH?
HEY, I DIDN'T SAY THAT...
...BUT YEAH!
HA HA HA HA!

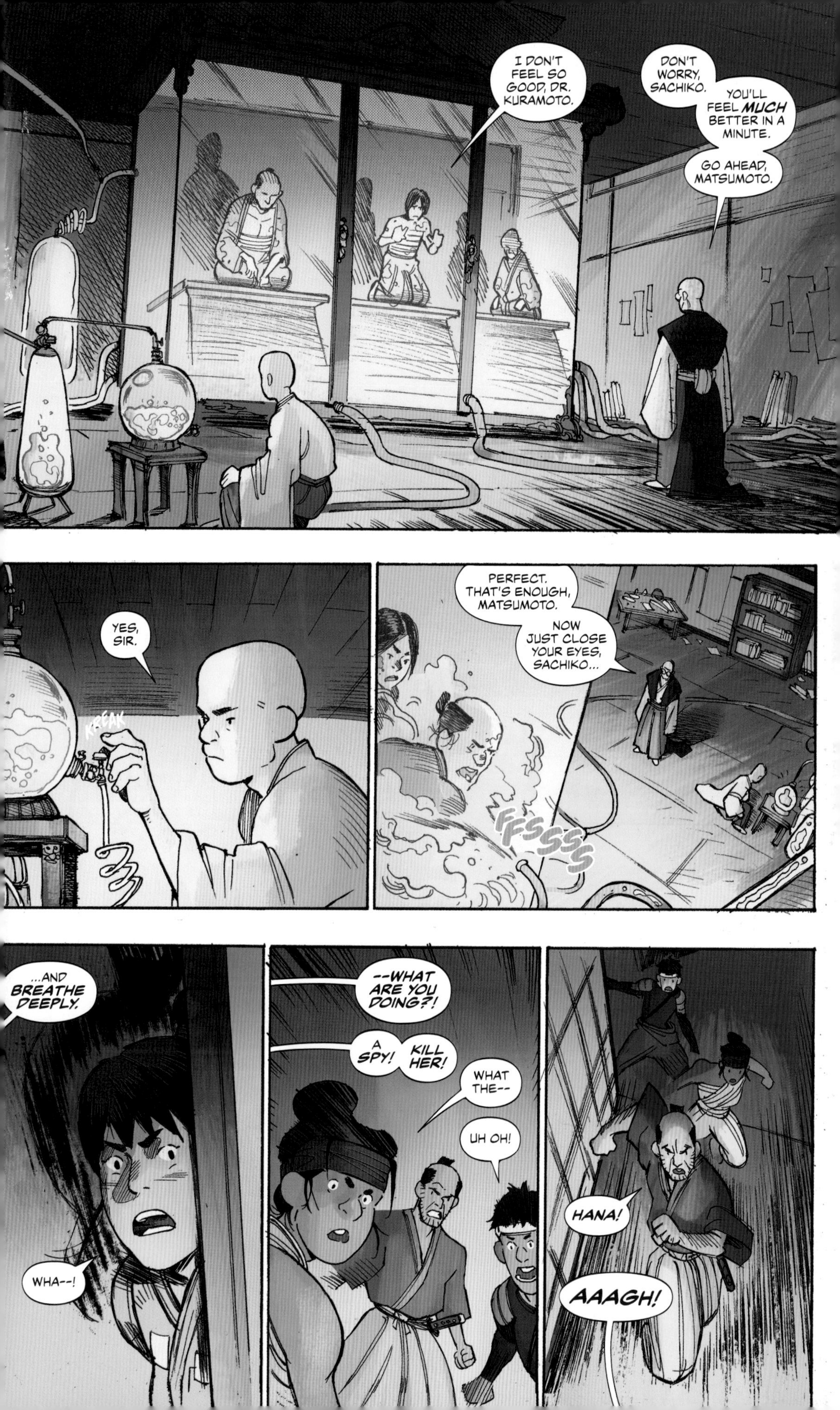
I DON'T FEEL SO GOOD, DR. KURAMOTO.
DON'T WORRY, SACHIKO.
YOU'LL FEEL MUCH BETTER IN A MINUTE.
GO AHEAD, MATSUMOTO.
YES, SIR.
KREAK
PERFECT. THAT'S ENOUGH, MATSUMOTO.
NOW JUST CLOSE YOUR EYES, SACHIKO...
FFSSSS
...AND BREATHE DEEPLY.
WHA--!
--WHAT ARE YOU DOING?!
A SPY!
KILL HER!
WHAT THE--
UH OH!
HANA!
AAAGH!

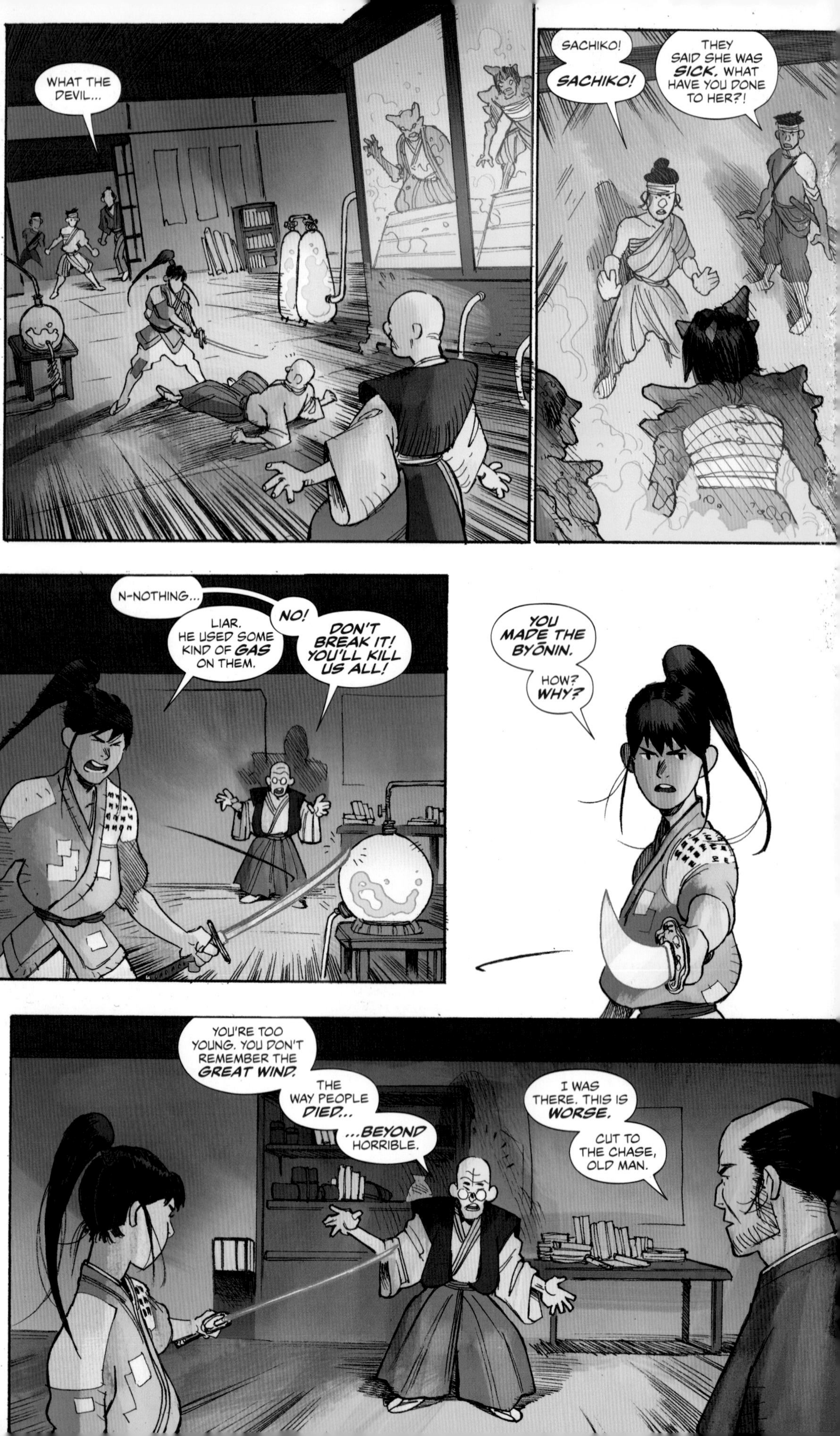
WHAT THE DEVIL...
SACHIKO!
SACHIKO!
THEY SAID SHE WAS SICK. WHAT HAVE YOU DONE TO HER?!
N-NOTHING...
LIAR. HE USED SOME KIND OF GAS ON THEM.
NO!
DON'T BREAK IT! YOU'LL KILL US ALL!
YOU MADE THE BYŌNIN.
HOW? WHY?
YOU'RE TOO YOUNG. YOU DON'T REMEMBER THE GREAT WIND.
THE WAY PEOPLE DIED...
...BEYOND HORRIBLE.
I WAS THERE. THIS IS WORSE.
CUT TO THE CHASE, OLD MAN.

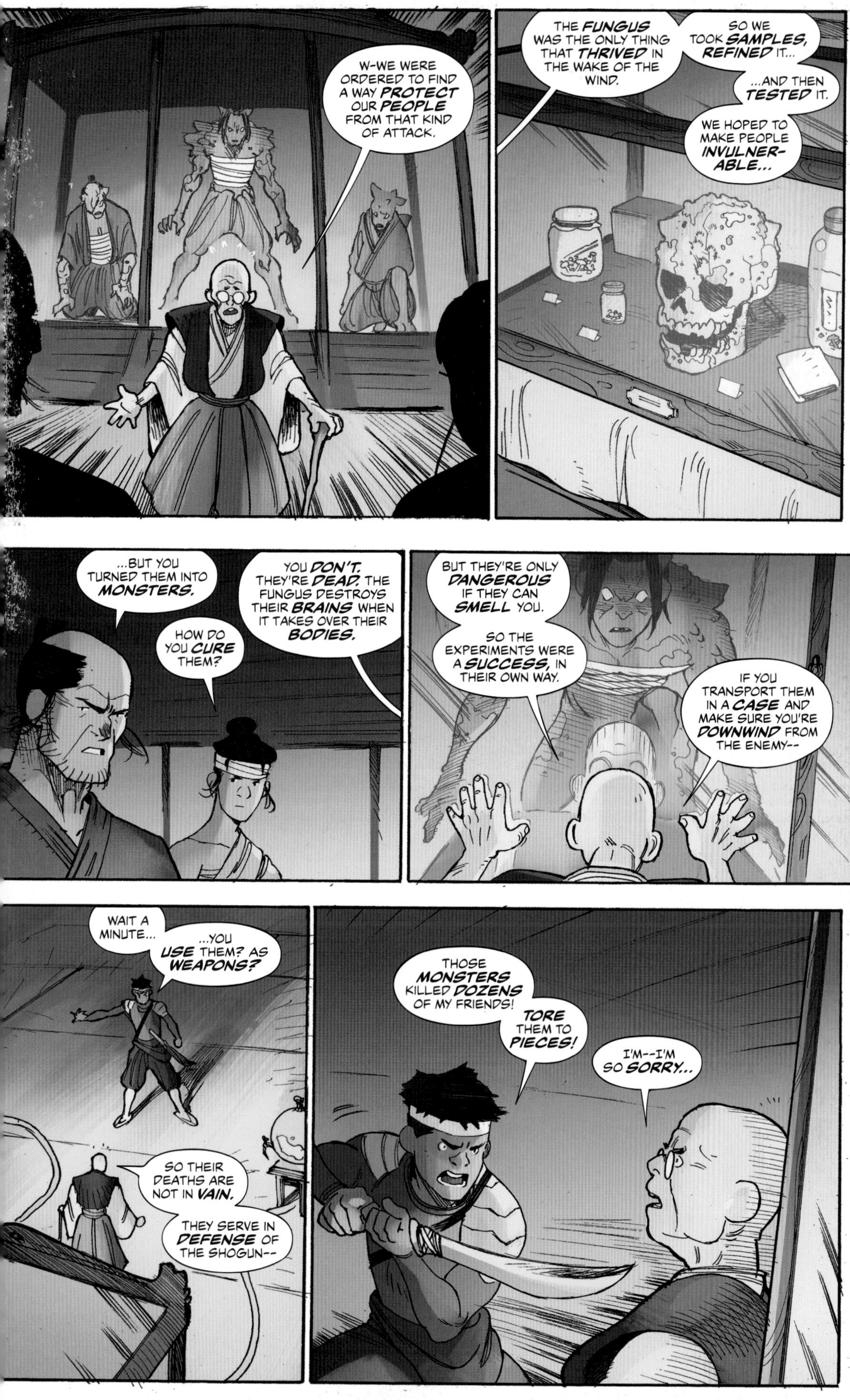
W-WE WERE ORDERED TO FIND A WAY PROTECT OUR PEOPLE FROM THAT KIND OF ATTACK.
THE FUNGUS WAS THE ONLY THING THAT THRIVED IN THE WAKE OF THE WIND.
SO WE TOOK SAMPLES, REFINED IT...
...AND THEN TESTED IT.
WE HOPED TO MAKE PEOPLE INVULNER-ABLE...
...BUT YOU TURNED THEM INTO MONSTERS.
HOW DO YOU CURE THEM?
YOU DON'T. THEY'RE DEAD. THE FUNGUS DESTROYS THEIR BRAINS WHEN IT TAKES OVER THEIR BODIES.
BUT THEY'RE ONLY DANGEROUS IF THEY CAN SMELL YOU.
SO THE EXPERIMENTS WERE A SUCCESS, IN THEIR OWN WAY.
IF YOU TRANSPORT THEM IN A CASE AND MAKE SURE YOU'RE DOWNWIND FROM THE ENEMY--
WAIT A MINUTE...
...YOU USE THEM? AS WEAPONS?
SO THEIR DEATHS ARE NOT IN VAIN.
THEY SERVE IN DEFENSE OF THE SHOGUN--
THOSE MONSTERS KILLED DOZENS OF MY FRIENDS!
TORE THEM TO PIECES!
I'M--I'M SO SORRY...

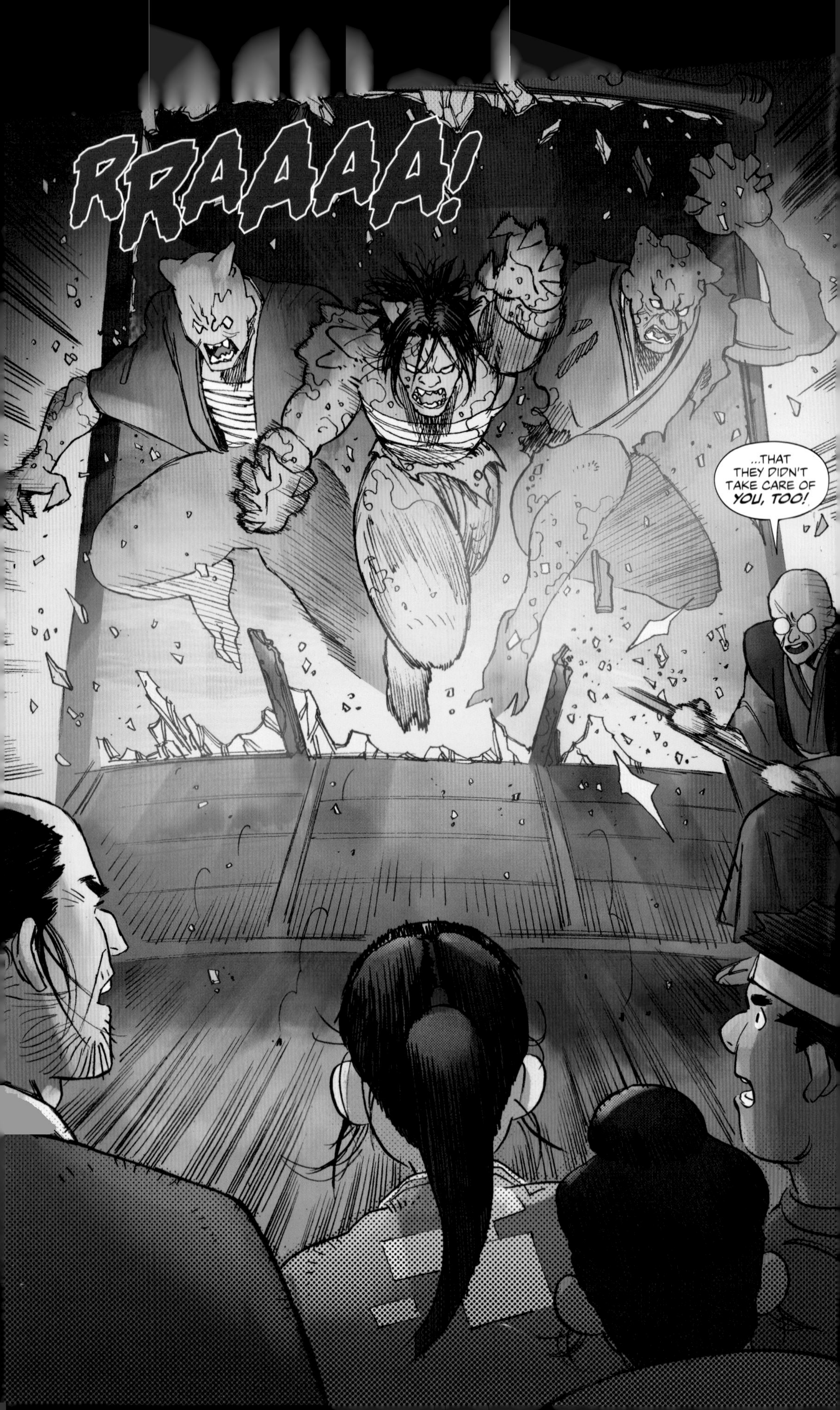
RRAAAA!
...THAT THEY DIDN'T TAKE CARE OF YOU, TOO!

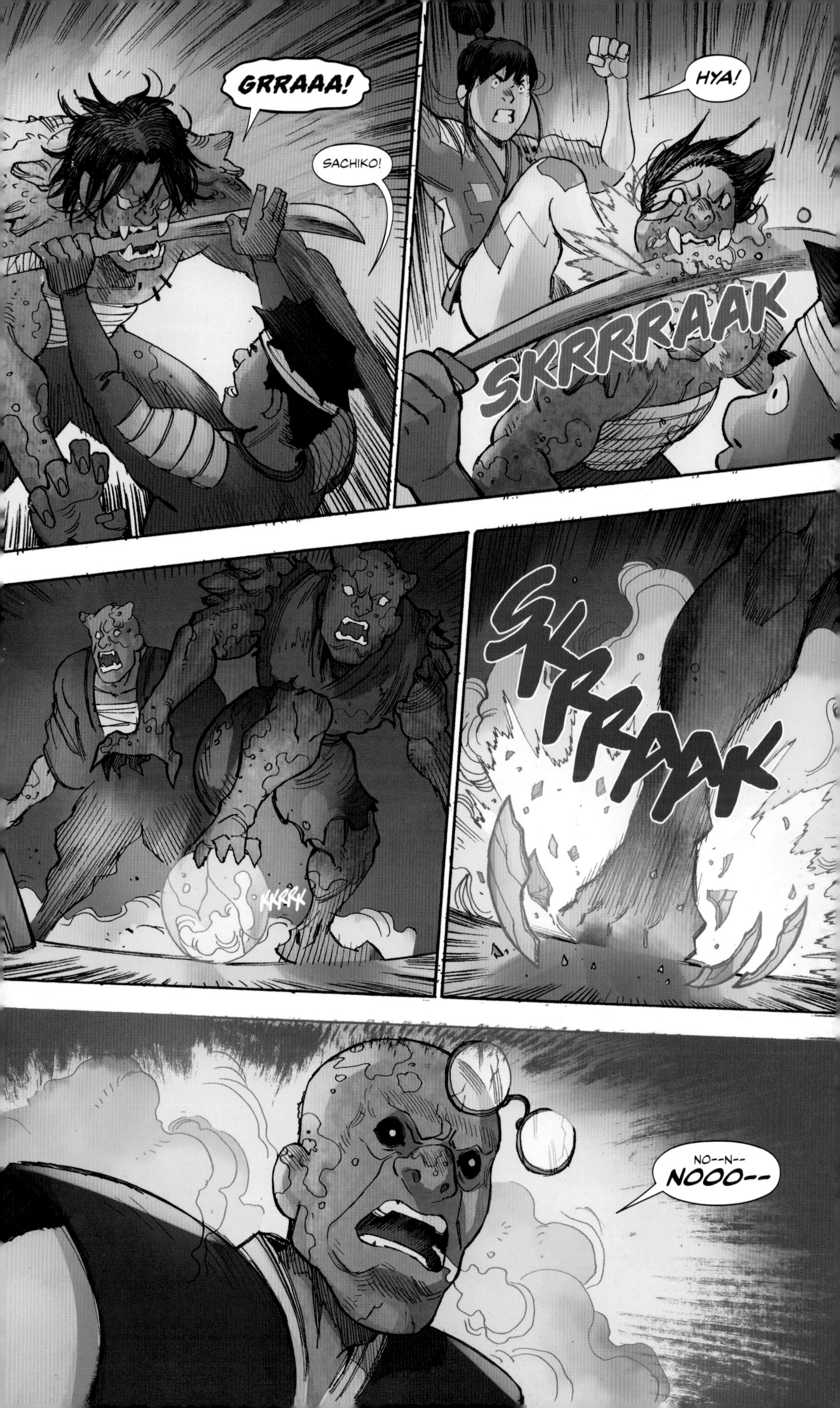
GRRAAA!
SACHIKO!
HYA!
SKRRRAAK
KKRRK
SKRRRAAK
NO--N--
NOOO--

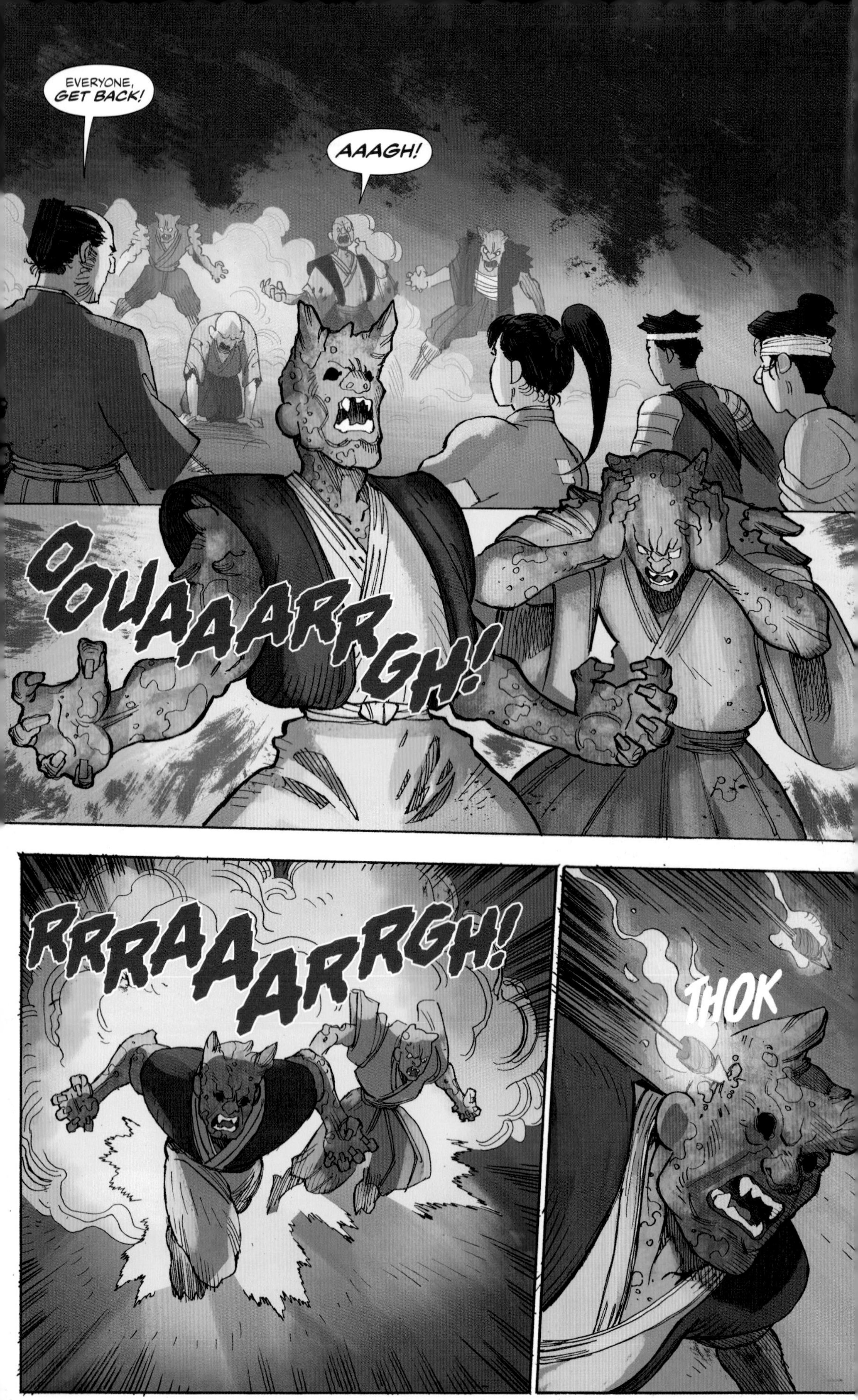
EVERYONE, GET BACK!
AAAGH!
OOUAAARRGH!
RRRAAAARRRGH!
THOK

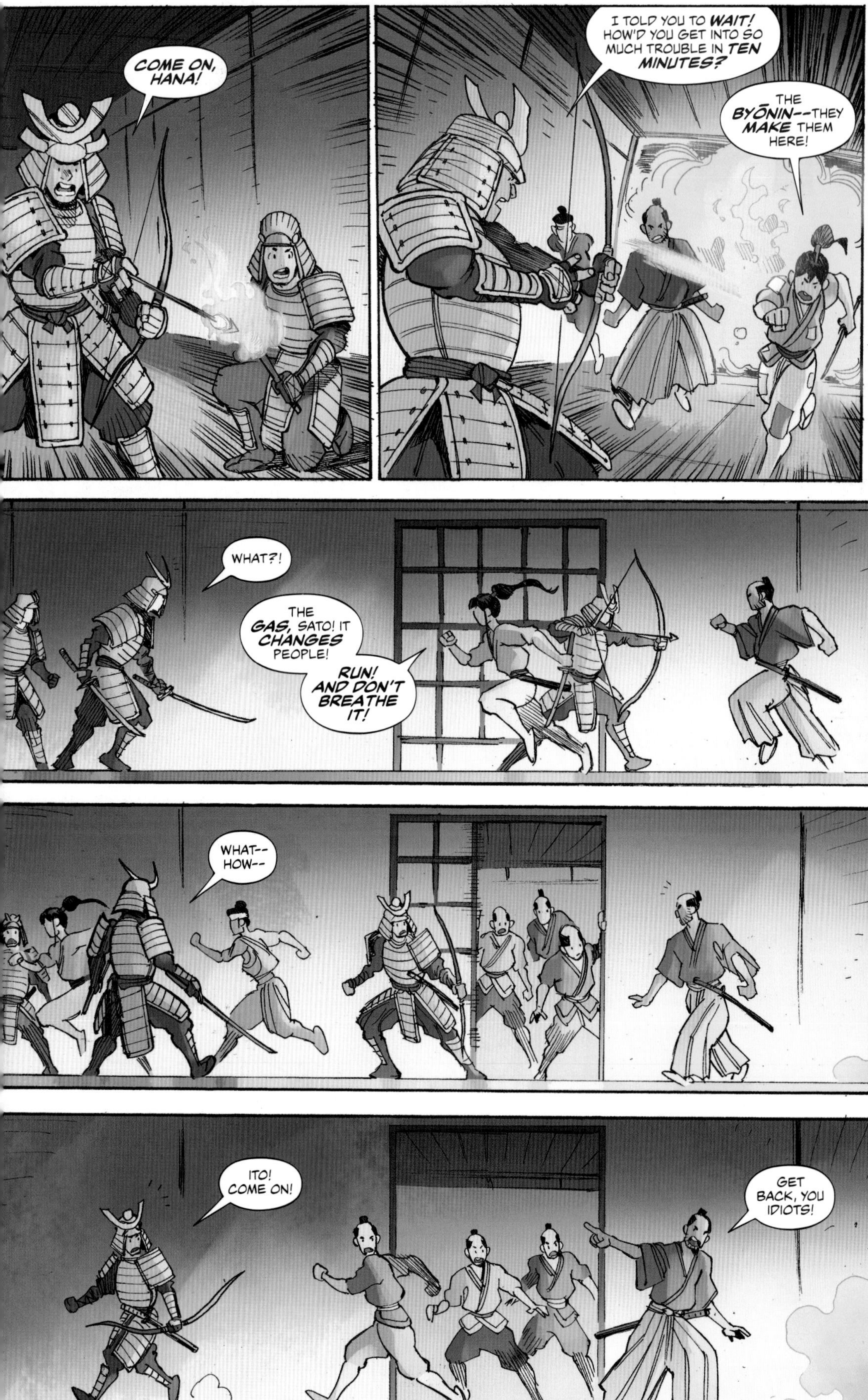
COME ON, HANA!
I TOLD YOU TO WAIT! HOW'D YOU GET INTO SO MUCH TROUBLE IN TEN MINUTES?
--THE BYŌNIN--THEY MAKE THEM HERE!
WHAT?!
THE GAS, SATO! IT CHANGES PEOPLE!
RUN! AND DON'T BREATHE IT!
WHAT--HOW--
ITO! COME ON!
GET BACK, YOU IDIOTS!

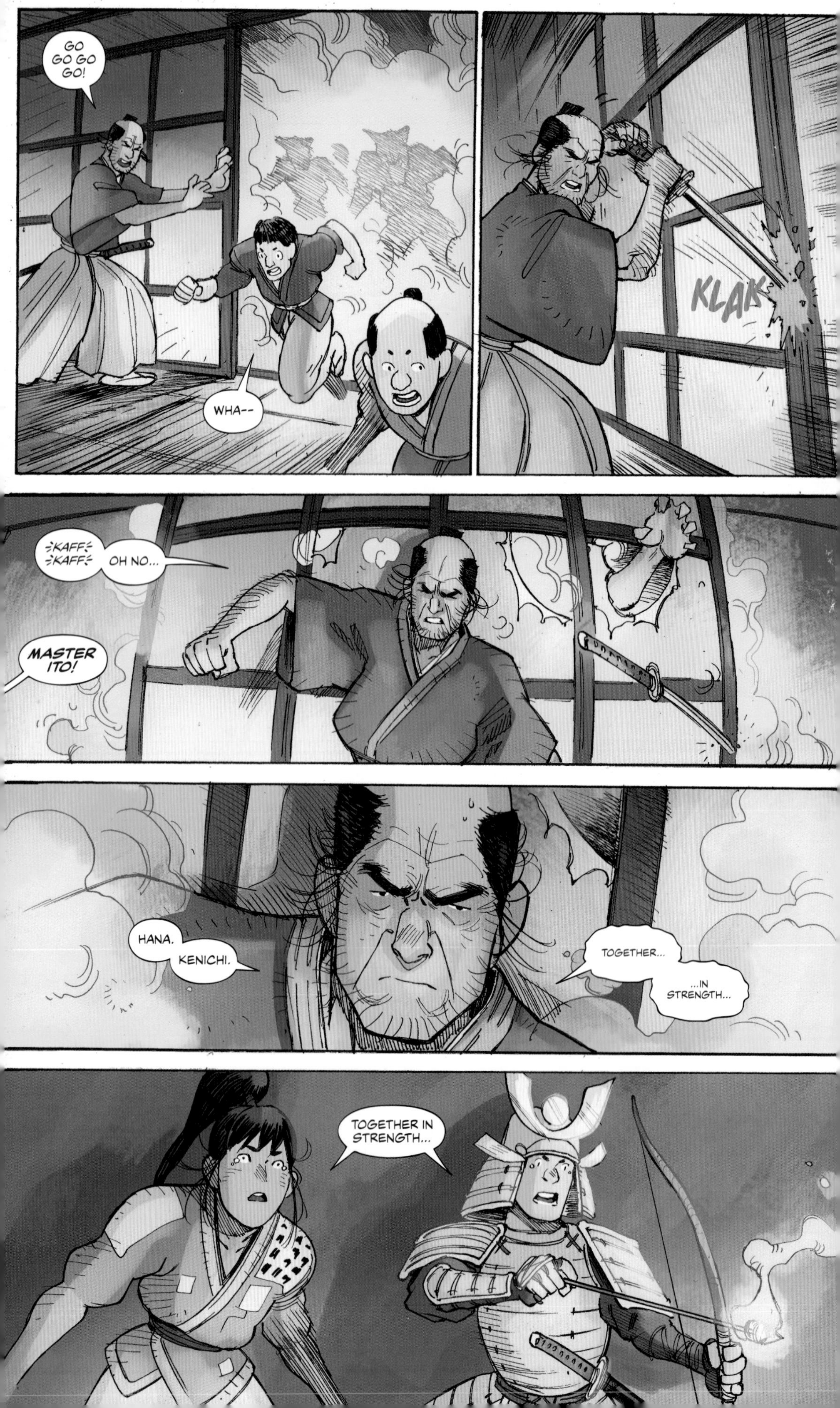
GO GO GO GO!
WHA--
KLAK
-KAFF- -KAFF-
OH NO...
MASTER ITO!
HANA.
KENICHI.
TOGETHER...
...IN STRENGTH...
TOGETHER IN STRENGTH...

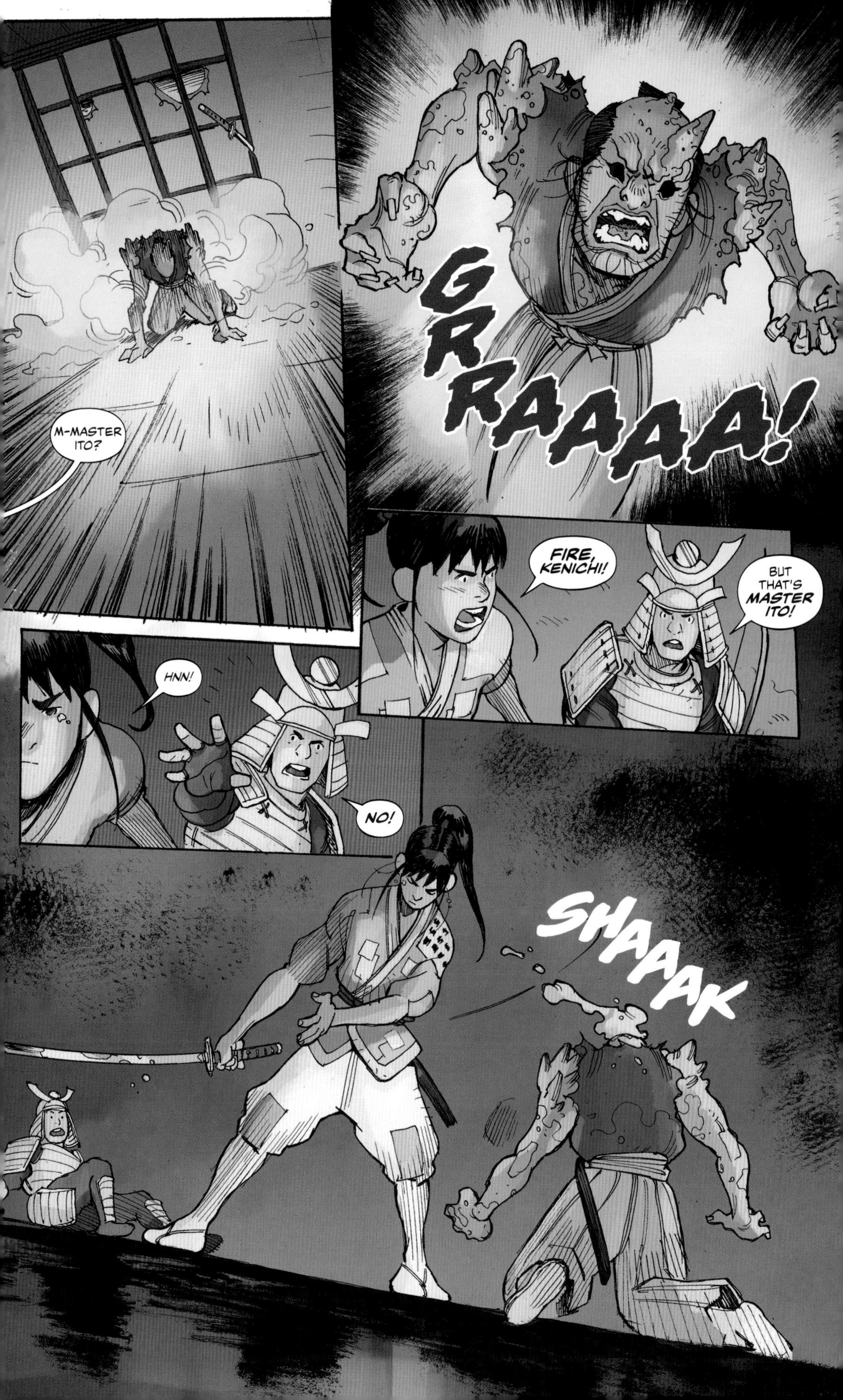
M-MASTER ITO?
GRRAAAAA!
FIRE, KENICHI!
BUT THAT'S MASTER ITO!
HNN!
NO!
SHAAAK

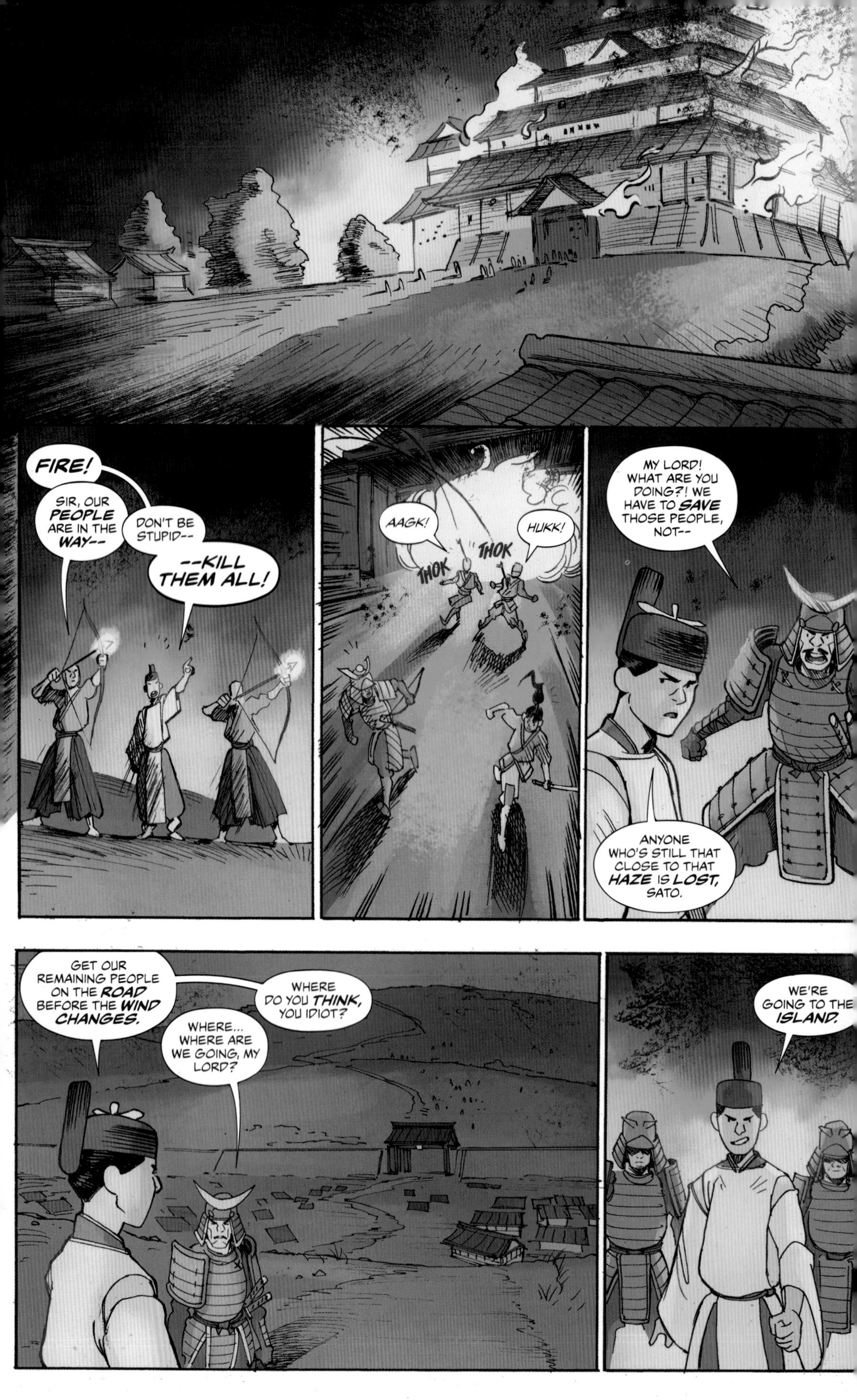
FIRE!
SIR, OUR PEOPLE ARE IN THE WAY--
DON'T BE STUPID--
--KILL THEM ALL!
AAGK!
HUKK!
THOK
THOK
MY LORD! WHAT ARE YOU DOING?! WE HAVE TO SAVE THOSE PEOPLE, NOT--
ANYONE WHO'S STILL THAT CLOSE TO THAT HAZE IS LOST, SATO.
GET OUR REMAINING PEOPLE ON THE ROAD BEFORE THE WIND CHANGES.
WHERE... WHERE ARE WE GOING, MY LORD?
WHERE DO YOU THINK, YOU IDIOT?
WE'RE GOING TO THE ISLAND.

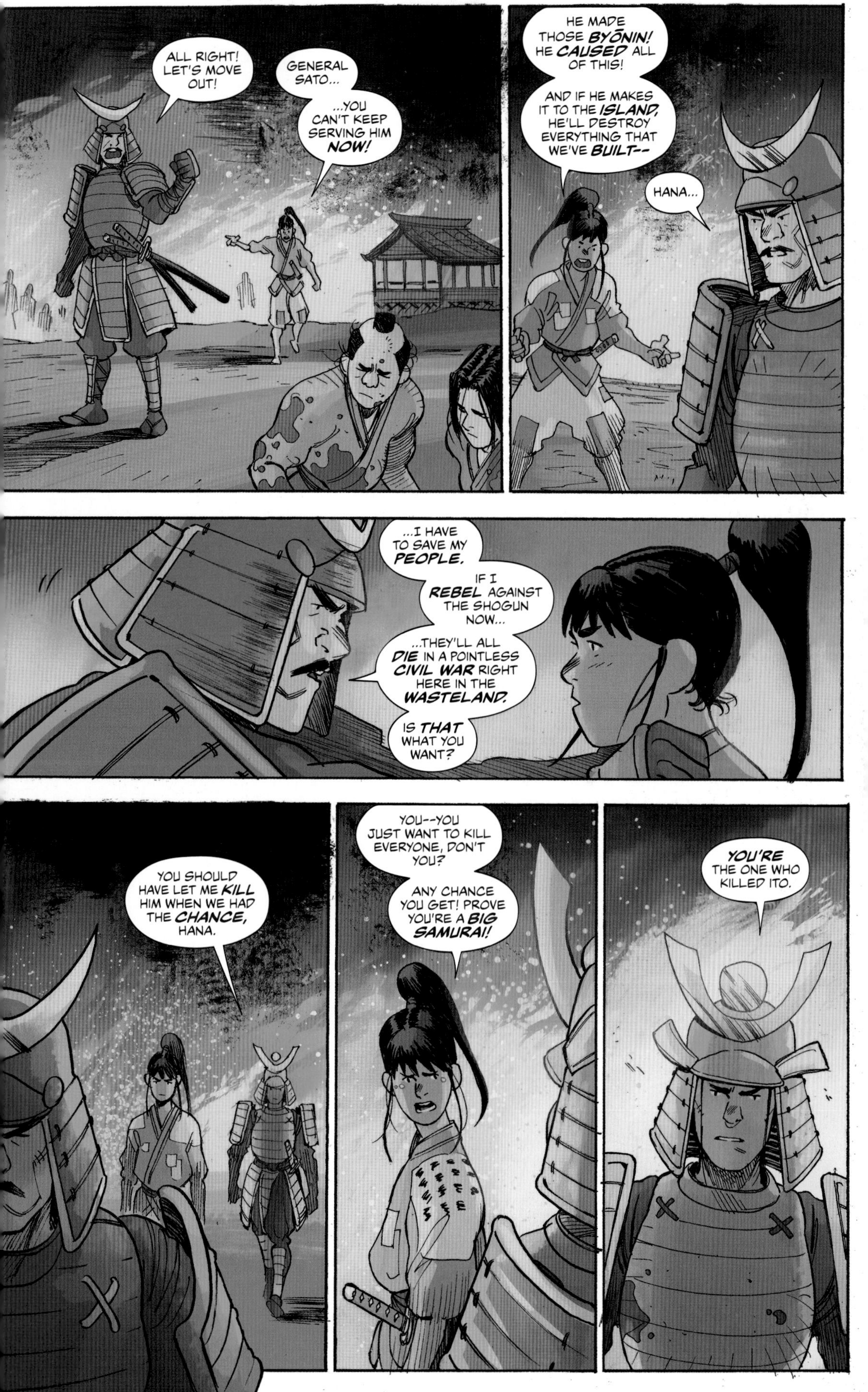
ALL RIGHT! LET'S MOVE OUT!
GENERAL SATO...
...YOU CAN'T KEEP SERVING HIM NOW!
HE MADE THOSE BYŌNIN! HE CAUSED ALL OF THIS!
AND IF HE MAKES IT TO THE ISLAND, HE'LL DESTROY EVERYTHING THAT WE'VE BUILT--
HANA...
...I HAVE TO SAVE MY PEOPLE.
IF I REBEL AGAINST THE SHOGUN NOW...
...THEY'LL ALL DIE IN A POINTLESS CIVIL WAR RIGHT HERE IN THE WASTELAND.
IS THAT WHAT YOU WANT?
YOU SHOULD HAVE LET ME KILL HIM WHEN WE HAD THE CHANCE, HANA.
YOU--YOU JUST WANT TO KILL EVERYONE, DON'T YOU?
ANY CHANCE YOU GET! PROVE YOU'RE A BIG SAMURAI!
YOU'RE THE ONE WHO KILLED ITO.

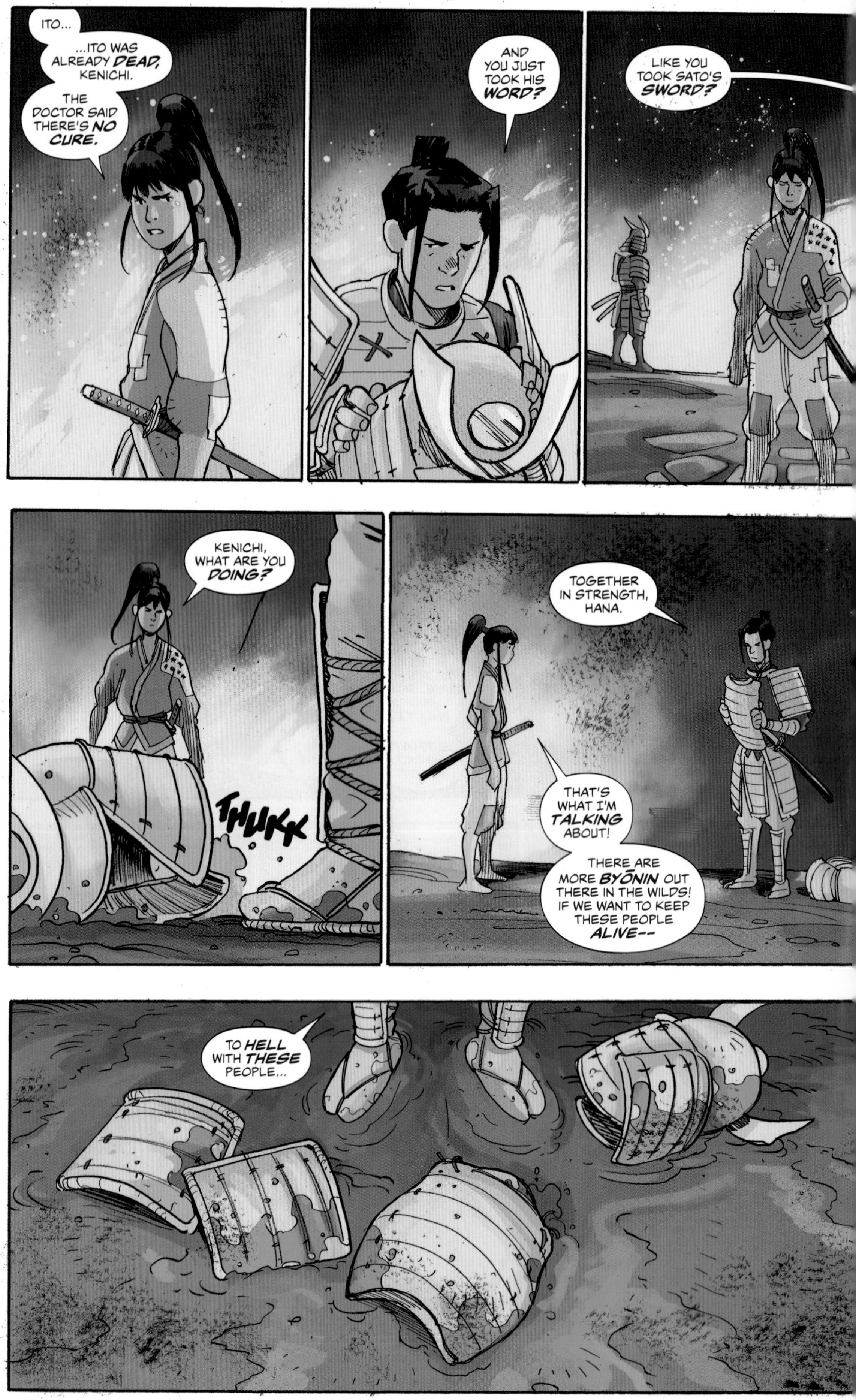
ITO...
...ITO WAS ALREADY DEAD, KENICHI.
THE DOCTOR SAID THERE'S NO CURE.
AND YOU JUST TOOK HIS WORD?
LIKE YOU TOOK SATO'S SWORD?
KENICHI, WHAT ARE YOU DOING?
THUKK
TOGETHER IN STRENGTH, HANA.
THAT'S WHAT I'M TALKING ABOUT!
THERE ARE MORE BYŌNIN OUT THERE IN THE WILDS! IF WE WANT TO KEEP THESE PEOPLE ALIVE--
TO HELL WITH THESE PEOPLE...

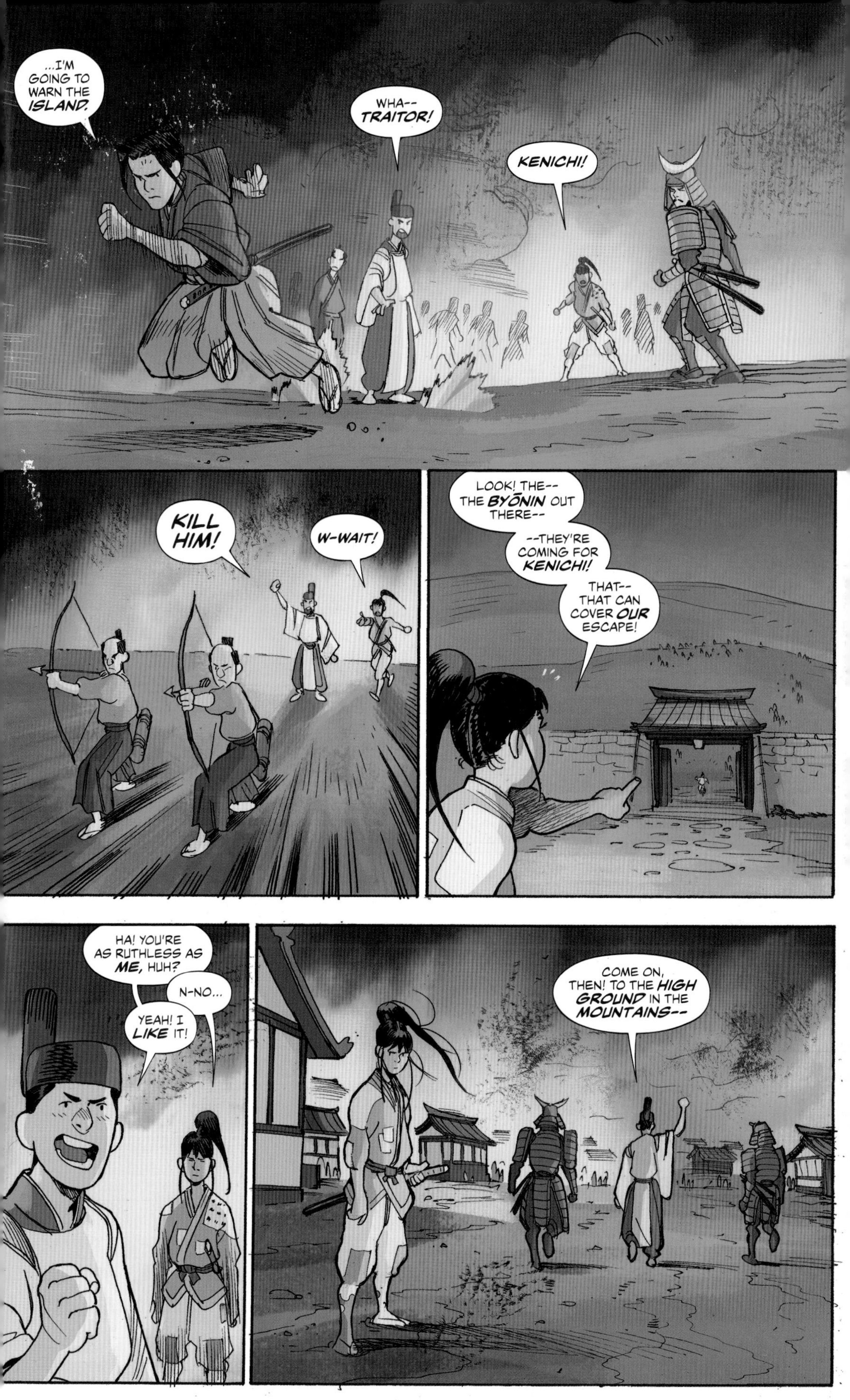

...I'M GOING TO WARN THE ISLAND.
WHA-- TRAITOR!
KENICHI!
KILL HIM!
W-WAIT!
LOOK! THE-- THE BYŌNIN OUT THERE--
--THEY'RE COMING FOR KENICHI!
THAT-- THAT CAN COVER OUR ESCAPE!
HA! YOU'RE AS RUTHLESS AS ME, HUH?
N-NO...
YEAH! I LIKE IT!
COME ON, THEN! TO THE HIGH GROUND IN THE MOUNTAINS--

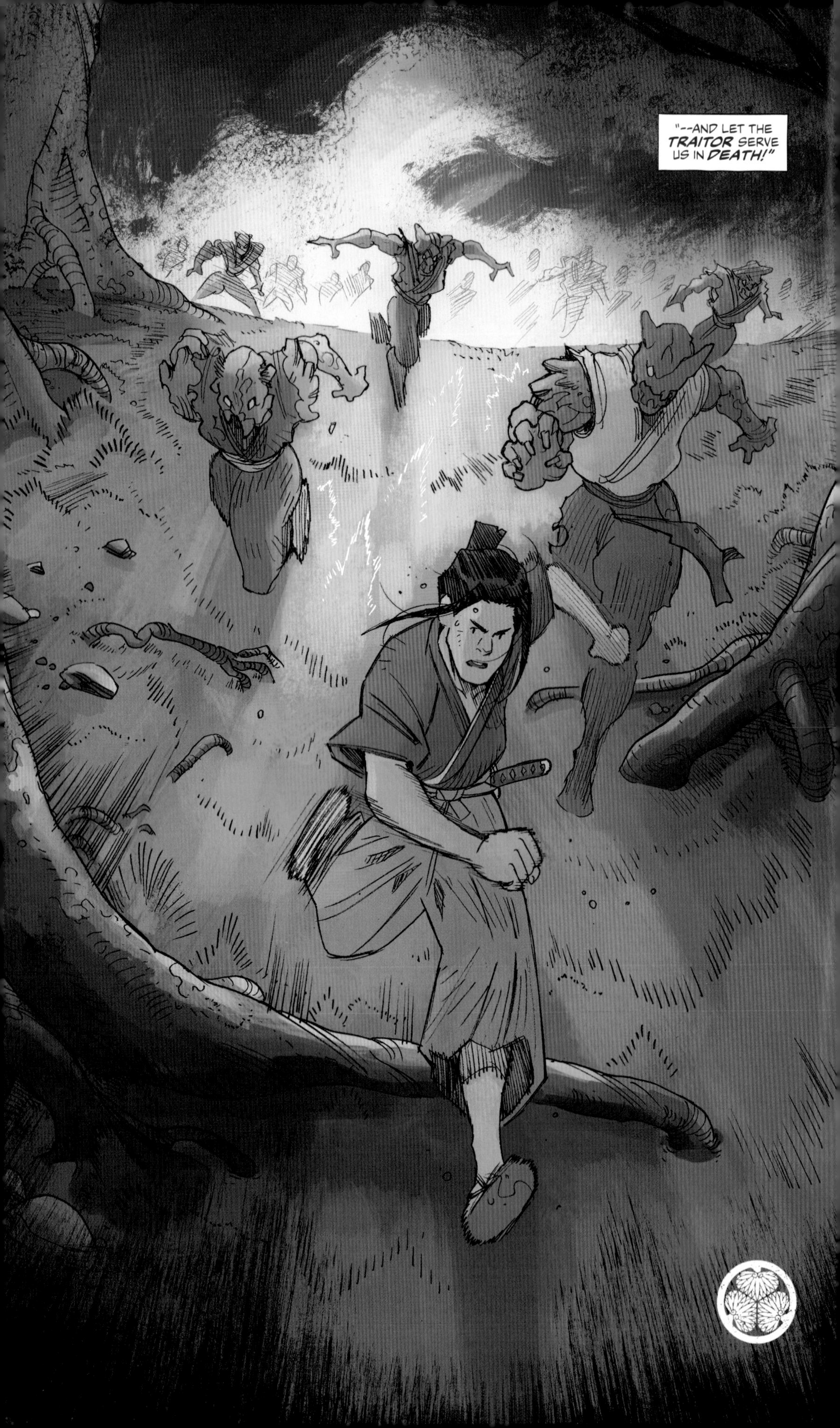
"--AND LET THE *TRAITOR* SERVE US IN *DEATH!*"

Issue Four Cover by **Ethan**

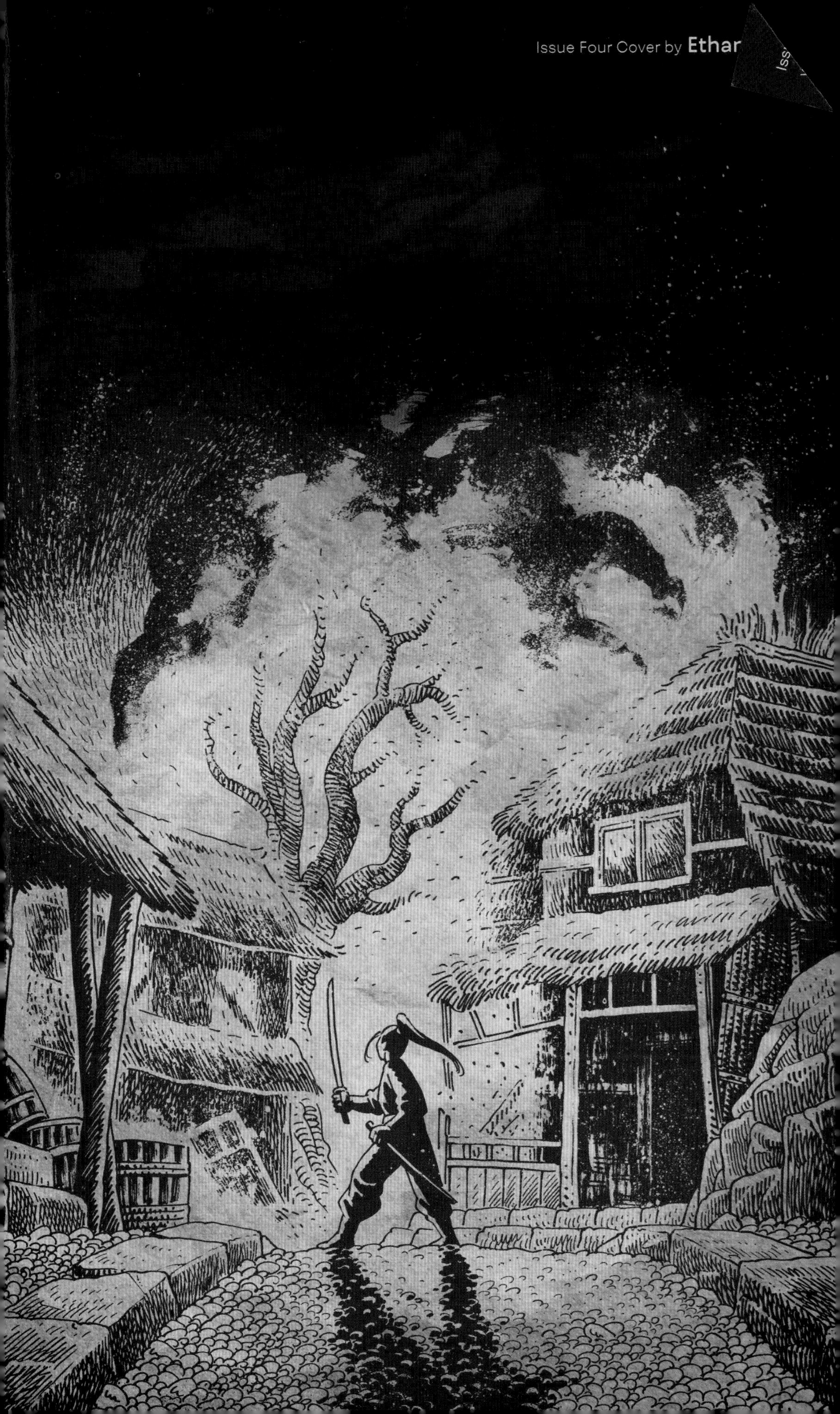

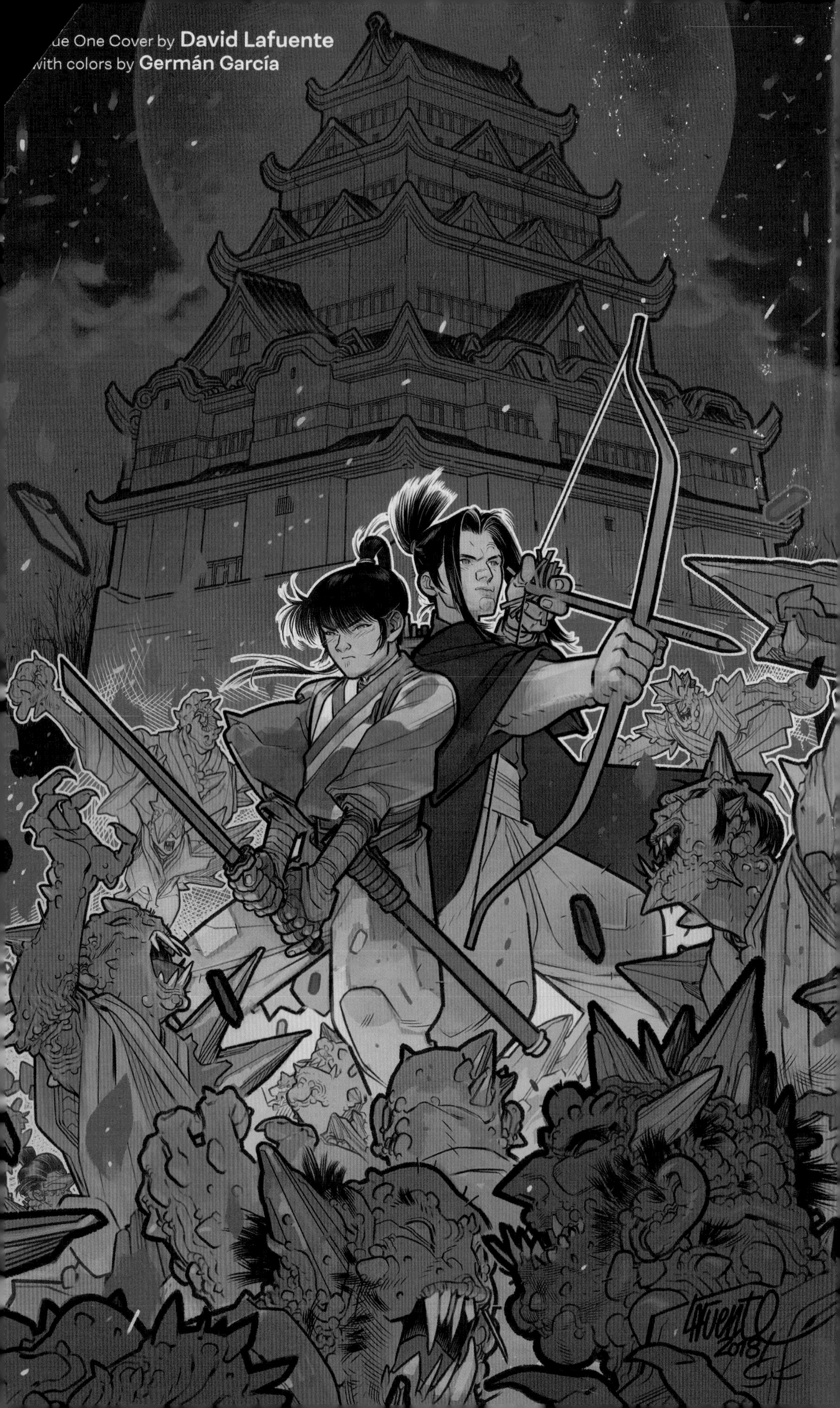

ue One Cover by **David Lafuente**
with colors by **Germán García**

Issue One Cover by **Kris Anka**

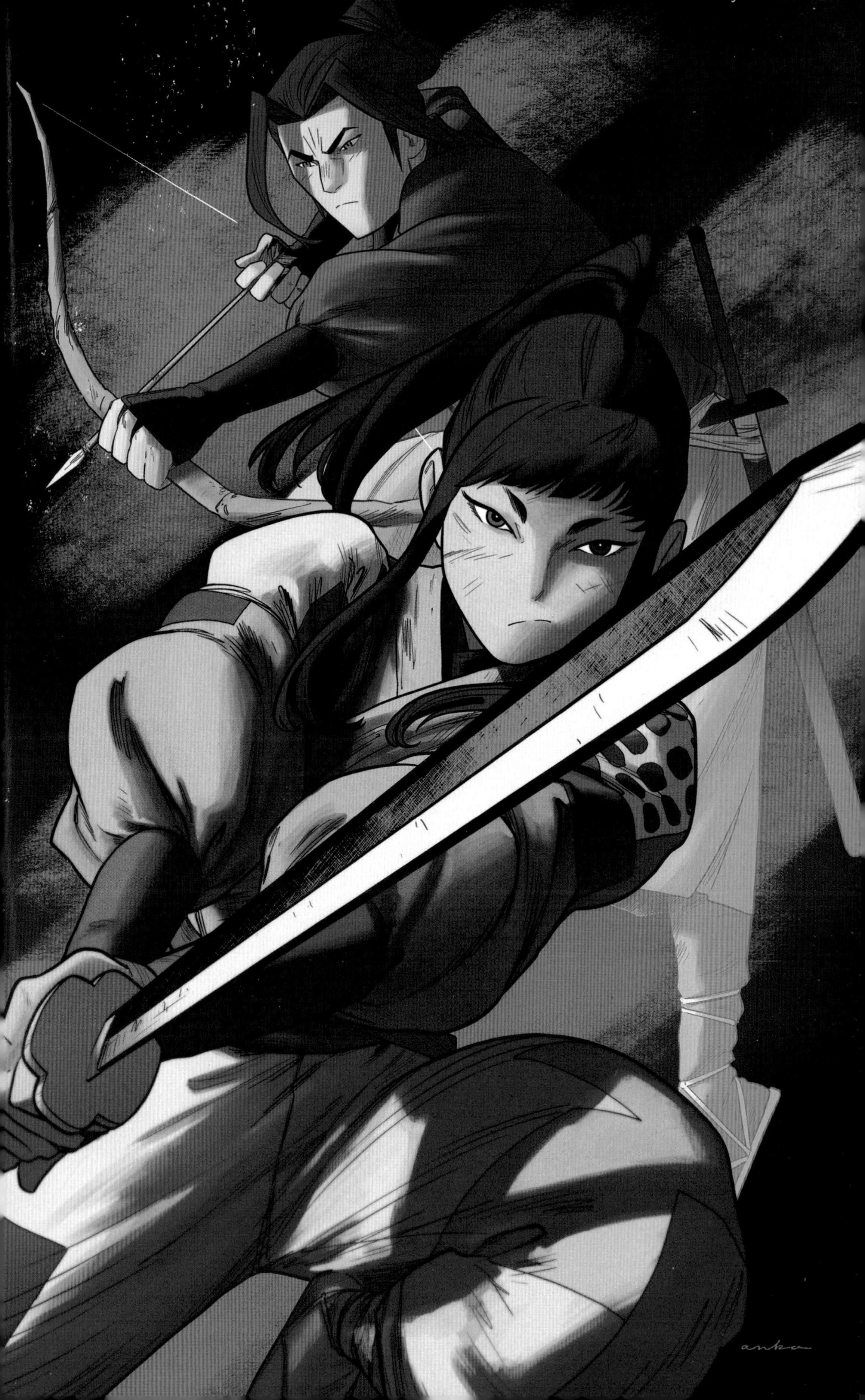
anka

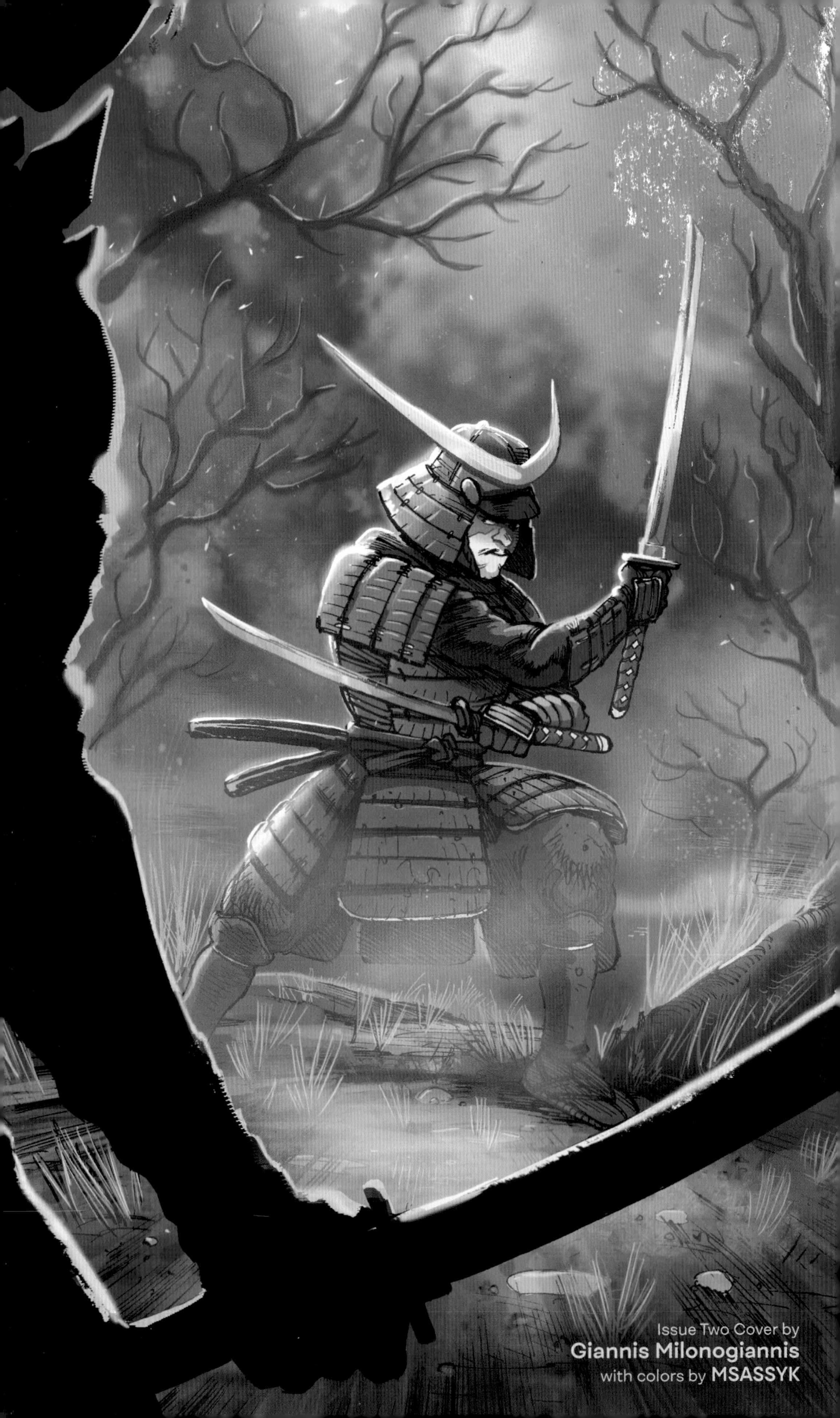

Issue Two Cover by
Giannis Milonogiannis
with colors by **MSASSYK**

Issue Three Cover by **Giannis Milonogiannis**
with colors by **MSASSYK**

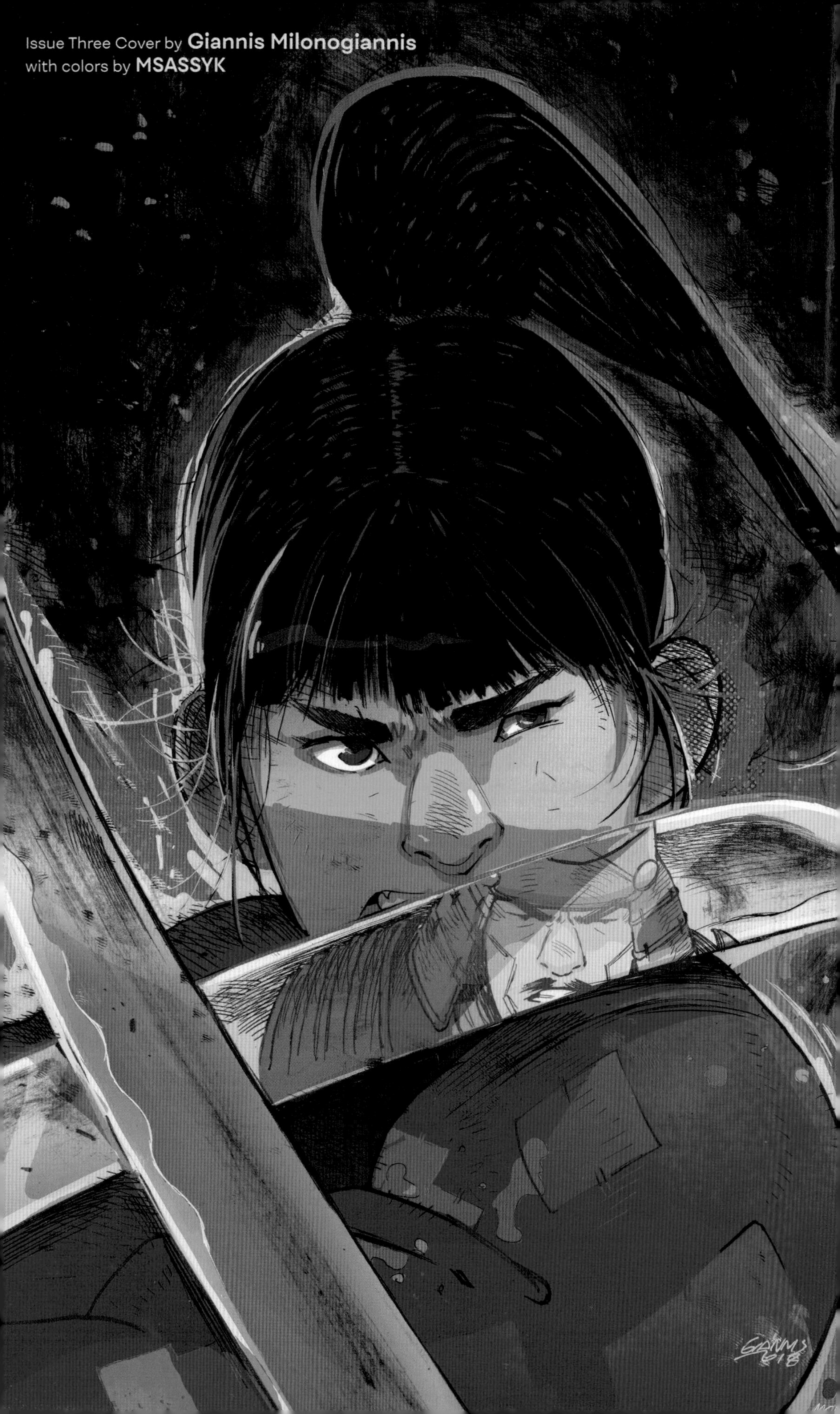

Issue Two 2nd Print Cover by **Giannis Milonogiannis**
with colors by **Irma Kniivila**

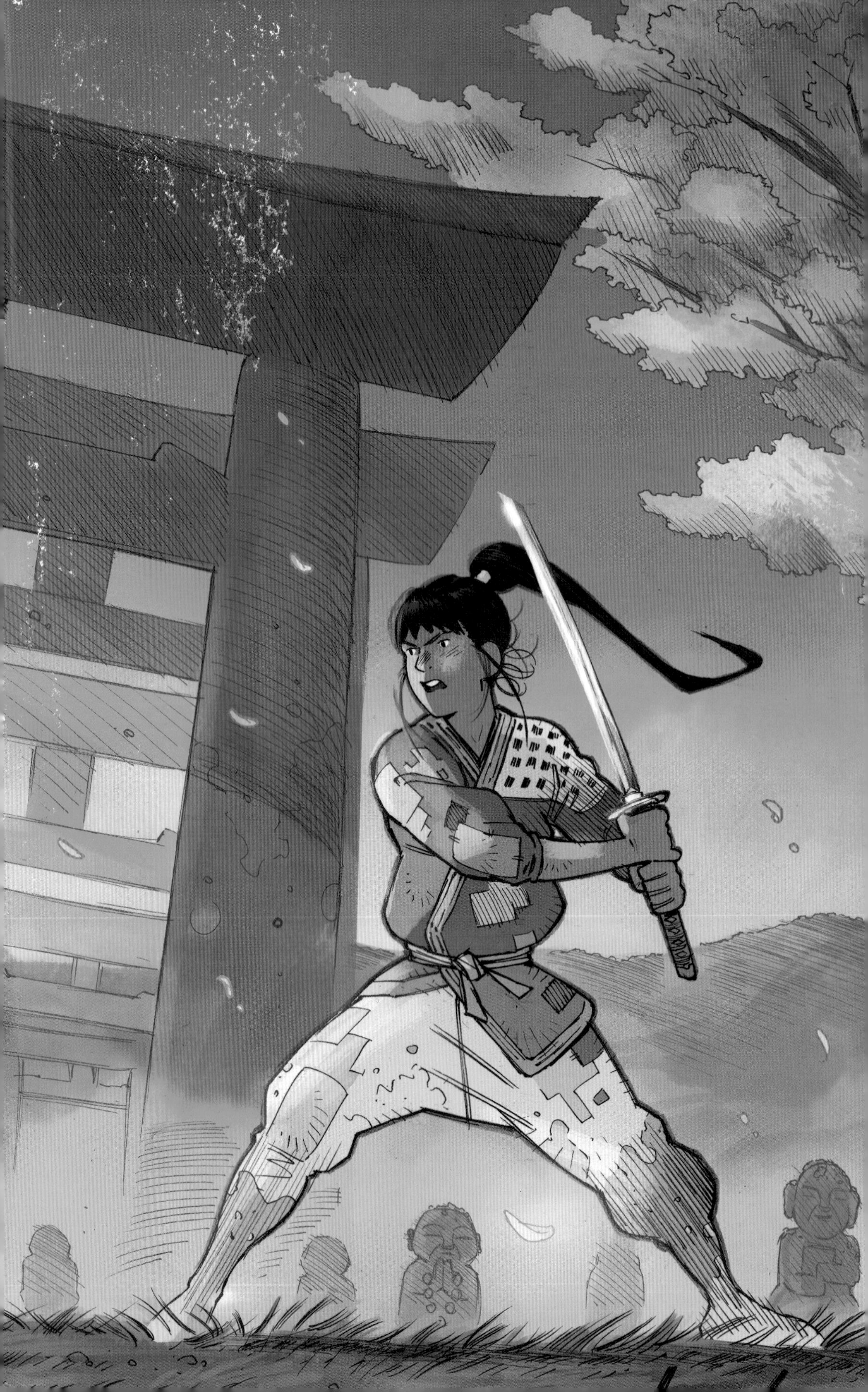

Issue One 2nd Print Cover by **Giannis Milonogiannis**
with colors by **Irma Kniivila**

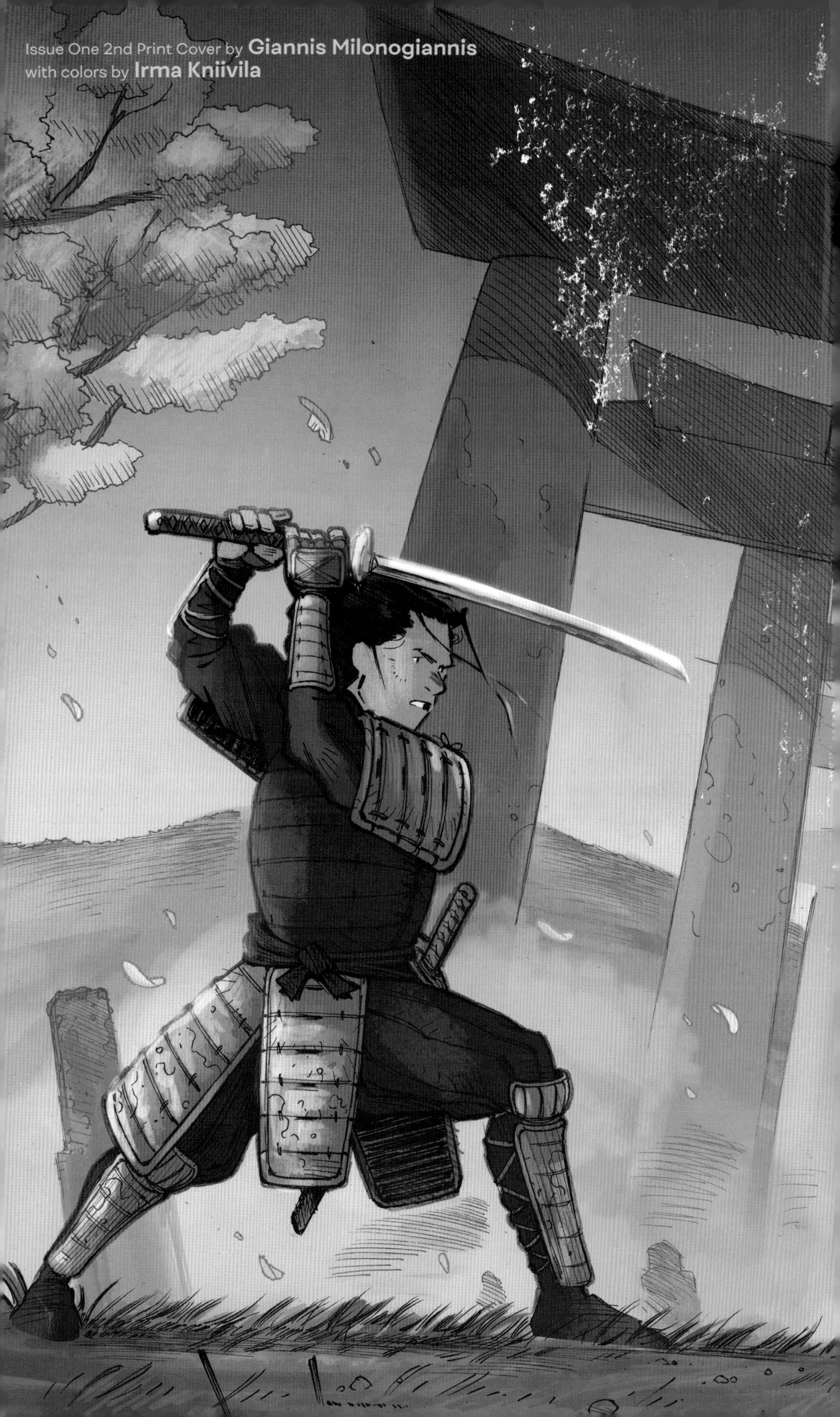

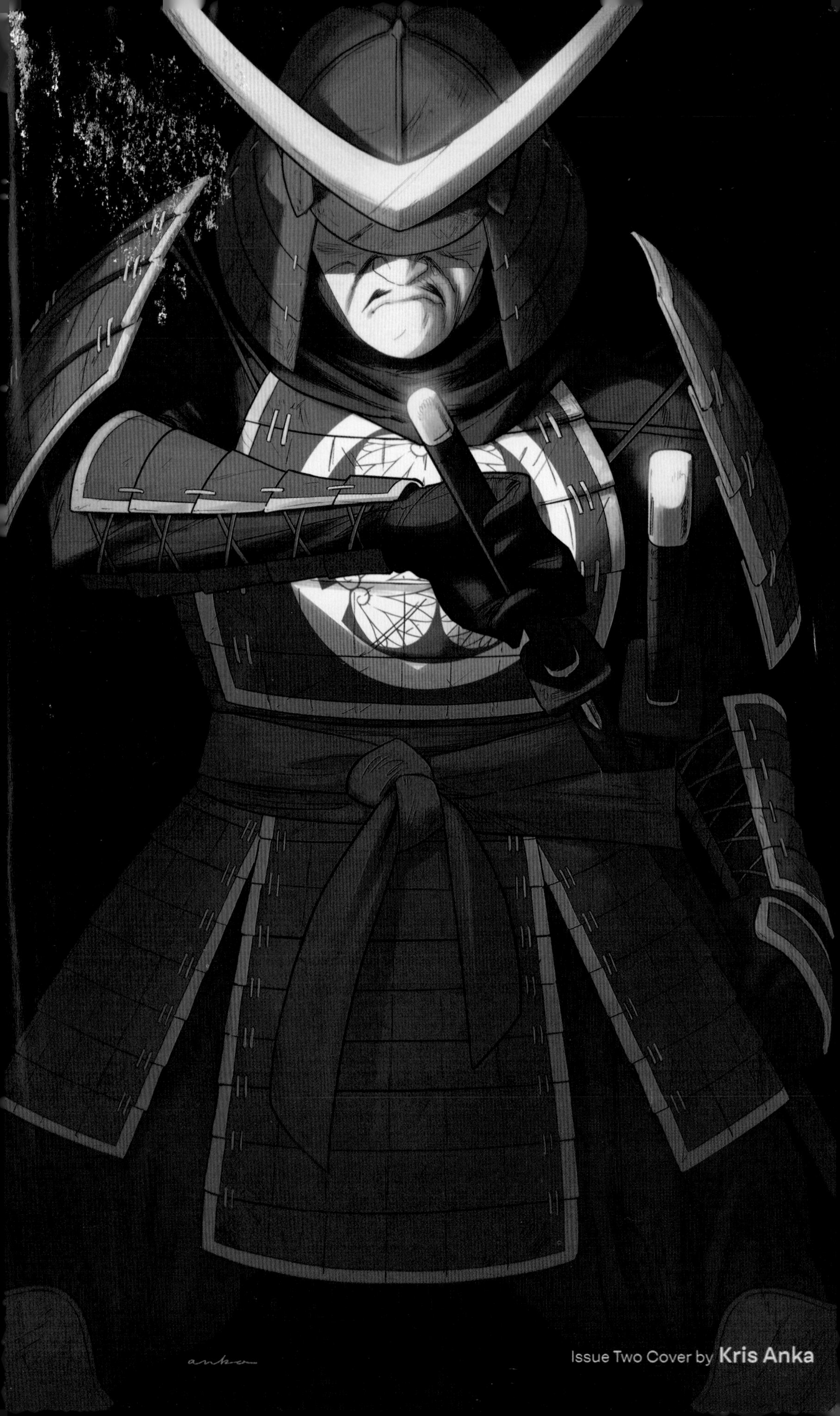
anka

Issue Two Cover by **Kris Anka**